Lecture Notes in Computer Science   12394

More information about this series at http://www.springer.com/series/7409

Andrea Kő · Enrico Francesconi ·
Gabriele Kotsis · A Min Tjoa ·
Ismail Khalil (Eds.)

Electronic Government and the Information Systems Perspective

9th International Conference, EGOVIS 2020
Bratislava, Slovakia, September 14–17, 2020
Proceedings

 Springer

Editors
Andrea Kő ⓘ
Department of Information Systems
Corvinus University of Budapest
Budapest, Hungary

Gabriele Kotsis
Johannes Kepler University of Linz
Linz, Oberösterreich, Austria

Ismail Khalil
Johannes Kepler University of Linz
Linz, Oberösterreich, Austria

Enrico Francesconi
National Research Council
Florence, Italy

A Min Tjoa
Vienna University of Technology
Vienna, Wien, Austria

ISSN 0302-9743   ISSN 1611-3349   (electronic)
Lecture Notes in Computer Science
ISBN 978-3-030-58956-1   ISBN 978-3-030-58957-8   (eBook)
https://doi.org/10.1007/978-3-030-58957-8

LNCS Sublibrary: SL3 – Information Systems and Applications, incl. Internet/Web, and HCI

This Springer imprint is published by the registered company Springer Nature Switzerland AG
The registered company address is: Gewerbestrasse 11, 6330 Cham, Switzerland

Preface

The 9th International Conference on Electronic Government and the Information Systems Perspective (EGOVIS 2020), took place online in the time zone of Bratislava, Slovakia, during September 14–17, 2020. The conference belongs to the 31st DEXA conference series.

EGOVIS focuses on information systems and ICT aspects of e-government. Information systems are a core enabler for e-government/governance in all its dimensions: e-administration, e-democracy, e-participation, and e-voting. EGOVIS aims to bring together experts from academia, public administrations, and industry to discuss e-government and e-democracy from different perspectives and disciplines, i.e., technology, policy and/or governance, and public administration.

The Program Committee accepted 16 papers from recent research fields such as artificial intelligence, machine learning, e-identity, e-participation, open government and e-government architectures for e-government, intelligent systems, and semantic technologies for services in the public sector. Beyond theoretical contributions, papers cover e-government practical applications and experiences.

These proceedings are organized into five sections according to the conference sessions.

Chairs of the Program Committee wish to thank all the reviewers for their valuable work; the reviews raised several research questions discussed at the conference. We would like to thank Ismail Khalil for the administrative support and stimulating us in proper scheduling.

We wish pleasant and beneficial learning experiences for the readers and hope that discussion continued after the conference between the researchers, contributing to building a global community in the field of e-government.

September 2020

Enrico Francesconi
Andrea Kő

Organization

General Chair

Roland Traunmüller   Johannes Kepler University Linz, Austria

Program Committee Chairs

Andrea Kő   Corvinus University of Budapest, Hungary
Enrico Francesconi   Italian National Research Council, Italy

Steering Committee

Gabriele Kotsis   Johannes Kepler University Linz, Austria
Ismail Khalil   Johannes Kepler University Linz, Austria
A Min Tjoa   Technical University of Vienna, Austria

Program Committee and Reviewers

Francesco Buccafurri   UNIRC, Italy
Alejandra Cechich   Universidad Nacional del Comahue, Argentina
Wojciech Cellary   Poznan University of Economics and Business, Poland
Wichian Chutimaskul   King Mongkut's University of Technology Thonburi, Thailand
Peter Cruickshank   Edinburgh Napier University, UK
Vytautas Čyras   Vilnius University, Lithuania
Ivan Futo   Multilogic Ltd., Hungary
Andras Gabor   Corvinno Technology Transfer Center Nonprofit Public Ltd., Hungary
Fernando Galindo   University of Zaragoza, Spain
Francisco Javier García Marco   University of Zaragoza, Spain
Stefanos Gritzalis   University of Piraeus, Greece
Christos Kalloniatis   University of the Aegean, Greece
Nikos Karacapilidis   University of Patras, Greece
Evangelia Kavakli   University of the Aegean, Greece
Bozidar Klicek   University of Zagreb, Croatia
Hun Yeong Kwon   Kwangwoon University, South Korea
Christine Leitner   Centre for Economics and Public Administration Ltd. (CEPA), Austria
Herbert Leitold   Secure Information Technology Center Austria, Austria
Peter Mambrey   Fraunhofer, University of Duisburg-Essen, Germany
Mara Nikolaidou   Harokopio University, Japan

Javier Nogueras Iso	University of Zaragoza, Spain
Monica Palmirani	CIRSFID, Italy
Aljosa Pasic	Atos Origin, France
Aires Rover	Universidade Federal de Santa Catarina, Brazil
Christian Rupp	Joint eGovernment and Open Data Innovation Lab, Austria
Erich Schweighofer	University of Vienna, Austria
Henning Sten-Hansen	Aalborg University, Denmark
A Min Tjoa	Vienna University of Technology, Austria
Julián Valero-Torrijos	University of Murcia, Spain
Costas Vassilakis	University of the Peloponnese, Greece
Gianluigi Viscusi	EPFL-CDM-CSI, Switzerland
Christopher C. Wills	Caris Research Ltd., UK
Robert Woitsch	BOC Asset Management, Austria
Chien-Chih Yu	National Chengchi University, Taiwan

Organizers

Institute for
Telecooperation

International Organization for

www.iiwas.org

Information Integration and
Web-based Applications & Services

Contents

Knowledge Representation
and Modeling in e-Government

Hybrid Refining Approach of PrOnto Ontology

Monica Palmirani[1]([⊠]) [iD], Giorgia Bincoletto[1] [iD], Valentina Leone[2] [iD],
Salvatore Sapienza[1] [iD], and Francesco Sovrano[3] [iD]

[1] CIRSFID, University of Bologna, Bologna, Italy
{monica.palmirani,giorgia.bincoletto2,
salvatore.sapienza}@unibo.it
[2] Computer Science Department, University of Turin, Turin, Italy
leone@di.unito.it
[3] DISI, University of Bologna, Bologna, Italy
francesco.sovrano2@unibo.it

Abstract. This paper presents a refinement of PrOnto ontology using a validation test based on legal experts' annotation of privacy policies combined with an Open Knowledge Extraction (OKE) algorithm. To ensure robustness of the results while preserving an interdisciplinary approach, the integration of legal and technical knowledge has been carried out as follows. The set of privacy policies was first analysed by the legal experts to discover legal concepts and map the text into PrOnto. The mapping was then provided to computer scientists to perform the OKE analysis. Results were validated by the legal experts, who provided feedbacks and refinements (i.e. new classes and modules) of the ontology according to MeLOn methodology. Three iterations were performed on a set of (development) policies, and a final test using a new set of privacy policies. The results are 75,43% of detection of concepts in the policy texts and an increase of roughly 33% in the accuracy gain on the test set, using the new refined version of PrOnto enriched with SKOS-XL lexicon terms and definitions.

Keywords: Legal ontology · GDPR · OKE · Refinement

1 Introduction

We have already published several papers about PrOnto ontology [24, 26–28] which aims to model the concepts and their relationships presented in the GDPR (General Data Protection Regulation EU 2016/679). PrOnto is a core ontology that started with a top-down method, using MeLOn methodology, based on a strong legal informatics analysis of GDPR normative provisions and their interpretations issued by Art. 29 WP (now, European Data Protection Board) through its opinions. PrOnto intends to represent data types and documents, agents and roles, processing purposes, legal bases (Art. 6 GDPR), processing operations, and deontic operations for modelling rights (Chapter 3, Artt. 12–23 GDPR) and duties (Chapter 4, Artt. 24–43 GDPR). The goals of PrOnto are:

© Springer Nature Switzerland AG 2020
A. Kő et al. (Eds.): EGOVIS 2020, LNCS 12394, pp. 3–17, 2020.
https://doi.org/10.1007/978-3-030-58957-8_1

i. supporting legal reasoning;
ii. compliance checking by employing defeasible logic theory (i.e., the LegalRuleML standard and the SPINDle engine [25]);
iii. helping the legal design visualisation based on robust theoretical legal conceptualisation [32];
iv. supporting information retrieval.

Taken together, these goals also contribute to the ongoing research on legal and regulatory aspects of data protection and privacy, in particular as regards the promotion of wide access to trustworthy legal information. In the previous papers the validation was carried out by legal experts (e.g., PhD students and researchers) and through SPARQL[1] queries on the basis of some RDF[2] triples. This article presents a different validation process of PrOnto ontology using – following the application of a robust theoretical and foundational top-down methodology – a bottom-up approach, starting from the language adopted in real examples of Privacy Policies. The research investigates:

i. if the existing PrOnto classes are sufficiently exhaustive to support NLP tools in detecting GDPR concepts directly from Privacy Policies;
ii. if some classes are missing with respect to the pragmatic language forms;
iii. if some frequent terminology could be added to the conceptualisation modelling using e.g., SKOS-XL[3] and so help the Open Knowledge Extraction (OKE) tools to support search engine goals;
iv. whether it is possible to create a ML tool that is capable of detecting GDPR concepts in the Privacy Policies and so to classify them with PrOnto creating RDF triples.

The paper first examines the used methodology; secondly, it presents the legal analysis of the Privacy Policies chosen for the validation and the related mapping of the linguistic terminology in the PrOnto classes; then, the work describes the ML technique applied to detect the PrOnto concepts from the other Privacy Policies and its results; finally, the conclusion discusses the refinements made to the PrOnto ontology thanks to the validation with the Privacy Policies.

2 Methodology

PrOnto was developed through an interdisciplinary approach called MeLOn (Methodology for building Legal Ontology) and it is explicitly designed in order to minimise the difficulties encountered by the legal operators during the definition of a legal ontology. MeLOn applies a top-down methodology on legal sources. It is strongly based on reusing

---

[1] https://www.w3.org/TR/sparql11-query/, last accessed 2020/06/19.

[2] https://www.w3.org/TR/rdf11-concepts/, last accessed 2020/06/19.

[3] https://www.w3.org/TR/skos-reference/skos-xl.html, last accessed 2020/06/19.

ontology patterns [15][4] and the results are evaluated using foundational ontology (e.g., DOLCE [11]) and using OntoClean [14] method. Finally, the validation is made by an interdisciplinary group that includes engineers, lawyers, linguists, logicians and ontologists. Hence, the legal knowledge modelling is performed rapidly and accurately while integrating the contributions of different disciplines.

For these reasons, the methodology of this research is based on the following pillars taking inspiration from other research in the legal data analytics [2, 3, 37]:

1. two legal experts selected ten privacy policies from US-based companies providing products and services to European citizens; so, the GDPR is applied according to its territorial scope (Art. 3);
2. the privacy policies were analysed using the comparative legal method to discover the frequent concepts mentioned in the texts and how they express the legal bases (Art. 6 GDPR), the purposes, the data subject's rights and the duties of the controller, some particular processes like information society services for children (Art. 8 GDPR), profiling and automatic decision-making systems (Art. 22 GDPR), processing of sensitive data (Art. 9 GDPR) and data transfer to third countries (Chapter 5 GDPR);
3. selected portions of text were mapped into the PrOnto ontology with also different linguistic variations, including syntagma. A table summarising the main linguistic expressions related to each PrOnto classes was set up;
4. this mapping was provided to the computer science team that used Open Knowledge Extraction technique starting from the GDPR lexicon, PrOnto ontology and the literal form variants to annotate the Privacy Policies;
5. results were validated by the legal team that returned the feedbacks to the technical team. In the meantime, they also discussed on some possible refinements of PrOnto ontology, following the MeLOn methodology, in order to better model the legal concepts (e.g., they proposed to add classes for Legal Basis);
6. the steps from 2 to 5 were iterated three times using the results of the algorithm in order to refine the ontology and the software model;
7. finally, new Privacy Policies were selected by the legal experts[5] in order to evaluate the effectiveness of the refined algorithm and ontology.

3   Legal Analysis of the Privacy Policies

We have selected ten Privacy Policies from an equal number of companies. The policies were extracted from the dedicated sections of the companies' websites made available to European visitors. We chose these companies due to their international dimension, their relevance in their market sectors and the diversity of data processing techniques.

---

[4] PrOnto reuses existing ontologies ALLOT [4] FRBR [19], LKIF [6] we use in particular lkif:Agent to model lkif:Organization, lkif:Person and lkif:Role [6], the Publishing Workflow Ontology (PWO) [13], Time-indexed Value in Context (TVC) and Time Interval [30]. Now with this work we include also SKOS-XL [5, 8].

[5] Rover, Parkclick, Springer, Zalando, Louis Vuitton, Burger King, Microsoft-Skype, Lufthansa, Booking, Zurich Insurance.

The Privacy Policies were analysed using the following macro-areas to follow a comparative method: sale of goods, supply of services and sharing economy. We compared for each macro-area the linguistic terms and we distinguished between the legal strict terminologies (e.g., data subject) and the communicative language (e.g., customer or user) (Table 1).

Table 1. List of the privacy policies analysed.

Sale of goods	Amazon	Dell	McDonalds	Nike
Supply of services	American Airlines	TripAdvisor	Hertz	Allianz U.S.
Sharing economy	AirBnb	Uber		

The legal experts have manually reviewed the Privacy Policies to discover the concepts of legal relevance for data protection domain (provisions, legal doctrine, Art. 29 WP/EDPB and case law) that are remarkably recurrent in the text. The interpretation has also kept into account the existing version of PrOnto ontology, in particular to identify the different wording that expresses the same concept recognised through a legal analysis at an equal level of abstraction. Occasionally these terms present different forms as the companies work in different sectors and across multiple jurisdictions. Thus, these forms have been analysed, compared and eventually included in the PrOnto ontology, using techniques like SKOS-XL for adding the different linguistic forms (e.g., skosxl:leteralForm). This extension of PrOnto definitely improves the capacity of the OKE tools to detect the correct fragment of text and to isolate the legal concept as well as populating the PrOnto ontology. We also noted that the Privacy Policies tend to use the ordinary, everyday language for reasons of transparency and comprehensibility of the texts. Despite the advantage for the costumer/user, the analysis underlined that certain terminologies are not accurate from a legal perspective. When a manual or NLP-assisted analysis is performed, such legal nuance is more difficult to detect. For instance, the expression "giving permission" is a communicative substitute of "giving consent" and "obtain consent", which implies the freely given, informed, unambiguous and specific nature of the data subject's agreement. This choice is probably made to simplify the expression and highlighting transparency. Another example is the sentence "you can also update your personal data" which does not convey the deontic specification of the right to request rectification of personal data (Art. 16 GDPR).

Moreover, after the analysis it can be argued that some terminologies are misused because the ordinary language in the policy does not reflect the legal sense. As an example, in the sentence "*otherwise anonymized (anonymous data), aggregate or anonymous information*" the type "anonymous data" (Recital 26 GDPR) is not in the scope of the Regulation and it is misled with "anonymised data". This type is a personal data handled to become anonymous by means of a sophisticated technical process (e.g., generalisation, aggregation, permutation, etc.). The same issue can be found in the statement "*when collecting or transferring sensitive information, such as credit card details*": the definition of sensitive or special category of data does not include any kind of financial information (Recital 10, 51, Art. 9 GDPR). In these cases, the PrOnto ontology should steer the technical detection of the legal concepts. Furthermore, we found that certain terminology is borrowed from the computer science domain and goes beyond the legal provisions. For instance, the forms *"to hash"*, *"log files"*, *"use encryption"* convey a technical meaning that is not used by GDPR requirements as the Regulation has been drafted in a technically neutral way.

4   PrOnto Mapping and New Modules

Following this analysis, we have mapped the synthesis of the different lexicon expressions with the PrOnto classes and this table was the basis for creating mapping between lexicon (terms and definitions) and taxonomy of concepts (classes). This step immediately allowed to detect some missing modules that are described below.

4.1   Legal Basis Module

Under the GDPR, personal data processing (Art. 4.1(2) GDPR) is lawful only if motivated by a purpose that must be legitimated by a legal basis (see Art. 6 GDPR on the lawfulness of processing). Therefore, a lawfulness status was needed and was thus added as a Boolean data property of the `PersonalDataProcessing` class. However, from the validation using Privacy Policies, it is extremely important to elicit the `LegalBasis` class because several other implications (rights, obligations, actions) depends to the kind of legal basis (e.g., Art. 22 GDPR). For this reason, we have modelled the following new module (see Fig. 1 the new classes are displayed in orange).

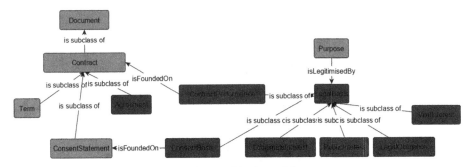

Fig. 1. Legal basis module.

4.2   Purpose Module

"Archiving" and "Services" are encountered frequently among the purposes of processing described in the Privacy Policies and they are added to the `Purpose` module, with also an important kind of service (`InformationSocietyService`) relevant in the child privacy management (Art. 8 GDPR) (see Fig. 2).

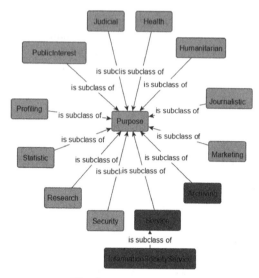

Fig. 2. Purpose module.

4.3 Obligations and Rights Module

The Privacy Policies underlined some rights with the related obligations, like the `ObligationToProvideHumanIntervention` connected with `RightToHaveHumanIntervention` and related with `AutomaticDecisionMaking` that is a new action added to the `Action` module (see Fig. 3).

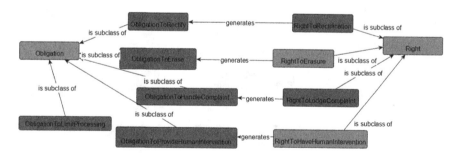

Fig. 3. New rights and obligations.

5   Open Information Extraction for Legal Domain

Taking inspiration from the PrOnto ontology, we extracted GDPR concepts from Privacy Policies through a tool conceptually based on ClausIE [9]. ClausIE is a clause-based approach to Open Information Extraction (Open IE), that exploits linguistic knowledge about the grammar of the English language to first detect clauses in an input sentence and to subsequently identify the type of each clause according to the grammatical function of its constituents. The goal of Open IE is to build information graphs representing natural language text in the form of SVO (Subject, Verb, Object) triples (please note that this is slightly different from building RDF graphs).

The main difference between our tool and ClausIE is that our tool extracts SVO triples by using a Spacy's[6] state-of-the-art dependency parser based on Neural Networks.

One of the main issues arising from exploiting such dependency parser might be that the parser has been trained on common language rather than legislative texts and rhetoric sentences, thus making it less effective in a legal context. Despite this, we argue that our choice is meaningful and correct for our specific application, since policy's text is usually simpler and it uses common language to be more understandable.

Identifying SVO triples through dependency parsers based on Neural Networks was used in other relevant works and several problems arise:

i.   linguistic variants of the same legal concept inside the agreement/contract text are numerous and they include some overlapping of meaning; Thus, it is hard to understand whether two different words have the same meaning.
ii. Legal provisions sometime are written in passive form in order to make more emphasis on prescriptiveness when addressing the command. This sometimes complicates the extraction of SVO triples.
iii. Legal text has normative references that affect the knowledge extraction.
iv. Legal concepts change over time.
v.   frequency is not a good indicator of relevance [35].

The main difference between many classical Open IE techniques and ClausIE is that the latter makes use of the grammatical dependencies extracted through an automatic dependency parser, to identify the SVO triples. ClausIE is able to identify SVO triples, but we need also to correctly associate them to ontology terms and their literal variants provided by the legal expert-team. Let the GDPR and the Privacy Policies be our corpus C. In order to perform the automatic text annotation of our corpus with PrOnto concepts, we follow these steps:

1. we firstly identify a list of all the terms (subjects, objects, verbs) in C, by using a simple variant of ClauseIE. The identified terms are said to be possible classes (in the case of subjects and objects) or possible properties (in the case of verbs);
2. we extract PrOnto's labels of classes and properties, with additional mapping of linguistic and lexical variants;
3. we try to map every possible class/property in C to its closest class/property in PrOnto, by using the same algorithm used in a previous project[7] [34]. This algorithm exploits pre-trained linguistic deep models in order to be able to easily compute a similarity score between two terms.

---

[6] https://spacy.io, last accessed 2020/06/19.
[7] https://gitlab.com/CIRSFID/un-challange-2019, last accessed 2020/06/19.

Ontologies are a formal way to describe classes, relationships and axioms. For this work we focus mainly on classes and properties and their literal forms, without taking into account the other types of knowledge usually coded into an ontology (e.g., Tbox).

Furthermore, especially in the case of Privacy Policies, we may expect important concepts not to be distributed uniformly across the whole text. Some important concepts (a.k.a *local*) are usually mentioned only in very specific document areas (e.g., chapters), while others (a.k.a *global*) are scattered throughout the whole text. If the Privacy Policies were marked up using Akoma Ntoso we could use the structure of the XML nodes for better detecting the concepts and properly apply the characteristics *local/global*.

6   PrOnto Refinement

The Privacy Policies linguistic analysis with OKE gives some inputs that produce important enhancements in PrOnto ontology.

6.1   Child Class

In the Privacy Policies is frequently mentioned "*child*" that is a particular "data subject" missing in the PrOnto ontology. Initially, we intended to use rules to define child concept because the definition changes for each jurisdiction according to the local implementation of the EU Regulation[8]. However, in light of the important rights and obligations defined in the GDPR for the minors, we decided finally to include a new class in the `Role` module as subclass of `DataSubject`. `Child` class is related with `ParentalResponsabilityHolder` (see Fig. 4).

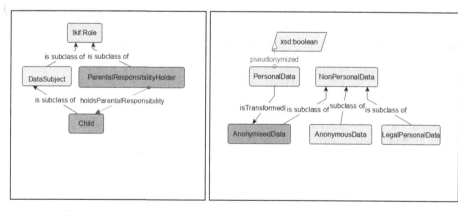

Fig. 4. Child class.   **Fig. 5.** Anonymised data class.

---

[8] https://www.betterinternetforkids.eu/web/portal/practice/awareness/detail?articleId=3017751, last accessed 2020/06/19.

6.2 Anonymous Data and Anonymised Data Classes

From the Privacy Policies linguistic analysis it emerges that "Anonymised Data"[9] and "Anonymous data" (Recital 26 GDPR)[10] are often misled and confused in the presentation of the data processing. The pragmatic language attempts to simplify the legal terminology and creates a mistake in the conceptualisation of those two classes of data that are ontologically different. For this reason, we modelled the relationship `Person-alData isTransformedIn AnonymisedData` in order to clarify the distinction from the legal point of view (See Fig. 5).

6.3 Action Module

The best manner to detect an action is through verbs. However, within OWL ontology, verbs play the role of predicates that connect domain and range. For this reason, the OKE suggested to modify the action's classes with the "ing" form. Some new actions are detected like `Collecting` and `Profiling`. The legal analysis collocates the `Profiling` class as subclass of `AutomatedDecisionMaking` following Art. 22 and the connected Recital 71. In this case, the OKE feedbacks offered a very good input to the legal experts that provided an improvement of the legal ontology by relying on their legal analysis (see Fig. 6).

7 Lexicon Modelling in PrOnto

After the validation with OKE, it was evident that it is important to connect the legal concepts to lexical forms. We have chosen to use SKOS and SKOS-XL that is a canonical method for connecting OWL and linguistic variants, using `skosxl:literalform`.

---

[9] COM (2019) 250 final "data which were initially personal data, but were later made anonymous. The 'anonymisation' of personal data is different to pseudonymisation (see above), as properly anonymised data cannot be attributed to a specific person, not even by use of additional data and are therefore non-personal data".

[10] Recital 26 GDPR "5. The principles of data protection should therefore not apply to anonymous information, namely information which does not relate to an identified or identifiable natural person or to personal data rendered anonymous in such a manner that the data subject is not or no longer identifiable. 6. This Regulation does not therefore concern the processing of such anonymous information, including for statistical or research purposes".

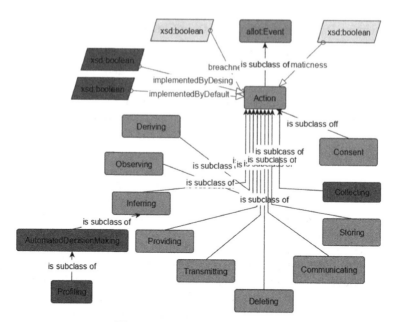

Fig. 6. Action module refinement.

```
PrOnto:Controller rdf:type owl:Class;
rdfs:subClassOf PrOnto:Role;
rdfs:subClassOf skos:Concept.

PrOnto:DataController rdf:type PrOnto:Controller;
skosxl:prefLabel PrOnto:controller_1;
skosxl:altLabel
PrOnto:altController_1,PrOnto:altController_2,
PrOnto:altController_3.

PrOnto:controller_1 rdf:type skosxl:Label;
skosxl:literalForm "controller"@en;
dct: created "2018-05-28"^^xsd:date;
dct: modified "2019-09-15"^^xsd:date.

PrOnto:altcontroller_1 rdf:type skosxl:Label;
skosxl:literalForm "data controller"@en.
PrOnto:altcontroller_2 rdf:type skosxl:Label;
skosxl:literalForm "company data controller"@en.
PrOnto:altController_3 rdf:type skosxl:Label;
  skosxl:literalForm "company that is responsible for your in-
formation"@en.
```

In this manner, it is possible to connect PrOnto Core Ontology with other existing lexicon-controlled vocabulary [18].

8   Related Work

We have at least four main related works to exam in this research.

Privacy Ontology. UsablePrivacy and PrivOnto [23] are ontologies oriented to provide linguistic tools in order to define glossaries and taxonomies for the privacy domain, basically starting from the bottom-up annotation of the privacy policies (crowdsourcing annotation). GDPRtEXT [29] lists concepts presented in the GDPR text without really entering the modelling of the norms and the legal axioms (e.g., the actions performed by the processor, the obligations of the controller and the rights of the data subject). GDPRov aims at describing the provenance of the consent and data lifecycle in the light of the Linked Open Data principles such as Fairness and Trust [30]. GConsent is an ontology for modelling the consent action, statement and actors [16]. The SPECIAL Project[11] develops tools for checking compliance in the privacy domain.

Deontic Ontology. ODRL provides predicates and classes for managing obligations, permission, prohibitions, but several parts of the deontic logic are missing (e.g., right and penalty classes). LegalRuleML ontology was included in PrOnto.

Lexicon Ontology. Controlled vocabularies, thesauri and lexical databases are some examples of linguistic ontologies. They express the terminology concerning a domain of interest by organising terms according to few semantic relations (e.g. hierarchical and associative ones). EUROVOC[12] and IATE[13] are some examples of linguistic ontologies released by the European Union to semantically structure the terminology of documents issued by EU institutions and bodies [33]. However, these resources do not clarify the distinction between legal concepts and their instances [20].

By contrast, the legal domain requires the modelling of legal core concepts, capable to overcome the vagueness of legal jargon that makes the meaning of legal terms subject to interpretation [20]. Thus, the modelling of legal core ontologies is a complex task involving knowledge grounded on legal theory, legal doctrine and legal sociology [10].

Several models have been proposed as natural language interfaces to fill the gap between the high-level ontological concepts and their low-level, context-dependent lexicalisations [22]. In particular, interesting works about SKOS-XL[14][8] and OntoLex [5] [17] are included in this version of PrOnto for combining ontology and linguistic literal forms, in support for NLP and search engines.

Open Knowledge Extraction. Open Information Extraction (Open IE) is to Open Knowledge Extraction (Open KE) as NLP (processing) and NLU (understanding). Open IE is capable to extract information graphs from natural language. Remarkable examples of Open IE tools are ClausIE [9], OpenCeres [21] and Inter-Clause Open IE [1], Open KE builds over Open IE in order to align the identified subjects, predicates and

---

[11] https://www.specialprivacy.eu/, last accessed 2020/06/19.

[12] https://publications.europa.eu/en/web/eu-vocabularies/th-dataset/-/resource/dataset/eurovoc, last accessed 2020/06/19.

[13] https://iate.europa.eu/, last accessed 2020/06/19.

[14] https://www.w3.org/TR/skos-reference/skos-xl.html, last accessed 2020/06/19.

objects (SVOs) to pre-defined ontologies. FRED [13] uses different NLP techniques for processing text and for extracting a raw ontology based on FrameNet situations. The challenge of Open KE is that the SVOs alignment requires to understand the meaning of ambiguous and context-dependent terms [36]. The algorithm we designed tackles the Open KE problem by exploiting pre-trained linguistic deep models in order to map information to knowledge.

PrOnto includes an exhaustive strong top-down modelling reinforced with a bottom-up linguistic approach. This approach guarantees the modelling of institutions of law with a robust theoretical approach not prone to the variants of the language (that can change by country, context, historical period). In the meantime, this work refined the classes (e.g., `Child`), the relationships (e.g., `holdsParentalResponsibility`) and the correlated terminology (e.g., customer/user) using the OKE.

9   Conclusions and Future Work

We have validated the PrOnto ontology with a sample of Privacy Policies and with a robust legal analysis following the MeLOn methodology, in order to manually check the completeness of the classes and relationships for representing the main content of the policies texts. This exercise detected some new needs in the PrOnto ontology (e.g., the `LegalBasis` module) that originally the team decided to not to include. The legal team detected some inconsistencies in the terminologies between the legislative text and the pragmatic language, which may prevent a clear interpretation of the legal terms frequently used in the context of privacy policies especially by authorities and public institutions. For this reason, the legal team produced a map of lexicon variants, then modelled using SKOS-XL. PrOnto and these extensions fill up an Open Knowledge Extraction algorithm to detect concepts in the Privacy Policies. The method was iterated three times and at the end we obtained an increase of 33% in the detection of concepts (accuracy gain) on the test set (a.k.a. 2nd set of privacy policies; or new policies), with respect to the first interaction that record an increase of 22%. We are capable to detect the 75% of the concept in the new privacy policies using the new version of PrOnto enriched with SKOS-XL terms. For the future, we intend to perform the same experiment using Consent Statements and also Code of Conducts. This work confirmed the robustness of PrOnto main modules, pattern-oriented and aligned with foundational ones, and in the future this work will be used in order to validate (e.g., with different type of legal documents), refine (e.g., extend with new modules like national customised-US), update (e.g., due to legislative modifications of the GDPR) the PrOnto schema design. This method is also relevant to annotate legal texts with PrOnto and so to create RDF triples for supporting applications (e.g., search engine, legal reasoning, checking compliance).

Acknowledgements. This work was partially supported by the European Union's Horizon 2020 research and innovation programme under the Marie Skłodowska-Curie grant agreement No 690974 "MIREL: MIning and REasoning with Legal texts".

Appendix

In this section we will provide additional data (technical results and measurements) resulting from the experiments described in this paper. More precisely, we present the statistics obtained from the experiments on both the first and the second set of privacy policies.

First Set of Privacy Policies (Development Set)

PrOnto version	SKOS support	Found ontology concepts	Ontology concepts	Presence	Accuracy gain
8	No	87	139	62,65%	0%
9	No	111	172	64,91%	27,58%
9	Yes	123	172	71,92%	41,37%

Second Set of Privacy Policies (Test Set)

PrOnto version	SKOS support	Found ontology concepts	Ontology concepts	Presence	Accuracy gain
8	No	97	139	69,78%	0%
9	No	119	172	69,59%	22,68%
9	Yes	129	172	75,43%	32,98%

Where:

- The "**Accuracy Gain**" is computed as (x2 - x1)/x1, where x1 is the number of "**Found Ontology Concepts**" with PrOnto v8 without SKOS support and x2 is the number of "**Found Ontology Concepts**" of any of the other versions of PrOnto.
- The "**Presence**" is computed as the ratio of "**Found Ontology Concepts**" and "**Ontology Concepts**".
- "**Ontology Concepts**" is the total number of concepts in the ontology.
- "**Found Ontology Concepts**" is the number of concepts of the ontology that have been identified by the OKE tool in the set of policies. "**Found Ontology Concepts**" is always lower than "**Ontology Concepts**".
- "**SKOS Support**" is a boolean indicating whether it has been used SKOS support or not.
- "**PrOnto Version**" indicates the version of PrOnto.

References

1. Angeli, G., Premkumar, M.J.J., Manning, C.D.: Leveraging linguistic structure for open domain information extraction. In: Proceedings of the 53rd Annual Meeting of the Association for Computational Linguistics and the 7th International Joint Conference on Natural Language Processing, vol. 1: Long Papers, pp. 344–354 (2015)

2. Ashley, K.D.: Artificial intelligence and Legal Analytics: New Tools for Law Practice in the Digital Age. Cambridge University Press, Cambridge (2017)
3. Bandeira, J., Bittencourt, I.I., Espinheira, P., Isotani, S.: FOCA: a methodology for ontology evaluation. Eprint ArXiv (2016)
4. Barabucci, G., Cervone, L., Di Iorio, A., Palmirani, M., Peroni, S., Vitali, F.: Managing semantics in XML vocabularies: an experience in the legal and legislative domain. In: Proceedings of Balisage: The Markup Conference, vol. 5 (2010)
5. Bosque-Gil, J., Gracia, J., Montiel-Ponsoda E.: Towards a module for lexicography in OntoLex. In: Proceedings of the LDK Workshops: OntoLex, TIAD and Challenges for Wordnets at 1st Language Data and Knowledge Conference (LDK 2017), Galway, Ireland, vol. 1899, pp. 74–84. CEUR-WS (2017)
6. Breuker, J., et al.: OWL Ontology of Basic Legal Concepts (LKIF-Core), Deliverable No. 1.4. IST-2004-027655 ESTRELLA: European project for Standardised Transparent Representations in order to Extend Legal Accessibility (2007)
7. Cer, D., et al.: Universal sentence encoder. arXiv preprint arXiv:1803.11175 (2018)
8. Declerck, T., Egorova, K., Schnur, E.: An integrated formal representation for terminological and lexical data included in classification schemes. In: Proceedings of the Eleventh International Conference on Language Resources and Evaluation (LREC-2018) (2018)
9. Del Corro, L., Gemulla, R.: ClausIE: clause-based open information extraction. In: Proceedings of the 22nd International Conference on World Wide Web, pp. 355–366. ACM (2013)
10. Fernández-Barrera, M., Sartor, G.: The legal theory perspective: doctrinal conceptual systems vs. computational ontologies. In: Sartor, G., Casanovas, P., Biasiotti, M., Fernández-Barrera, M. (eds.) Approaches to Legal Ontologies. Law, Governance and Technology Series, vol. 1, pp. 15–47. Springer, Dordrecht (2011). https://doi.org/10.1007/978-94-007-0120-5_2
11. Gangemi, A., Guarino, N., Masolo, C., Oltramari, A., Schneider, L.: Sweetening ontologies with DOLCE. In: Gómez-Pérez, A., Benjamins, V.R. (eds.) EKAW 2002. LNCS (LNAI), vol. 2473, pp. 166–181. Springer, Heidelberg (2002). https://doi.org/10.1007/3-540-45810-7_18
12. Gangemi, A., Peroni, S., Shotton, D., Vitali, F.: The publishing workflow ontology (PWO). Semant. Web **8**, 703–718 (2017). https://doi.org/10.3233/SW-160230
13. Gangemi, A., Presutti, V., Reforgiato Recupero, D., Nuzzolese, A.G., Draicchio, F., Mongiovì, M.: Semantic web machine reading with FRED. Semant. Web **8**(6), 873–893 (2017)
14. Guarino, N., Welty, C.A.: An overview of OntoClean. In: Staab, S., Studer, R. (eds.) Handbook on Ontologies. International Handbooks on Information Systems, pp. 151–171. Springer, Heidelberg (2004). https://doi.org/10.1007/978-3-540-24750-0_8
15. Hitzler, P., Gangemi, A., Janowicz, K., Krisnadhi, A. (eds.): Ontology Engineering with Ontology Design Patterns: Foundations and Applications. Studies on the Semantic Web. IOS Press, Amsterdam (2016)
16. http://openscience.adaptcentre.ie/ontologies/GConsent/docs/ontology. Accessed 19 June 2020
17. http://www.w3.org/2016/05/ontolex. Accessed 19 June 2020
18. https://www.w3.org/ns/dpv#data-controller. Accessed 19 June 2020
19. IFLA Study Group on the Functional Requirements for Bibliographic Records. Functional Requirements for Bibliographic Records. IFLA Series on Bibliographic Control. De Gruyter Saur (1996)
20. Liebwald, D.: Law's capacity for vagueness. International Journal for the Semiotics of Law-Revue internationale de Sémiotique juridique **26**(2), 391–423 (2012)
21. Lockard, C., Shiralkar, P., Dong, X.L.: OpenCeres: when open information extraction meets the semi-structured web. In: Proceedings of the 2019 Conference of the North American Chapter of the Association for Computational Linguistics: Human Language Technologies, vol. 1 (Long and Short Papers), pp. 3047–3056 (2019)

22. McCrae, J., Spohr, D., Cimiano, P.: Linking lexical resources and ontologies on the semantic web with lemon. In: Antoniou, G., et al. (eds.) ESWC 2011. LNCS, vol. 6643, pp. 245–259. Springer, Heidelberg (2011). https://doi.org/10.1007/978-3-642-21034-1_17

23. Oltramari, A., et al.: PrivOnto: a semantic framework for the analysis of privacy policies. Semant. Web, 1–19 (2016)

24. Palmirani, M., Bincoletto, G., Leone, V., Sapienza, S., Sovrano, F.: PrOnto ontology refinement through open knowledge extraction. In: Jurix 2019 Proceedings, pp. 205–210 (2019)

25. Palmirani, M., Governatori, G.: Modelling legal knowledge for GDPR compliance checking. In: JURIX 2018 Proceedings, pp. 101–110 (2018)

26. Palmirani, M., Martoni, M., Rossi, A., Bartolini, C., Robaldo, L.: PrOnto: privacy ontology for legal reasoning. In: Kő, A., Francesconi, E. (eds.) EGOVIS 2018. LNCS, vol. 11032, pp. 139–152. Springer, Cham (2018). https://doi.org/10.1007/978-3-319-98349-3_11

27. Palmirani, M., Martoni, M., Rossi, A., Bartolini, C., Robaldo, L.: Legal ontology for modelling GDPR concepts and norms. In: JURIX 2018 Proceedings, pp. 91–100 (2018)

28. Palmirani, M., Martoni, M., Rossi, A., Bartolini, C., Robaldo, L.: PrOnto: privacy ontology for legal compliance. In: Proceedings of the 18th European Conference on Digital Government ECDG 2018, Reading UK, Academic Conferences and Publishing International Limited, 2018, pp. 142–151 (2018)

29. Pandit, H.J., Fatema, K., O'Sullivan, D., Lewis, D.: GDPRtEXT - GDPR as a linked data resource. In: Gangemi, A., et al. (eds.) ESWC 2018. LNCS, vol. 10843, pp. 481–495. Springer, Cham (2018). https://doi.org/10.1007/978-3-319-93417-4_31

30. Pandit, H.J., Lewis, D.: Modelling provenance for gdpr compliance using linked open data vocabularies. In: Proceedings of the 5th Workshop on Society, Privacy and the Semantic Web - Policy and Technology (PrivOn2017) co-located with the 16th International Semantic Web Conference (ISWC 2017) (2017)

31. Peroni, S., Palmirani, M., Vitali, F.: UNDO: the united nations system document ontology. In: d'Amato, C., et al. (eds.) ISWC 2017. LNCS, vol. 10588, pp. 175–183. Springer, Cham (2017). https://doi.org/10.1007/978-3-319-68204-4_18

32. Rossi, A., Palmirani, M.: DaPIS: an ontology-based data protection icon set. In: Peruginelli, G., Faro, S. (eds.) Knowledge of the Law in the Big Data Age. Frontiers in Artificial Intelligence and Applications, vol. 317. IOS Press (2019)

33. Roussey, C., Pinet, F., Kang, M.A., Corcho, O.: An introduction to ontologies and ontology engineering. In: Falquet, G., Métral, C., Teller, J., Tweed, C. (eds.) Ontologies in Urban Development Projects. Advanced Information and Knowledge Processing, vol. 1, pp. 9–38. Springer, London (2011). https://doi.org/10.1007/978-0-85729-724-2_2

34. Sovrano, F., Palmirani, M., Vitali, F.: Deep learning based multi-label text classification of UNGA resolutions. arXiv preprint arXiv:2004.03455 (2020)

35. van Opijnen, M., Santos, C.: On the concept of relevance in legal information retrieval. Artif. Intell. Law 25(1), 65–87 (2017). https://doi.org/10.1007/s10506-017-9195-8

36. Welty, Chris, Murdock, J.W.: Towards knowledge acquisition from information extraction. In: Cruz, Isabel, Decker, Stefan, Allemang, Dean, Preist, Chris, Schwabe, Daniel, Mika, Peter, Uschold, Mike, Aroyo, Lora M. (eds.) ISWC 2006. LNCS, vol. 4273, pp. 709–722. Springer, Heidelberg (2006). https://doi.org/10.1007/11926078_51

37. Wilson, S., et al.: Analyzing privacy policies at scale: from crowdsourcing to automated annotations. ACM Trans. Web 13, 1 (2018)

Ranking E-government Ontologies on the Semantic Web

Jean Vincent Fonou-Dombeu[(⌨)]

School of Mathematics, Statistics and Computer Science,
University of KwaZulu-Natal, King Edward Avenue,
Scottsville, Pietermaritzburg 3209, South Africa
`fonoudombeuj@ukzn.ac.za`

Abstract. The field of e-government has been an attractive area of ontology development in the past years, resulting in an increase in the number of e-government ontologies on the web. The availability of these ontologies gives the opportunity to reuse them in future e-government projects rather than trying to develop similar ontologies *de novo*. This study aims to promote the selection and reuse of e-government ontologies on the web, through the provision of a ranked list of existing e-government ontologies on the basis of their quality metrics. A number of 23 e-government ontologies are downloaded on the web and their quality metrics are computed with the OntoMetrics online ontology evaluation environment. Thereafter, a decision making algorithm is applied to rank the e-government ontologies based on the aggregation of their quality metrics. The decision scheme is constituted of the 23 e-government ontologies or alternatives and their 11 quality metrics or attributes. The experimental results yielded an ordered list of the 23 inputs e-government ontologies ranked according to their quality metrics. This may provide some insights on the selection and reuse of these ontologies in future e-government projects.

Keywords: E-government · ELECTRE · Ontology · Ontology ranking · OntoMetrics

1 Introduction

The field of e-government has been an attractive area of ontology development in the past years. This is evidenced by recent studies on ontology development in e-government [1–3] as well as extensive reviews of previous use of ontologies in e-government [4,5]. Furthermore, the advent of linked/open data and open government have increased the number of e-government ontologies on the web [6]. The fact that some of the existing e-government ontologies are readily available for download on the internet today provides an opportunity to select and reuse them in other e-government projects rather than trying to reinvent the wheel by building similar ontologies *de novo*.

© Springer Nature Switzerland AG 2020
A. Kő et al. (Eds.): EGOVIS 2020, LNCS 12394, pp. 18–30, 2020.
https://doi.org/10.1007/978-3-030-58957-8_2

The benefits of reusing existing e-government ontologies would be the reduction of the time and cost for developing semantic-based e-government applications as well as the number of experts needed. In fact, it is argued in the ontology engineering literature that the development of a new ontology from scratch demands the involvement of experts, is expensive and tedious [7]. Experts may be required to approve the ontology design in terms of its concepts and semantic relations or to assist in the encoding of the new ontology in a format that can be processed by computers with formal languages such as the Resource Description Framework (RDF) and Web Ontology Language (OWL). Furthermore, the scale of the domain of interest may require the experts to work collaboratively from various geographical locations; this may also bring some challenges in terms of coordination and delay. Moreover, the fact that the existing ontologies have already been tested and approved in other projects may guarantee the quality of the new applications that are reusing them.

In spite of the advantages of ontology reuse, the users or ontology engineers must be able to select the suitable ontologies they want to reuse from the available ontologies in a domain. This is a challenging task to date because of the growing number of ontologies that are being created and loaded onto the web. This increase in the number of ontologies over the web is supported by the emergence of topics such as linked/open/big data, ontologies libraries as well as the growing use of semantic technologies in industries, organizations and governments. The problem of choosing the right ontologies for reuse amongst the available ontologies in a domain is a decision making problem [8,9]. To deal with this problem, one of the approaches has been the ranking of ontologies on the basis of a certain criteria. However, most of the existing ontology ranking solutions [10,11] did not use the advanced and popular methods such as the decision-making techniques [12]. Furthermore, none of the previous studies on ontology ranking has focused on the ranking of e-government ontologies.

In light of the above, this study aims to promote the selection and reuse of e-government ontologies on the web, through the provision of a ranked list of existing e-government ontologies on the basis of their quality metrics. A number of 23 e-government ontologies are downloaded from various repositories on the web and their quality metrics are computed with the OntoMetrics online ontology evaluation environment. Thereafter, a decision making algorithm, namely, Elimination and Choice Translating REality (ELECTRE) is applied to rank the e-government ontologies based on the aggregation of their quality metrics. The decision scheme is constituted of the 23 e-government ontologies or alternatives and their 11 quality metrics or attributes. The experimental results yielded an ordered list of the 23 inputs e-government ontologies ranked according to their quality metrics. This may provide some insights on the selection and reuse of these ontologies in future e-government projects.

The rest of the paper is structured as follows. Section 2 discusses the related studies on ontology ranking. The materials and methods used in the study are described in Sect. 3. Section 4 presents the experiments and results and a conclusion ends the paper in Sect. 5.

2   Related Work

Authors have investigated various techniques for ranking ontologies [10,11,13–17]. The AKTiveRank method was proposed in [13]. It uses criteria including centrality, class match, density and betweenness to weight and rank ontologies on the semantic web. Each criterion is applied to each ontology to calculate a score based on how best it matches input user's concepts. The ranking result for each ontology is the weighted sum of all the scores obtained for the four ranking criteria.

Another approach for ranking ontologies, namely, ARRO is proposed in [15]. The ARRO uses features such as the semantic relations and hierarchy structure of classes to weight and rank ontologies. The similarity between the ARRO and AKTiveRank is that they both rank the candidate ontologies based on how best they match the terms in the user's query. The OntologyRank technique proposed in [14] measures the semantic relationships between the classes of ontologies to weight and rank them; the classes considered are those that match the user's query terms.

In [16], the OS_Rank method is proposed as an improvement of ARRO. It ranks ontologies based on their coverage of user's concepts using criteria including class name, ontology structure and semantic. Another method, namely, content-based is proposed in [17]. In the content-based method, each ontology is matched to a corpus of terms built from the user's query; the matching scores are then used to rank the candidate ontologies. In [10] the Content-OR method is proposed. The Content-OR combines the OntologyRank [14] and the content-based methods [17] in that, the Content-OR first applies the content-based method and uses the output in the OntologyRank method to rank the ontologies. A recent study in [11] proposed the DWRank method. It uses the concepts of centrality and authority to learn the weights of concepts/classes of ontologies that match the user's query terms and rank the ontologies.

The above mentioned ontologies ranking techniques use the conceptual features of ontologies to weight and rank them based on how best they match the user's query terms. None of these ontologies ranking methods has used existing metrics that measure the quality of ontologies [18] in the ranking criteria. Furthermore, none of the previous ontology ranking techniques discussed above has neither used a decision-making method in the ranking process nor focused on the ranking of e-government ontologies.

The early attempts to use decision making in ontology ranking was in [8] and [9]. The authors in [9] implemented ELECTRE I&III with a set of criteria adapted from the AKTiveRank [13], whereas, [8] implemented the Analytic Hierarchy Process (AHP) with criteria adapted from OntologyRank [14] to rank ontologies. Therefore, [8] and [9] have applied decision making to rank ontologies based of their conceptual features as in the previous ontology ranking methods. In recent studies, our contributions have been the implementation of various Multi-Criteria Decision Making (MCDM) algorithms including Weighted Linear Combination Ranking Technique (WLCRT) [19], Weighted Sum Model (WSM), Weighted Product Model (WPM) and Technique for Order Preference by

Similarity to Ideal Solution (TOPSIS) [20] to rank biomedical ontologies based on their design complexity metrics. This study further implements ELECTRE I on a set of quality metrics of ontologies adopted from the OntoMetrics framework [18] with the aim of ranking the e-government ontologies on the web based on their qualities rather than their conceptual features as in the related studies [8,9].

3   Materials and Methods

This section presents the quality metrics adopted from the OntoMetrics framework [18] as attributes to rank e-government ontologies as well as the ELECTRE decision making algorithm.

3.1   Quality Metrics of Ontologies

Eleven quality metrics of ontologies including Average Population (AP), Absolute Root Cardinality (ARC), Absolute Leaf Cardinality (AC), Average Depth (AD), Maximum Depth (MD), Average Breadth (AB), Maximum Breadth (MB), Attribute Richness (AR), Inheritance Richness (IR), Relationship Richness (RR) and Class Richness (CR) are used as attributes in the ELECTRE algorithm to rank e-government ontologies in this study. These metrics characterise the schema, knowledge base and graph properties of ontologies. The OntoMetrics framework provides an online environment where these quality metrics of ontologies can be automatically generated given input ontologies' codes. In a recent study [21], we applied the OntoMetrics framework to evaluate the quality of the e-government ontologies to be ranked in this study. A detailed review of the OntoMetrics framework, its quality metrics suite as well as the mathematical definitions of these metrics are provided in [21] and will not be repeated here due to space constraints. Interested readers may refer to [21] for more information.

3.2   ELECTRE Method

Multi-criteria decision making (MCDM) methods are useful in decision processes in many scientific and business domains. ELECTRE is a family of MCDM methods that was introduced in 1968 [9]. It consists in implementing pairwise comparisons between alternatives based on their performances against different criteria. The pairwise comparison between two alternatives allows to determine the outranking relationship between them. The outranking relationship between two alternatives A_r and A_s is defined as the dominance of the alternative A_r over the alternative A_s. The outranking relationships between alternatives are determined from the analysis of the concordance and discordance indexes. The former are defined as the set of evidences that an alternative A_r dominates the alternative A_s while the later provides proof that A_s is dominated by A_r. The initial version of the ELECTRE family of MCDM methods was ELECTRE I;

since, then, subsequent versions including ELECTRE II, III, VI & TRI have been introduced as the improvements of ELECTRE I [9].

In many decision making methods, the decision process requires the lists of alternatives $(A_1, A_2, A_3, ..., A_M)$ and criteria/attributes of the alternatives $(C_1, C_2, C_3, ..., C_N)$. In this study, a set of ontologies constitute the alternatives, whereas, a number of quality metrics are used as the criteria/attributes of the ontologies. The set of alternatives and criteria are used to build the decision matrix as in Eq. 1.

$$D = \begin{matrix} & \begin{matrix} C_1 & C_2 & C_3 \ldots & C_N \end{matrix} \\ \begin{matrix} A_1 \\ A_2 \\ A_3 \\ \vdots \\ \vdots \\ A_M \end{matrix} & \begin{pmatrix} d_{11} & d_{12} & d_{13} \ldots & d_{1N} \\ d_{21} & d_{22} & d_{23} \ldots & d_{2N} \\ d_{31} & d_{32} & d_{33} \ldots & d_{3N} \\ \vdots & \vdots & \vdots & \vdots \\ \vdots & \vdots & \vdots & \vdots \\ d_{M1} & d_{M2} & d_{M3} \ldots & d_{MN} \end{pmatrix} \end{matrix} \tag{1}$$

where d_{ij} is the performance of the alternation A_i evaluated against the attributes/criteria $C_j, 1 \leq i \leq M$ and $1 \leq j \leq N$.

Furthermore, a set of criteria weights $(w_1, w_2, w_3, ..., w_N)$ is computed from the decision matrix D such that $\sum_j w_j = 1$. There are different techniques for computing the criteria weights as in [22]. On the basis of the decision matrix and criteria weights, the ELECTRE I algorithm [23] executes the seven steps below.

1. **Normalize the Decision Matrix** - The decision matrix D in Eq. 1 is normalized into a new matrix R with Eq. 2.

$$r_{ij} = \frac{d_{ij}}{\sqrt{\sum_i^M d_{ij}^2}}, 1 \leq i \leq M \text{ and } 1 \leq j \leq N \tag{2}$$

2. **Construct the Weighted Normalized Matrix** - A weighted normalized matrix V is built from R as in Eq. 3 by multiplying each column of R by the weight of the associated criterion.

$$V_{ij} = r_{ij}.w_j, 1 \leq i \leq M \text{ and } 1 \leq j \leq N \tag{3}$$

3. **Determine the Sets of Concordance and Discordance** - The set of concordances Con_{rs} between two alternatives A_r and A_s includes the criteria where A_r is considered to be more performing than A_s in the normalised weighted matrix V in Eq. 3. The set of concordances is defined in Eq. 4.

$$Con_{rs} = \{j, V_{sj} \geq V_{rj}\}, j = 1, 2, 3, ..., N \tag{4}$$

Similarly, Eq. 5 defines the set of discordances Dis_{rs} between the alternatives A_r and A_s as the complementary of Con_{rs}; it corresponds to the set of criteria where A_r is less performing than A_s in the normalised weighted matrix V in Eq. 3.

$$Dis_{rs} = \{j, V_{sj} \leq V_{rj}\}, j = 1, 2, 3, ..., N \tag{5}$$

4. **Compute the Concordance and Discordance Matrixes** - The concordance matrix is a MxM matrix where each element C_{rs} ($s \neq r$) is the concordance index of A_r when compared to an alternative A_s. The concordance index of the alternatives A_r and A_s is the sum of the weights of elements in their concordance set as in Eq. 6.

$$C_{rs} = \sum_{j \in Con_{rs}} W_j \tag{6}$$

The discordance matrix is a MxM matrix where each element is the discordance index of the alternative A_r compared to A_s, obtained by dividing the maximum value of the discordance set of the alternatives A_r and A_s by the maximum discordance value of the whole set as in Eq. 7 [23].

$$D_{rs} = \frac{\max_{j \in Dis_{rs}} |V_{sj} - V_{rj}|}{\max_{j} |V_{sj} - V_{rj}|} \tag{7}$$

5. **Compute the Concordance and Discordance Dominance Matrices** - The concordance dominance matrix CD is an MxM matrix where each element cd_{rs} is either 1 or 0. The elements of the CD matrix represent the outcome of the comparison of the concordance indexes of two alternatives A_r and A_s against the threshold value $\bar{c}$ of the concordance matrix. The threshold value of the concordance matrix is given in Eq. 8.

$$\bar{c} = \frac{\sum_{s=1}^{M} \sum_{r=1}^{M} C_{rs}}{M(M-1)} \tag{8}$$

Each element cd_{rs} of the matrix CD is then obtained by comparing the element C_{rs} of the concordance matrix to the threshold value as in Eq. 9.

$$\begin{cases} cd_{rs} = 1 \Rightarrow C_{rs} \geq \bar{c} \\ cd_{rs} = 0 \Rightarrow C_{rs} \leq \bar{c} \end{cases} \tag{9}$$

A similar process is followed with Eqs. 10 and 11 to compute the discordance dominance matrix DD. The threshold value $\bar{d}$ of the discordance matrix is calculated in Eq. 10.

$$\bar{d} = \frac{\sum_{s=1}^{M} \sum_{r=1}^{M} D_{rs}}{M(M-1)} \tag{10}$$

Each element dd_{rs} of the DD matrix is obtained by comparing the element D_{rs} to the threshold value $\bar{d}$ as in Eq. 11.

$$\begin{cases} dd_{rs} = 1 \Rightarrow D_{rs} \geq \bar{d} \\ dd_{rs} = 0 \Rightarrow D_{rs} \leq \bar{d} \end{cases} \tag{11}$$

6. **Compute the Aggregate Dominance Matrix** - An element e_{rs} of the aggregate dominance matrix AD is obtained by multiplying each element cd_{sr} of the CD matrix to the element dd_{rs} of matrix DD as in Eq. 12.

$$e_{rs} = cd_{sr}.dd_{rs} \tag{12}$$

7. **Rank Alternatives** - At this stage the scores of each alternative is computed as in Eq. 13 [12].

$$Score_k = \sum_{i=1}^{N} e_{ki} - \sum_{j=1}^{N} e_{jk}, k = 1, 2, 3, ..., M \tag{13}$$

Thereafter, the scores are sorted in increasing order to rank the alternatives [12].

4   Experiments

This section presents the dataset and the experimental results of the study.

4.1   Dataset

The dataset in this study is constituted of 23 ontologies of the e-government domain. Each ontology in the dataset is assigned an index $O_i, 1 \leq i \leq 23$ to ease its reference in the discussions. Table 1 shows the list of ontologies in the dataset with their names and source files. The extensions of these e-government ontologies' files reveal their formats including XML, OWL and KOAN. The XML files are web documents that include the RDF/OWL files of the corresponding ontologies. It is shown in Table 1 that the majority of e-government ontologies downloaded are in OWL format, which is the *state-of-the-art* language for building ontologies. It can also be noticed that the ontologies O_{14} and O_{20} in Table 1 have the same names and different source file extensions; these are two different ontologies developed by different authors.

Due to space constraints the web links where the ontologies in Table 1 are located could not be provided in this study. However, these web links are provided in [21]. The names of some ontologies such as $CPSV - AP\_IT.owl$ and $quontoV2.owl$ in Table 1 are not self-explanatory. The $CPSV - AP\_IT.owl$ is the Core Public Service Vocabulary Application Profile ontology of the Italian government, whereas, the $quontoV2.owl$, where the acronym QUONTO stands for Quality Ontology is an ontology that formalizes the knowledge needed for a multi-perspective and adaptive evaluation of e-government portals.

Table 1. E-government ontologies in the dataset

Index	Ontology	Source file
O_1	Public contracts ontology	vocabulary_2.xml
O_2	geographica ontology	vocabulary_69.xml
O_3	OntoGov ontology	vocabulary_89.xml
O_4	GovStat ontology	vocabulary_40.xml
O_5	Central Government ontology	central-government.owl
O_6	Government core ontology	gc.owl
O_7	Government ontology	oe1gov.owl
O_8	US government ontology	us1gov.owl
O_9	geopolitical ontology	geopolitical.owl
O_{10}	Quonto quality ontology	quontoV2.owl
O_{11}	Domain ontology	DomainOntology.kaon
O_{12}	Legal ontology	LegalOntology.koan
O_{13}	Life cycle ontology	LifeCycleOn tology.koan
O_{14}	Life event ontology	lifeEventOntology.koan
O_{15}	Organisational ontology	OrganisationalOntology.kaon
O_{16}	CPSV-AP_IT ontology	CPSV-AP_IT.owl
O_{17}	gPAP ontology	administration.owl
O_{18}	Municipal Ontology	ontology.owl
O_{19}	Open 311 ontology	open311.owl
O_{20}	Life event ontology	leo.owl
O_{21}	Web portal ontology	WebPortalOntology.owl
O_{22}	User model ontology	UserModel.owl
O_{23}	Problem ontology	problemsOntologyV2.owl

4.2   Results and Discussions

The 11 quality metrics of the 23 e-government ontologies in Table 1 were gathered by iteratively loading their source codes into the OntoMetrics online system. Table 2 provides the resulting quality metrics of all the e-government ontologies in the dataset. There are no values for some metrics of the ontology O_{18} in Table 2 because these metrics were unavailable in the OntoMetrics outputs. Furthermore, some metrics are zeros for a number of ontologies across Table 2; however, the majority of metrics where successfully gathered for all the ontologies in the dataset. As shown in Table 2, the metrics are small numbers; only the graph metric AC (third column in Table 2) is higher for some ontologies, reaching hundred for the ontologies O_7, O_{14} and O_{19}.

Table 2 constitutes the decision matrix for the ELECTRE algorithm in this study. The first step of implementation of the ELECTRE algorithm on the decision matrix in Table 2 consisted to compute the weighted normalized decision

Table 2. Quality metrics of E-government ontologies

	ARC	AC	AD	MD	AB	MB	AP	CR	AR	IR	RR
O_1	19	19	1,136364	2	5,5	19	0,681818	0,090909	0,59099	0,136364	0,930233
O_2	7	10	3,033333	5	2,142857	7	0,526316	0,105263	0,315789	0,736842	0,222222
O_3	2	10	3,285714	5	2,33333	4	0,352941	0,058824	0	1	0,346154
O_4	3	10	2,076923	3	3,25	6	0	0	0,076923	1,230769	0,407407
O_5	15	42	2,836066	6	3,388889	15	0,016949	0,016949	0,067797	0,779661	0,577982
O_6	3	2	1,5	2	1,5	3	1,166667	0,333333	0,666667	1,333333	0,5
O_7	26	112	3,419162	6	3,604317	33	0,134831	0,02809	0,033708	1,601124	0,2711
O_8	3	2	1,5	2	1,5	3	1,166667	0,333333	0,666667	1,333333	0,5
O_9	1	8	3,416667	4	2,4	4	26	0,583333	7,416667	7,333333	0,169811
O_{10}	26	92	2,447368	4	4,956522	26	1,386364	0,530303	0,106061	1,515152	0,602386
O_{11}	2	7	2,727273	4	2,2	3	4,727273	0,272727	0,363636	0,818182	0,25
O_{12}	2	6	2,375	3	2,666667	5	1,375	0,125	0,375	0,75	0,4
O_{13}	2	6	2,25	3	2,666667	4	1,875	0,125	0,75	0,75	0,333333
O_{14}	2	107	3,801587	4	6,3	17	0,992063	0,007937	0	0,984127	0
O_{15}	2	10	3,285714	5	2,333333	4	0,352941	0,058824	0	1	0,346154
O_{16}	22	22	1,3125	2	2,909091	22	0,54	0,12	0,36	2,12	0,341615
O_{17}	16	56	3,009709	6	2,575	16	0,652174	0,434783	0,217391	1,978261	0,172727
O_{18}							0	0	0,042231	1,130279	0,003862
O_{19}	8	112	3,639706	5	5,666667	25	0	0	0,133333	1,148148	0,093567
O_{20}	8	26	1,84375	3	4,571429	9	1,90625	0,5	0,4375	0,75	0,813956
O_{21}	2	7	1,75	2	4	6	2,375	0,75	0	0,75	0,727273
O_{22}	5	7	1,375	2	4	5	0	0	0,25	0,375	0,571429
O_{23}	3	26	3,125	5	4,571429	14	0	0	0,21875	0,90625	0,09375

matrix (V) (Eq. 3). Thereafter, the matric V was used to calculate the concordance and discordance matrixes (Eqs. 4 and 5); these resulted in 23×23 matrixes. The next step consisted to compute the concordance and discordance dominance matrixes. These were matrixes of 23×23 binary elements (0 or 1). Thereafter, the concordance and discordance binary matrixes were used to generate the aggregate dominance matrix (Eq. 12); this matrix allowed to get the dominance status (the number of dominating ontologies) of each ontology in the dataset. Each row of the dominance matrix D represents the dominance relationships of an alternative to all the other alternatives. A value 1 in a row of D indicates that the corresponding alternative is dominated by the alternative

Table 3. Dominance statuses of alternatives

Index	Dominance	Index	Dominance	Index	Dominance	Index	Dominance
O_1	0	O_7	0	O_{13}	0	O_{19}	18
O_2	0	O_8	1	O_{14}	0	O_{20}	0
O_3	1	O_9	9	O_{15}	1	O_{21}	0
O_4	0	O_{10}	3	O_{16}	12	O_{22}	0
O_5	2	O_{11}	0	O_{17}	1	O_{23}	13
O_6	1	O_{12}	0	O_{18}	0		

in the column, whereas, a value 0 indicates the dominance of this alternative on the other alternative in column. Therefore, the alternative(s) with the less number of values 1 in their rows are considered to be more favourable than the ones with large number of values 1.

Table 3 shows the dominance status of each ontology or alternative; it is a number obtained by counting the number of cells with 1 in the aggregate dominance matrix. In Table 3 the dominance statuses of ontologies including O_1, O_2, O_4, O_7, O_{11}, O_{12}, O_{13}, O_{14}, O_{18}, O_{20}, O_{21} and O_{22} are zeros; this indicates that these ontologies share the same level of preference and that they dominate the rest of ontologies. Table 3 was further utilised to calculate the scores of the alternatives with Eq. 13.

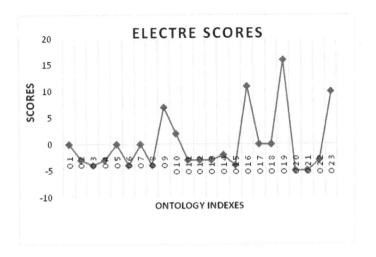

Fig. 1. ELECTRE scores for ontologies in the dataset

Figure 1 displays the chart of the ELECTRE scores for all the e-government ontologies or alternatives in the dataset. It is shown in Fig. 1 that the majority of ontologies in the dataset (13 out of 23 ontologies) including those with null dominance statuses in Table 3 have low score values, indicating that they are more favorable than the rest of the ontologies. In other words, these 13 ontologies are of good quality compared to the rest of e-government ontologies in the dataset. The ELECTRE ranking results of the 23 e-government ontologies in the dataset was obtained by further sorting the ELECTRE scores (Fig. 1) in increasing order. Table 4 displays the ELECTRE ranking results.

Table 4. ELECTRE ranking results

O_{20}	O_{21}	O_3	O_6	O_8	O_{15}	O_2	O_4	O_{11}	O_{12}	O_{13}	O_{22}	O_{14}	O_1	O_5	O_7	O_{17}	O_{18}	O_{10}	O_9	O_{23}	O_{16}	O_{19}
1	2	3	4	5	6	7	8	9	10	11	12	13	14	15	16	17	18	19	20	21	22	23

The top row of Table 4 includes the ontologies' indices and the bottom row the order in which the ontologies appear in the ranking result (1 to 23). As expected, the first 13 positions in the ELECTRE ranking results in Table 4 correspond to the ontologies with low ELECTRE scores in Fig. 1; this indicates that ELECTRE has successfully ranked the e-government ontologies in the dataset base on their quality metrics.

As mentioned earlier in this study, the quality metrics in Table 2 were used in [21] to discuss the quality of e-government ontologies in terms of the extend to which the ontologies model the e-government domain (accuracy), how easy it is to understand the e-government ontologies (understandability), the level of relatedness amongst the classes of the e-government ontologies (cohesion) and the level of utility of the knowledge represented in the ontologies (conciseness). A further analysis of the quality metrics (Table 2) of ontologies in the ranking results in Table 4 suggests that ELECTRE has ordered the e-government ontologies in the dataset based on their performances in the four quality dimensions of accuracy, understandability, cohesion and conciseness. This finding may provide some insights on the selection and reuse of the e-government ontologies (Table 1) in future e-government research and/or projects.

Furthermore, the research reported in this study can be replicated in any other knowledge domain to rank ontologies for the purpose of selection for reuse. The results of the study can also serve as inputs to existing content-based ontology ranking techniques, whereby, selected ranked e-government ontologies are further subjected to content analysis based on users' preferences for further selection.

5   Conclusion

In this study, 23 e-government ontologies were ranked based on their quality metrics. A decision scheme based on the set of ontologies and their quality metrics was constructed to rank the e-government ontologies with the ELECTRE decision making algorithm. The results provided a list of e-government ontologies ordered according to their quality metrics.

The future direction of research would be to improve the dataset to include more e-government ontologies' codes and to perform a clustering/classification of these ontologies with Machine Learning techniques.

References

1. Alazemi, N., Al-Shehab, A.J., Alhakem, H.A.: Semantic-based e-government framework based on domain ontologies: a case of Kuwait region. J. Theor. Appl. Inf. Technol. **96**, 2557–2566 (2018)
2. Distinto, I., d'Aquin, M., Motta, E.: LOTED2: an ontology of European public procurement notices. Semant. Web J. **7**, 1–15 (2016)
3. Ferneda, E., et al.: Potential of ontology for interoperability in e-government: discussing international initiatives and the Brazilliang case. Braz. J. Inf. Stud. Res. Trends **10**, 47–57 (2016)

4. Fonou-Dombeu, J.V., Huisman, M.: Engineering semantic web services for government business processes automation. In: Kő, A., Francesconi, E. (eds.) EGOVIS 2015. LNCS, vol. 9265, pp. 40–54. Springer, Cham (2015). https://doi.org/10.1007/978-3-319-22389-6_4

5. Ouchetto, H., Ouchetto, O., Roudies, O.: Ontology-oriented e-gov services retrieval. Int. J. Comput. Sci. Issues **2**, 99–107 (2012)

6. Petrusic, D., Segedinac, M., Konjovic, Z.: Semantic modelling and ontology integration of the open government systems. Tehnicki Vjesnik **23**, 1631–1641 (2016)

7. Lonsdale, D., Embley, D.W., Ding, Y., Xu, L., Hepp, M.: Reusing ontologies and language components for ontology generation. Data Knowl. Eng. **69**, 318–330 (2010)

8. Groza, A., Dragoste, I., Sincai, I., Jimborean, I., Moraru, V.: An ontology selection and ranking system based on the analytical hierarchy process. In: The 16th International Symposium on Symbolic and Numerical Algorithms for Scientific Computing, Timisoara, Romania (2014)

9. Esposito, A., Zappatore, M., Tarricone, L.: Applying multi-criteria approaches to ontology ranking: a comparison with AKtiveRank. Int. J. Metadata Semant. Ontol. **7**, 197–208 (2012)

10. Subhashini, R., Akilandeswari, J., Haris, S.: An integrated ontology ranking method for enhancing knowledge reuse. Int. J. Eng. Technol. (IJET) **6**, 1424–1431 (2014)

11. Butt, A.S., Haller, A., Xie, L.: DWRank: learning concept ranking for ontology search. Semant. Web **7**, 447–461 (2016)

12. Lee, H.C., Chang, C.: Comparative analysis of MCDM methods for ranking renewable energy sources in Taiwan. Renew. Sustain. Energy Rev. **92**, 883–896 (2018)

13. Alani, H., Brewster, C., Shadbolt, N.: Ranking ontologies with AKTiveRank. In: 5th International Conference on the Semantic Web, Athens, Greece, pp. 1–15 (2006)

14. Park, J., Ohb, S., Ahn, J.: Ontology selection ranking model for knowledge reuse. Expert Syst. Appl. **38**, 5133–5144 (2011)

15. Yu, W., Cao, J., Chen, J.: A Novel Approach for Ranking Ontologies on the Semantic Web. In: 1st International Symposium on Pervasive Computing and Applications, Urumchi, Xinjiang, China, pp. 608–612 (2006)

16. Yu, W., Chen, J.: Ontology ranking for the semantic web. In: 3rd International Symposium on Intelligent Information Technology Application, NanChang, China, pp. 573–574 (2009)

17. Jones, M., Alani, H.: Content-based ontology ranking. In: 9th International Protégé Conference, Stanford, CA, USA, pp. 1–4 (2006)

18. Lantow, B.: OntoMetrics: putting metrics into use for ontology evaluation. In: Proceedings of the 8th International Joint Conference on Knowledge Discovery, Knowledge Engineering and Knowledge Management (IC3K 2016), Joaquim Filipe, Portugal, pp. 186–191 (2016)

19. Fonou-Dombeu, J.V., Viriri, S.: CRank: a novel framework for ranking semantic web ontologies. In: Abdelwahed, E.H., Bellatreche, L., Golfarelli, M., Méry, D., Ordonez, C. (eds.) MEDI 2018. LNCS, vol. 11163, pp. 107–121. Springer, Cham (2018). https://doi.org/10.1007/978-3-030-00856-7_7

20. Fonou-Dombeu, J.V.: A comparative application of multi-criteria decision making in ontology ranking. In: Abramowicz, W., Corchuelo, R. (eds.) BIS 2019. LNBIP, vol. 353, pp. 55–69. Springer, Cham (2019). https://doi.org/10.1007/978-3-030-20485-3_5

21. Fonou-Dombeu, J.V., Viriri, S.: OntoMetrics evaluation of quality of e-government ontologies. In: Kő, A., Francesconi, E., Anderst-Kotsis, G., Tjoa, A.M., Khalil, I. (eds.) EGOVIS 2019. LNCS, vol. 11709, pp. 189–203. Springer, Cham (2019). https://doi.org/10.1007/978-3-030-27523-5_14
22. Roszkowska, E.: Rank ordering criteria weighting methods - a comparative review. Optimum Studia Ekonomicze NR **5**, 14–33 (2013)
23. Pang, J., Zhang, G., Chen, G.: ELECTRE I decision model of reliability design scheme for computer numerical control. J. Softw. **6**, 894–900 (2011)

Framework for Data Analysis in the Context of the Smart Villages

Jorge Martinez-Gil[1(✉)], Mario Pichler[1], Muhamed Turkanović[2], Tina Beranič[2],
Mitja Gradišnik[2], Gianluca Lentini[3], Alessandro Lué[3], Alberto Colorni Vitale[3],
Guillaume Doukhan[4], and Claire Belet[4]

[1] Software Competence Center Hagenberg GmbH,
Softwarepark 21, 4232 Hagenberg, Austria
jorge.martinez-gil@scch.at
[2] Faculty of Electrical Engineering and Computer Science, University of Maribor,
Koroška cesta 46, 2000 Maribor, Slovenia
[3] Poliedra-Politecnico di Milano, via G. Colombo 40, 20133 Milan, Italy
[4] ADRETS, 69 rue Carnot, 05000 Gap, France

Abstract. In recent times, the digitalization of urban areas has got considerable attention from the public. As a side effect, there has also been great interest in the digitalization of the rural world or the so-called Smart Villages. Smart Villages refer to the improvement of infrastructure management and planning to fight against depopulation and low population density as well as the cuts and centralization of services supported by digitalization efforts. In this work, we present our research to build a framework for the analysis of data generated around the project Smart Villages, which is a joint effort to digitalize rural areas in the context of the Alpine Space. Our goal is to build a system to help local authorities to pilot a smooth transition into this new concept of the village.

Keywords: Data analysis · Digitalization · Smart villages

1 Introduction

It is widely assumed that the digital revolution and new technology's prospects have fundamentally changed the way we live in recent decades. In this regard, it is worth noting a recent and growing interest in the concept of digitalization of urban and rural areas [7]. Although until now almost all research activity has been focused in the urban areas, e.g. the so-called Smart Cities [3], little attention has been paid to the rural world [21]. The truth is that the Smart Cities are able to generate a huge amount of data that makes the discipline very attractive for dealing with problems related to Big Data and Artificial Intelligence. Some practical examples are the intelligent regulation of traffic lights, the automatic management of parking spaces, the intelligent management of urban solid waste, the optimization of mechanisms for energy saving on a large scale, the development of methods for collaborative transport, the intelligent communication between vehicles, the automatic methods for smart surveillance, etc.

A. Kő et al. (Eds.): EGOVIS 2020, LNCS 12394, pp. 31–45, 2020.
https://doi.org/10.1007/978-3-030-58957-8_3

All these problems, due to their data-intensive nature, have no direct application in the rural world, where data generation is not so frequent and is much more dispersed and fragmented. This makes the challenges of different villages having different conceptual frameworks [24]. For example, the rural world is experiencing a series of problems that if managed in time can be prevented from getting worse [15]. To name just a few problems, depopulation as a consequence of rural exodus, where many people leave the place where they have lived during many years in search of new opportunities in the urban world. The aging of the population, related to the previous point, as young people consider that other more populated places can be more attractive and offer more professional opportunities. Or the disappearance of public services, because it becomes very expensive to offer a service that will not have a large number of users.

The main goal of this work is to build a data framework associated with an online platform[1] intended to trigger the revitalization of rural services through digital and social innovation. In fact, our work is intended to support the automated analysis of a wide range of scenarios related to rural services such as how health care [8], social services [22], technology [11], energy [20], employment [12], transport [18] or retail [14] can be improved and made more sustainable through the use of information technology tools as well as community initiatives.

As an outcome of this analysis phase, it should be possible to proceed with the dissemination of practical guidelines that can be used in the conceptualization and development of smart villages. In parallel, the platform for linking the various initiatives is being maintained with the purpose of becoming an open space where to discuss and exchange ideas that can contribute to the correct development of rural areas. Therefore, our contribution here is the design and implementation of a framework for data analysis to pilot an appropriate transition to the Smart Village concept. To do so, we make use of a set of tools as well as several external knowledge bases that help us to automatically analyze the current state of a specific village in relation to a key set of attributes defined by an international community of experts in the field.

The remainder of this work is as follows: Sect. 2 overviews the state-of-the-art regarding existing data analysis approaches in the context of the Smart Villages. Sect. 3 presents the technical details of our framework including how we have proceeded to implement some interesting functionality: self-assessment, matchmaking, fake form detection, clustering, similarity calculation, and ranking. Sect. 4 presents a discussion about the possibilities that our framework offers to improve many aspects related to smart villages and it exposes in a concise way the lessons learned that can be extrapolated to a number of application areas that present a similar context. Finally, we remark the major conclusions of this work and possible future lines of research in Sect. 5.

---

[1] https://smart-villages.eu.

2 State-of-the-Art

Firstly, it is necessary to remark that there is not one clear and global definition of what a smart village is. There have been several attempts to provide a definition. However, there is no common agreement among the authors as to which attributes should be covered by such a definition. Zavranik et al. state that the reason for not having a simple unique definition is related to the fact that the communities from the rural world are not just an entity, inanimate and unchangeable, and are thus always dependent on the environment and changes in social and cultural structures [25]. In this paper, we believe that a fairly simple but also effective definition could be to consider smart villages as communities in rural areas that use innovative solutions to improve their resilience by leveraging their local strengths and opportunities.

What does seem to be clear is a list (probably not exhaustive) of use cases or scenarios that should be possible to easily implement in a smart village. Some examples of these scenarios are: a) creating new housing alternatives and opportunities [6]; b) making both energy generation and consumption more accessible [17]; c) improving the sense of community [9]; d) preserving important environmental zones [10]; e) connecting new and existing developments [23], and so on.

It is necessary to remark that there are already many initiatives in the context of Smart Villages. For example, the IEEE Smart Village program aims reducing the urban-rural breach [4]. Intending to reduce the gap between rural and urban areas and promoting the rural economy, the European Commission has also given priority to the development of Smart Villages within its agricultural policies, as well as in other plans related to specific research programs, for example the SIMRA project[2] and the ERUDITE project[3]. Moreover, Digital India has put the focus in rendering services to citizens in India. This focus plans for convergence of all services through a digital hub [5].

Besides, it is possible to find some works in the technical literature that allow to envision some urban-rural collaboration. For example [2] and [16]. However, there is a lack of field-oriented systematic methods and tools to guide and monitor the evolutionary process of the villages to higher smartness maturity levels. In fact, at present, this process is so unstructured that most local authorities do not have a starting point and guidelines that support them in making adequate progress in terms of smartness maturity. Therefore, the contribution represented by our work aims to fill this gap.

Within the context of our previous work, we designed a pilot system that aims to help the rural world identify its strengths and weaknesses concerning the degree of innovation in several different but complimentary areas [1]. The reason for this pilot system was to provide an effective and efficient tool for local authorities in villages to later help them pilot their transition to much more sustainable and intelligent models that will help combat some of the problems they

---

[2] http://www.simra-h2020.eu/.

[3] https://www.interregeurope.eu/erudite/.

face. This system was based on the concept of a questionnaire. The latter was specifically designed by a European committee of experts and tries to measure in an objective way the degree of maturity of the area to be investigated from six points of view, which although different, have a great relationship between them. These perspectives are economy, governance, mobility, environment, people and living. Now, our recent development will allow local authorities to effectively interact with the village and facilities as well as to monitor the village's developments.

3 Towards a Framework for Data Analysis

In our previous work, we built an online community around a Digital Exchange Platform (DEP) which as its name suggests allows the exchange of information and communication between all the villages, municipalities, or towns that wish to register. This community can be very useful to communicate experiences, ask questions, or simply keep in touch with a multitude of peers that share the same concerns when it comes to digitalization. However, this platform lacks a framework for the analysis of the data generated by the users. Now we have designed and implemented this framework.

To do that, we have based our solution on an architecture oriented to the deployment of microservices [19]. The advantage of an architecture of this kind is the capability to deploy applications as collections of loosely coupled services. Some additional advantages of this kind of architecture are: the microservices are easier to maintain and test, and they can be independently deployed. In this way, our solution allows the rapid and reliable delivery of services. Let us see each of the implemented components.

3.1 Self-Assessment

The main goal of the smartness assessment component is to identify the smartness maturity level of a given village based on the six dimensions proposed by the smartness model [13]. Based on the smartness questionnaire and context metadata entered by an assessor, potential possibilities of improvement are identified. The key outcome of the smartness assessment lies in the possibility of capturing the current status of a village in terms of smartness, as defined by the six smartness dimensions and within the boundaries of the specific assessor's knowledge, and in the possibility of creating targets for improvement in terms of smart transformation, as detailed in the following sections.

Smartness Questionnaire. The smartness questionnaire is divided into two main parts, i.e. one devoted to the questions intended for collecting metadata, outlining the basic characteristics of the evaluated village, and evaluation questions. The second part is devoted to collect the metadata that outlines the basic characteristics of the village being evaluated and of the assessors themselves. The key attributes used in the questionnaire are:

(1) **name of the village,**
(2) **country** in which the village is located,
(3) **kind of village** (choice: city—village—municipality—local area),
(4) **number of inhabitants,**
(5) **assessor age** (choice: youth—elderly—students—active working people),
(6) **assessor type** (choice: policy maker—academia—business).

The second part of the smartness questionnaire is 24 evaluation questions, divided into six dimensions. For each question, the assessor chooses one of the four offered options, and optionally, also provide a comment. In this context, after having filled in the fields related to the metadata and all the questions related to the six dimensions under study, the result is calculated. The smartness model [13] is able to predict the following smartness dimensions: Smart People, Smart Governance, Smart Living, Smart Environment, Smart Economy, and Smart Mobility.

The result is used for two main purposes. On the one hand, to show the visualization of the assessment using a bar chart and calculate the statistics that will allow the local authority to have a much more detailed vision of the current situation of its village. And on the other hand, to start a matchmaking process with other villages or areas that are already included in the system.

The smartness assessment solution consists of independent systems (i.e. smartness assessment and matchmaking) and knowledge bases (i.e. the collection of good practices and toolbox methods). To provide flexible and technologically independent communication between subsystems and knowledge bases, REST API is used as an interface between subsystems of the solution. The use of REST API technology ensures a high degree of interoperability in terms of data exchange, while at the same time provides the independence in technology selection.

After the process is complete, the assessment model can be visualized, printed or exported. The smartness assessment process involves activities that offer a set of pre-established good practices and tools to bring similar practices into the real world.

3.2   Best Practice Recommendation

Another key feature of our framework is the matchmaking between villages whose information is entered into the system. The matchmaking is done after the village's information is inserted with the help of the smartness assessment questionnaire, the level of smartness that this village has is calculated. The smartness of the village is shown as a distribution around the six thematic dimensions, which is useful in order to expose the use cases or good practices. To do that, we have designed a mechanism based on a microservice-oriented architecture that is capable of calculating the most related scenarios.

In the end, the output of the matchmaking process is an ordered list of recommendations adapted to the profile of an assessor and the context of the smartness of the village. One or more suggested recommendations consist of good practices that have previously been established in the region and have been proven to work in real-life scenarios. Beside good practices, recommendations also offer useful methods and techniques that describe guided approaches to achieve the goals set. The results are represented as we can see below.

```
1  {
2  "metadata": {
3      "name": "string",
4      "country": "string",
5      "kind": "string",
6      "number_of_inhabitants": 0,
7      "assessor_age": "string",
8      "assessor_type": "string"
9  },
10  "smart_assessment": {
11      "smart_people": 0,
12      "smart_governance": 0,
13      "smart_living": 0,
14      "smart_environment": 0,
15      "smart_economy": 0,
16      "smart_mobility": 0
17  }
18  }
```

And then, we will get the answer:

```
1  {
2      "id_good_practices": ["id", "id",...],
3      "id_toolbox_method": ["id", "id",...]
4  }
```

Where the id is the unique key for each of the good practices so that

```
1  {
2  "goodpractices":[
3  {
4   "id":2202,
5   "title":"test",
6   "short description":"test",
7   "country":"Slovenia",
8   "region":"test",
9   "town": {
10      "address":"Koroska cesta 46, 2000 Maribor,
           Slovenia",
11          "latitude":46.5590355,
12          "longitude":15.6380735
13      }
14  }
```

The Matchmaking Process. This process of matchmaking is carried out following the sequential steps. Firstly, the process identifies the good practices that are oriented to the type of user who has filled in the form, and secondly, filters out good practices that are oriented to the subject matter in which the assessed village has obtained the worst results. In this way, the user has access to very valuable information that will allow them to inform themselves and reflect on why other villages or areas have been able to progress in that particular dimension. The output of the matchmaking process is a list of recommendations that are fitted to the profile of an assessor and the calculated smartness of the assessed village.

The suggested recommendations consist of good practices and methods and techniques. While good practices represent illustrative examples already established in the region that have been proven to work in real-life scenarios, methods and techniques describe guided approaches to achieve the goals set by the village.

The knowledge base of good practices represents a collection of good practices from the domain of smart villages that have been proven in practice over the years and collected in the regions of the special scope of the project. Each of the good practices in the catalog is described by mandatory and optional attributes. The key attributes are:

(1) **Title of the good practice** – meaningful title of the good practice,
(2) **Short description** – concise description of the good practice,
(3) **Country** – country of origin,
(4) **Region** – region of origin,
(5) **Town** – town of origin represented by the pin on a map,
(6) **Category of smart dimension** (choice: Smart Economy—Smart Environment—Smart Governance—Smart Living—Smart Mobility—Smart People),
(7) **Applicable in rural, non-city areas** (choice: Yes—Maybe—No),
(8) **Region level** (choice: NUTS 1—NUTS 2—NUTS 3),
(9) **Affecting – scale** (choice: Village—City—Municipality—Local Region),
(10) **Affecting – population** (choice: Youth—Elderly—Students—Active Working People),
(11) **Timescale** – start and end date of duration of good practice.

3.3 Fake Form Detection

One of the most severe problems we have to face when working with data from smart villages is being able to automatically discern the veracity of the information to be analyzed. For example, in our framework, we capture a lot of data and information through questionnaires specifically designed to determine the degree of smartness of a given village. These forms are open to the public, and anyone can fill out the information truthfully or can do so without much thought, in a hurry, or without knowing for sure if the information they are entering is completely true. For us, it is extremely important to have the most reliable information possible, otherwise, the conclusions of our analysis run the risk of not being accurate. For this reason, we have been working on an automatic mechanism capable of verifying the plausibility of the data inserted into the system using different machine learning techniques.

Our solution is based on the notion of automatic classification which is a process intended to predict the outcome from a dataset that has been previously labeled by an human expert. In this case, we face a binary classification problem since there are only two classes: the filled form is valid or is not valid. In order to do that, the method needs to use some training samples to understand how the given input variables relate to the output values. If the automatic classifier is trained properly, it can be used to detect the validity of new data inputs. In this context, there are many automatic classification methods publicly available but it is not possible to conclude which one is the best. Most of the time, it depends on the application and nature of the dataset. For this reason, we have tried several methods here with their standard configuration.

The Dataset. Our dataset[4] has been compiled from a sample of 210 forms that have been filled out online by anonymous users. Many of these questionnaires are not serious because it can be clearly seen that many questions have not been answered or that many comments are meaningless. Or even because such a village does not exist or the metadata provided does not correspond to that of the village in question. Therefore, we have eliminated the empty forms and the repeated forms, and we have manually labeled the rest with the possibility that it is valid or not. From that sample, we are already able to apply some machine learning techniques that are capable of recognizing the patterns of the valid forms, so that in the future only these are processed, and therefore, the conclusions drawn are not altered by erroneous information.

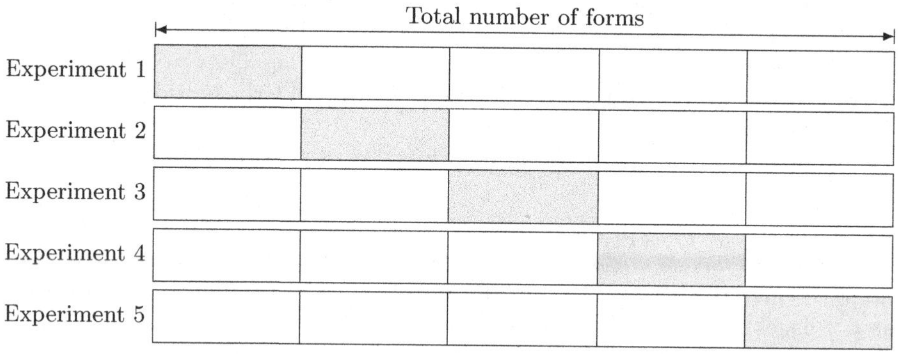

Fig. 1. Example of 5-fold cross validation

---

[4] https://smart-villages.eu/services/api/smartness.

It is necessary to note that over-fitting is a common problem that can occur in most trained models. To avoid that, k-fold cross-validation can be performed in order to verify that a given model is not over-fitted. In this work, our dataset has been randomly partitioned into 5 mutually exclusive subsets to assure the predictive capability. This kind of cross-validation is commonly used in practice to compare and select a model because it is easy to understand and provides results that generally have better predictive capabilities than other approaches. Figure 1 shows us an example of how to proceed.

Support Vector Machines (SVM) are a set of supervised learning methods used for classification. SVM aims to smartly generate a hyperplane which separates the instances into two different classes: legit or not legit. The advantages of support vector machines are that they are effective in high dimensional spaces which is actually our case.

The k-Nearest Neighbors (KNN) algorithm is a simple supervised machine learning algorithm that can be used to solve classification problems. It works by scoring the target sample with the most common value among its k-nearest neighbors.

Random Forests (RF) or random decision forests are a machine learning approach for automatic classification that operates by constructing a number of computational decision trees at training time and providing the result that is the mode of the results issued from all the decision trees.

Multi-layer Perceptron (MLP) classifiers stand for Multi-layer Perceptron classifiers. Unlike other automatic classification algorithms, it relies on an underlying Neural Network to perform the task of classification what usually leads to very good results although the interpretability, i.e. the ability to understand how the model works, is usually low.

Results. We present here the results that we have obtained from our experiments. These results have been obtained after ten independent executions of each of the classifiers. The results are shown in Fig. 2. As the process of dividing the dataset into training and test sets is done randomly, different results are obtained for each of the different executions. The way of representation through box plots allows visualizing efficiently the distribution of the obtained results.

As we can see in Fig. 2, it is not always possible to identify if a form is legit. However, our classification models are able to achieve quite good results, being able to exceed 90% accuracy most of the times and even reaching values close to 95% in some situations. Therefore, we can conclude that our methods are capable of identifying a valid form with a fairly high probability. This will increase the quality of the final results and, therefore, the veracity of the conclusions that can be drawn from those results.

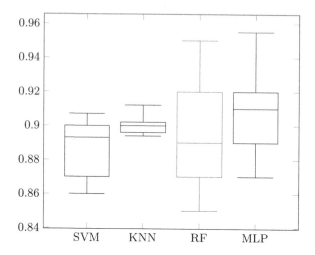

Fig. 2. Results of the four different classifiers for solving the problem of detecting fake questionnaires. SVM = Support Vector Machines, KNN = K-Nearest Neighbor, RF = Random Forests, and MLP = Multi-layer Perceptron

3.4 Clustering

One of the most interesting capabilities that our framework for data analysis can offer is to automatically calculate the clusters or logical aggregation of villages that share a similar degree of smartness either in general or in specific thematic areas. In our specific case, clustering is a data analysis technique whereby given a set of villages (represented by values stating the answers to the questionnaire), we can classify each village into a specific group. In this way, villages that are in the same group should have similar properties, while villages in different groups should have highly dissimilar features.

To do this, we proceed with the application K-means clustering algorithm that considers that each of the answers given by users is a different feature. Then, it aims to partition the villages into k clusters in which each village belongs to the cluster with the nearest mean. The set of answers given by each village represents the feature vector of that village from which the mean will be computed. It is possible to run the algorithm with different k parameters, and obtain results that have an obvious practical interest since it allows us to logically group the villages in the Alpine space that are more similar.

Figure 3 shows an example of 2-means clustering where it seems that the dimensions concerning economy and environment are not very overlapped. In general, it is possible to perform this kind of analysis to gain some valuable insights from our data by seeing what groups the villages fall into, and take decisions or elaborate policy tools accordingly.

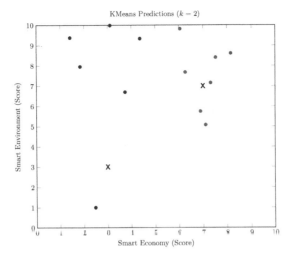

Fig. 3. Example of clustering of villages registered in our system

3.5   Similarity Calculation

Another feature we have implemented in our framework is the automatic calculation of the similarity between villages. Of course, this is not a physical similarity, but a type of similarity that measures the degree of maturity in relation to each of the six dimensions of study that we address in the framework of this work. The calculation of similarity is very useful because it allows the local authorities of the rural world to determine which places present some characteristics to those of the place in question, so it is possible to look at them as a third-person viewer and analyze what actions they are currently developing. The similarity can be calculated as follows (being $\mathbf{A}$ and $\mathbf{B}$ the answers associated to the source and target village respectively)

$$\text{similarity}(\mathbf{A}, \mathbf{B}) = \frac{\mathbf{A} \cdot \mathbf{B}}{\|\mathbf{A}\| \|\mathbf{B}\|} = \frac{\sum\limits_{i=1}^{n} A_i B_i}{\sqrt{\sum\limits_{i=1}^{n} A_i^2} \sqrt{\sum\limits_{i=1}^{n} B_i^2}}$$

The results of the comparison are something like we can see in the following portion of the code. Please note that the results are presented in a semi-structured format to facilitate automatic processing by a computer.

```
1  <?xml version="1.0" encoding="UTF-8"?>
2  <results>
3   <similarity>
4    <villageA>Maribor</villageA>
5    <villageB>Hagenberg</villageB>
6    <score>0.8359</score>
7   </similarity>
8  </results>
```

This similarity measure is just a statistical measures based on the calculation of the overlapping degree between answers given in the self-assessment test. Therefore, the resulting score does not have any additional connotation.

3.6 Ranking

The ranking functionality is related to the creation of an ordered list of villages to facilitate the understanding of specific factors. By reducing detailed features to a sequence of ordinal numbers, the ranking functionality makes it possible to assess interesting information according to some specific criteria. But since the results only show the perception that the local authorities have about their village, these results must be taken with caution.

The following listing shows us an example of a ranking for the category Smart Living extracted from our system. The listing has been generated in a semi-structured format to facilitate automatic processing.

```
1   <?xml version="1.0" encoding="UTF-8"?>
2   <SmartLiving>
3     <village name="Maribor" points=11 category="B"/>
4     <village name="Hagenberg" points=11 category="B"/>
5     <village name="Wattberg" points=10 category="B"/>
6     <village name="Linz" points=10 category="B"/>
7   </SmartLiving>
```

It should also be noted that the granularity of the results is not very large, so perhaps the category gives more information than the numerical value itself.

4 Discussion

Most rural areas in many developed countries are facing a major transition related to digitalization. Some of the most interesting aspects of this transition are how current facilities are going to be adapted to work with low-carbon demand or how some of the existing solutions can be integrated into the circular economy. In this context, it could be of great help some tools to guide the digital transformation of the rural economy, and even some guidelines to create positive relations between villages and cities

So far, most of the technological advances made in recent years have benefited urban areas. In this way, novel methods and tools based on Big Data techniques and Artificial Intelligence have greatly benefited the development of the so-called Smart Cities. However, rural areas have not benefited as much from technology until now. With our work, we have attempted to do our bit for the development of methods and tools to fight some of the problems that plague rural areas. We think that rural areas can benefit equally from all scientific and technological advances, but the right framework must be in place so that these solutions can make sense and help local authorities to manage a transition that is appropriate to their needs.

Also, the Smart Village model seeks to change conventional rural industries such as agriculture, livestock, mining, etc. by implementing innovative approaches for smart data processing. In this manner, new concepts linked to sustainability and productivity become very relevant and give rise to new types of business models.

5   Conclusions and Future Work

In this paper, we have presented our framework for data analysis in the context of the smart villages. Our goal is to develop novel methodologies and tools that will help local authorities in the rural world to pilot an appropriate transition to an effective and sustainable digitalization model that will handle some of the problems that they are currently facing.

In this context, we think that our framework can successfully help to manage a wide variety of data that can be captured from our online platform. Examples of these data are collections of the current status of a village, including metadata about the person that fills the questionnaire and the answers to the questions performed to prepare a smartness assessment report. Recommendation of good practices so that experiences that have taken place elsewhere could be applied in the place of the person or local authority receiving the recommendation. Fake form detection, because when working in an open environment, there may be situations where the information entered is not legit and therefore may lead to wrong conclusions about the situation of the village. Clustering of villages so that interest groups that share certain peculiarities and characteristics can be identified automatically and without human supervision, and for whom joint action could have meaning and great advantages. Calculation of the similarity between villages that are registered in the system, so that it is possible to better understand which places share common characteristics. And last but not least, the automatic creation of rankings to support decision-making aimed at improving the quality of life and the revitalization of rural environments.

We think that our work concerning the development of new methods, tools and frameworks for data analysis in this context will facilitate a transition into the concept of Smart Villages. At present, this transition lacks proper guidelines and tools, and it is so unstructured that most local authorities do not have a starting point nor software support to guide them in making adequate progress in terms of smartness maturity. However, this is only the first version of the framework. And we propose an iterative life cycle to improve it based on the experiences and suggestions provided by the users.

As future work, we would like to work on interoperability with a toolbox component. That toolbox component would be a repository to organize a number of existing tools or methods in the context of the digitalization of rural areas. The idea is to help local authorities to pilot a smooth transition into more sustainable models. In addition, we would like to add more collaborative features, at this time we can analyze a snapshot by village or test area, but we would like to design novel methods to determine the degree of smartness of a given village. We would like to collect a multitude of opinions from a wide range of inhabitants, including local authorities, neighbors, businesses, etc. In that way, we think that the analysis would reflect reality much more accurately.

Acknowledgements. Authors would like to thank the anonymous reviewers for their help towards improving this manuscript. This work has been developed within the SmartVillages project, Smart Digital Transformation of Villages in the Alpine Space, co-funded by Interreg Alpine Space (20182021). The authors would like to express the appreciation to SmartVillages project members for their contribution.

References

1. Beranič, T., et al.: Facilitating the digital transformation of villages. In: Central European Conference on Information and Intelligent Systems, pp. 281–288. Faculty of Organization and Informatics Varazdin (2019)
2. Bruni, E., Panza, A., Sarto, L., Khayatian, F., et al.: Evaluation of cities' smartness by means of indicators for small and medium cities and communities: a methodology for northern italy. Sustain. Cities Soc. **34**, 193–202 (2017)
3. Chourabi, H., et al.: Understanding smart cities: an integrative framework. In: 2012 45th Hawaii International Conference on System Sciences, pp. 2289–2297. IEEE (2012)
4. Coughlin, T.: IEEE consumer electronics society sponsors the smart village program [society news]. IEEE Consum. Electron. Mag. **4**(3), 15–16 (2015)
5. Das, R.K., Misra, H.: Digital India, e-governance and common people: how connected are these in access layer of smart village? In: Proceedings of the 10th International Conference on Theory and Practice of Electronic Governance, pp. 556–557 (2017)
6. Doloi, H., Green, R., Donovan, S.: Planning, Housing and Infrastructure for Smart Villages. Routledge, Abingdon (2018)
7. Fennell, S., et al.: Examining linkages between smart villages and smart cities: learning from rural youth accessing the internet in india. Telecommun. Policy **42**(10), 810–823 (2018)
8. Gahlot, S., Reddy, S., Kumar, D.: Review of smart health monitoring approaches with survey analysis and proposed framework. IEEE Internet Things J. **6**(2), 2116–2127 (2018)
9. Heap, R.: Smart villages: new thinking for off-grid communities worldwide. Essay Compilation, Banson (2015)
10. Holmes, J., Thomas, M.: Introducing the smart villages concept. Int. J. Green Growth Dev. **2**, 151 (2015)
11. Katara, S.K.: Envisioning smart villages through information and communication technologies – a framework for implementation in India. In: Chugunov, A.V., Bolgov, R., Kabanov, Y., Kampis, G., Wimmer, M. (eds.) DTGS 2016. CCIS, vol. 674, pp. 463–468. Springer, Cham (2016). https://doi.org/10.1007/978-3-319-49700-6_46
12. Martinez-Gil, J., Paoletti, A.L., Schewe, K.-D.: A smart approach for matching, learning and querying information from the human resources domain. In: Ivanović, M., Thalheim, B., Catania, B., Schewe, K.-D., Kirikova, M., Šaloun, P., Dahanayake, A., Cerquitelli, T., Baralis, E., Michiardi, P. (eds.) ADBIS 2016. CCIS, vol. 637, pp. 157–167. Springer, Cham (2016). https://doi.org/10.1007/978-3-319-44066-8_17
13. Martinez-Gil, J., et al.: Framework for assessing the smartness maturity level of villages. In: Welzer, T., et al. (eds.) ADBIS 2019. CCIS, vol. 1064, pp. 501–512. Springer, Cham (2019). https://doi.org/10.1007/978-3-030-30278-8_48

14. Müller, C., Struzek, D., Jung-Henrich, J.: Participatory design in the smart village: co-design of a public display in a rural village shop. In: Dachselt, R., Weber, G. (eds.) Mensch und Computer 2018 - Tagungsband, Dresden, Germany, 2–5 September 2018. Gesellschaft für Informatik e.V. (2018)
15. Paniagua, A.: Smart villages in depopulated areas. In: Patnaik, S., Sen, S., Mahmoud, M.S. (eds.) Smart Village Technology. MOST, vol. 17, pp. 399–409. Springer, Cham (2020). https://doi.org/10.1007/978-3-030-37794-6_20
16. Postránecký, M., Svítek, M.: Assessment method to measure smartness of cities. In: 2017 Smart City Symposium Prague (SCSP), pp. 1–5. IEEE (2017)
17. Prinsloo, G., Mammoli, A., Dobson, R.: Customer domain supply and load coordination: a case for smart villages and transactive control in rural off-grid microgrids. Energy **135**, 430–441 (2017)
18. Ramos, G., Dionísio, R., Pereira, P.: Linking sustainable tourism and electric mobility – moveletur. In: Machado, J., Soares, F., Veiga, G. (eds.) HELIX 2018. LNEE, vol. 505, pp. 985–991. Springer, Cham (2019). https://doi.org/10.1007/978-3-319-91334-6_135
19. Schwartz, A.: Microservices. Informatik-Spektrum **40**(6), 590–594 (2017). https://doi.org/10.1007/s00287-017-1078-6
20. van Gevelt, T., et al.: Achieving universal energy access and rural development through smart villages. Energy Sustain. Dev. **43**, 139–142 (2018)
21. Visvizi, A., Lytras, M.D.: Rescaling and refocusing smart cities research: from mega cities to smart villages. J. Sci. Technol. Policy Manag. **9**(2), 134–145 (2018)
22. Visvizi, A., Lytras, M.D., et al.: Sustainable smart cities and smart villages research: rethinking security, safety, well-being, and happiness. Sustainability **12**(1), 1–4 (2019)
23. Visvizi, A., Lytras, M.D., Mudri, G.: Smart Villages in the EU and Beyond. Emerald Publishing Limited, Bingley (2019)
24. Wolski, O., Wójcik, M.: Smart villages revisited: conceptual background and new challenges at the local level. In: Smart Villages in the EU and Beyond: People, Technology, and Wellbeing, pp. 29–48 (2019)
25. Zavratnik, V., Kos, A., Stojmenova Duh, E.: Smart villages: comprehensive review of initiatives and practices. Sustainability **10**(7), 2559 (2018)

e-Government Theoretical Background

A Conceptual Proposal for Responsible Innovation

Thais Assis de Souza[1,2(✉)] ⓘ, Rodrigo Marçal Gandia[1,2] ⓘ,
Bruna Habib Cavazza[1] ⓘ, André Grutzmann[1] ⓘ, and Isabelle Nicolaï[2] ⓘ

[1] Federal University of Lavras, Lavras, Minas Gerais 37200-000, Brazil
`assis.sthais@gmail.com`
[2] CentraleSupélec/Université Paris-Saclay, LGI - Laboratoire Génie Industriel,
Gif-sur-Yvette 91190, France

Abstract. The concept of Responsible Innovation holds that any innovation should take into account the balance of economic, ethical, social and sustainable aspects throughout the entire project in a manner that shows care for the future being constructed. However, as this concept is recent, originates in the context of the European Union and addresses issues of the Global North, critics have called for improvements in the way the concept is formulated. This article aims to establish a broader perspective to support the development of the concept of Responsible Innovation, which means discussing its main premises to highlight its critical aspects related to contextual terms, supporting a view to adapt it for use in different countries under various requirements and circumstances, thus facilitating its implementation on the path to innovation. Thus, an integrative review was developed. From an analysis of articles chosen based on research criteria, a useful theoretical framework was formed to fill the gaps in Responsible Innovation, comparing its perspectives to a traditional innovation, establishing a concept capable of yielding the expected benefits.

Keywords: Responsible innovation · Integrative review · Theoretical framework

1 Introduction

Innovation, as a concept, brings wide possibilities to delivering something substantially new, which generates some kind of value. The general premise is the combination of intellectual and practical creativity to bring about changes in what is known in the world. This transformation is therefore considered a creator of the future and can be conceived from incremental improvements to radical changes [2, 9].

Highlighting the change aspect promoted by an innovation, Jonas [10] discusses the "principle of responsibility" as an appropriate alternative for addressing technological impacts by indicating that modern technology must consider the effects of its action to influence human conditions; in this sense, action must be reflected and prudent.

The notion of responsibility has always been present in research and innovation practices, although this notion can be different in terms of time and place [24]. However,

© Springer Nature Switzerland AG 2020
A. Kő et al. (Eds.): EGOVIS 2020, LNCS 12394, pp. 49–63, 2020.
https://doi.org/10.1007/978-3-030-58957-8_4

the topic of Responsible Innovation (RI) is emergent and starts from the intention to create an approach with the purpose of reducing the uncertainties and ambiguities of an innovation while focusing on ethics, sustainability and social aspects [18, 24]. In this sense, RI is related to the intention to take care of the future through the management of innovation in the present [24].

Considering the European origin of the concept of Responsible Innovation, a forum was held in March 2014 in Campinas (Brazilian city), where Brazilian and UK researchers debated RI as a treaty in which there are specific considerations of realities in developed countries. For the researchers, it is necessary that the concept of RI be placed in debates on urban and economic development, institutional reforms, capacity building, transitions and social responsibility. To do so, it is essential to consider cultural, social and political aspects [13].

On the other hand, there are still criticisms and discussions about the concept of RI related to a lack of amplitude [21], a lack of practical indication [21, 32] and strong relations with political issues of the Global North [8, 24], which hinder its institutionalization [4].

In this sense, we understand the importance of considering the specificity of cultural and institutional contexts with respect to RI. Thus, it is crucial to seek a better conceptualization of RI so that its premises provide more beneficial results in the future. For Wodzisz [32], to discriminate against irresponsible innovations (referred to as traditional innovation in this work) is to avoid unnecessary effort in improving the impact of innovation, thereby simplifying the consideration of aspects of responsibility from the beginning of a project.

Given the aforementioned, this work is guided by the following questions: How is the field of studies in Responsible Innovation characterized? What are the approaches established by the concept of Responsible Innovation and its main characteristics? How can the concept of Responsible Innovation be configured to the detriment of a traditional innovation approach?

In this way, this work aims to identify characteristics and precepts established by the concept of Responsible Innovation and to discuss the exposed distinctions between responsible and traditional approaches to contribute to its applicability and construction of the state of the art.

This study can also be justified because it provides opportunities for academic and practical advances given that the theoretical field permeating RI is still incipient and under construction. Moreover, a bird's eye view on the applicability of a conceptualization and operationalization of Responsible Innovation allows it to be applied in different countries and based on different needs and realities facilitating its application in the innovation journey.

2   Responsible Innovation

Innovation, which is able to take many different forms, is a concept that deserves considerable exploration. In general, one can consider four main dimensions: product innovation, process innovation, position innovation, and paradigm innovation [7].

It has been said that innovation represents a challenge in that it is a moving target. The challenge is related to the finding that in dynamic environments, constant changes present new threats, new technologies, new markets and new regulatory frameworks. Thus, companies are concerned with ensuring their long-term survival [2].

In terms of results, it is not possible to argue that all innovations are essentially good, even if they propose to offer benefits. A well-known example is DDT, which was initially acclaimed as an innovation that would revolutionize the field of pesticides; however, significant negative impacts later came to light. Other negative impacts include nuclear energy and the development of "wonder" drugs. These considerations show the need to consider innovation options in a way that ensures an approach characterized by Responsible Innovation [2].

Before conceptualizing Responsible Innovation (RI), one must ask a plausible and necessary question: What qualifies as responsible? In the conceptual basis of Responsible Innovation, responsibility refers to the future that the innovation intends to create. Due to the wide range of possibilities for innovation and its goals, the nature of responsibility presents conceptual and practical difficulties [9].

RI is an emerging discourse through which various authors seek to reduce the uncertainties and ambiguities of an innovation through the concise construction of a promising framework [18, 24].

RI originates in the broader idea of Responsible Research and Innovation (RRI), which became an important expression in European political discourse because of its relation to future issues addressed in the European Union program "Horizon 2020," specifically with regard to the subject of research and innovation [11, 29]. RRI translates into a discourse containing a number of ideas that will most likely influence the way we will assess issues related to technological research and innovation in the future. As Stahl et al. [21] note, responsible research and innovation concept can be viewed as an umbrella used that includes orientation aspects to develop innovation, science, research and technology that turn into positive, desirable and socially acceptable outcomes.

In conceptual terms, there is no commonly held definition for RI, nor is there agreement on the best approach to implement it [29]. Owen, Macnaghten and Stilgoe [15] highlight some criticisms that consider RRI ambiguous in terms of its motivation, it needs a theoretical conceptualization more established and there is a lack of orientation to its translation into practice. Von Schomberg [28] considers it a process that focuses on transparency and the interaction of innovative social actors who bear in mind the mutual responsibility, acceptability, sustainability and social suitability of the process and the results of an innovation and its products.

Stahl et al. [22] discuss a concept of RI that focuses on socially desirable results. Owen et al. [16] highlight the collective and the importance of a responsive administration with a commitment to the present and awareness of the future. According to Pavie and Carthy [19], RI is the development of new products and services that combine growth, performance and responsibility. Blok and Lemmens [3] describe RI as a new approach to innovation.

According to Koops [11], the roots of RI can be found, separately and in combination, in science, technology and social studies along lines such as technological assessment and value-sensitive design, applied ethics, and governance and regulation studies. Thus, RI seeks to bring together a variety of ideas and traditions, considering interactions in the context of a complex process and constituting a broad and relevant approach that is applicable to innovations in institutions, social practices, regulations and technology.

3 Methodology

This study undertakes an integrative review of the literature on Responsible Innovation, specifically aiming to describe the field of RI research in management and business, identify specific central concepts, summarize the evidence found, and highlight relevant aspects that can guide a concept of RI. Figure 1 shows the study's methodological design.

An integrative review is useful to review the empirical and theoretical literature, as well as present the state of the art, for the purpose of developing an analysis of the results and summarizing contributions in an integrated manner [30].

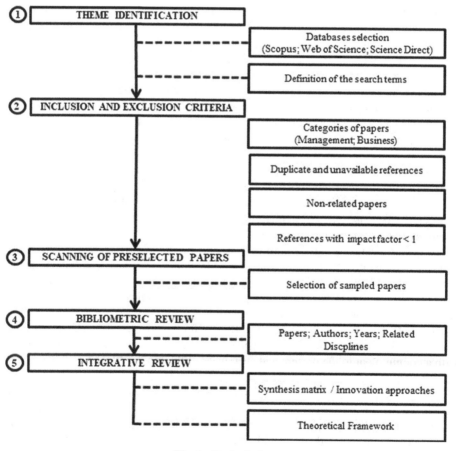

Fig. 1. Study design

Each methodological step developed is described below:

- Stage 1 – Theme identification. A search for articles was conducted in the Scopus, Web of Science (WoS) and Science Direct (SD) databases. The search covered all years. The search term was "responsible_innovation" with the underline Boolean operator and quotation marks to return results with this exact term. In the Scopus and Web of Science databases, the search was conducted in the "title" and "topic" fields, including abstracts and keywords. Since this option was not available in the Science Direct database, the search was conducted in all fields. The search found 351 articles in Scopus, 234 in WoS and 67 in Science Direct.
- Stage 2 – Inclusion and exclusion criteria. The first criterion was that the articles must be in English. In the Science Direct and Scopus databases, the search looked for articles in the business, management and accounting fields. In the WoS database, articles were sought in the fields of economics, business and management. The first filter returned 30 articles on the Web of Science and 105 in Scopus; since Science Direct did not offer an English language filter, all 67 articles from that database remained.

Tsujimoto et al. [25] applied a classification criterion to identify the most relevant journals in the field studied. Along these lines, an impact factor analysis (InCites) considered only journals with an impact factor greater than 1. Based on this and the other criteria defined for this study, the search excluded 76 articles found in Scopus, 24 articles in Science Direct and nine on the WoS. Another 33 studies were excluded because they were duplicates, and the titles and abstracts of the remaining 70 articles were then read to determine their relevance to this study. This phase excluded 52 articles.

- Stage 3 – Scanning of preselected papers: After step 2, we ended up with 18 papers for research and analysis. Those papers were preselected for in-depth reading and analysis. It is worth noting that we used peer review to reduce bias in interpretation.
- Stage 4 – Bibliometric review: To obtain a general overview of the field of Responsible Innovation, the publication years, primary authors and disciplines were identified.
- Stage 5 – Integrative review: For the purpose of establishing a broader conceptualization for operationalizing RI, an effort was made to identify aspects of its premises and conceptual elements. To this end, articles were placed on a synthesis matrix to organize them by topic: original basis, publication journal, impact factor, author, year, related country, abstract, keywords, research question, objectives, main RI concepts, theoretical and practical background, methodology, main contribution, specific details, gaps for future research, limitations and general observations. Based on the analysis of the synthesis matrix and the concepts and treatment of RI covered in the selected articles, this review highlights the considered approaches to innovation, the main concepts of RI, the main criticisms, and the related theories and practical approaches; it also presents a theoretical framework covering the main concepts and aspects discussed.

4   Analysis and Discussion

Beginning in 2010, discussion in the European Commission grew around the concept of the responsibility of science. A workshop in Brussels in May 2011 gave rise to the first public statements about RRI. This initially very broad concept was based on premises that focused on science and its relationship with society, treating risk management as the dominant paradigm [15].

Still in 2011, the term 'Responsible Innovation' (RI) gained ground in the discussion due to discomfort with the concept of RRI rooted in the European Union and science. The aim was therefore to question the public value of science and address the impact of research and open space for public participation in creating socially desirable innovation, which came to mean "innovation management" rather than "risk management" [15].

4.1 Evolution of Publications and Overview of Responsible Innovation

To provide a better understanding of the studies and movement of the field, Fig. 2 shows the evolution of publications over time. The sample consisted of studies from 2009 to 2018, with 2018 accounting for the largest number of publications (five). This evolution demonstrates and reinforces the overview of the initial discussions about RI and its status as an emerging field.

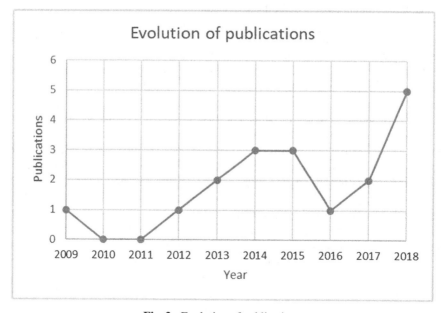

Fig. 2. Evolution of publications

Several authors stand out as having multiple works on this list; Jack Stilgoe, Richard Owen, Phil Macnaghten, Arnim Wiek, Rider W. Foley and Bernd Carsten Stahl account for two publications each. With regard to the related discipline, Fig. 3 shows the topics discussed in the sample of articles.

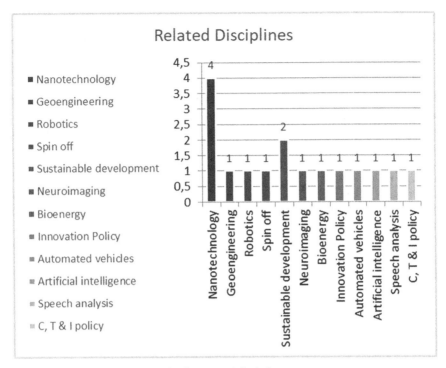

Fig. 3. Related disciplines.

Nanotechnology was cited in four articles as a practical example of innovation. On this point, it is worth noting that according to Genus and Iskandarova [8], empirical research on RI initially focused on nanotechnology, biomedical technologies, geoengineering and information technologies, and the emphasis in these articles underscores that nanotechnology in particular is widely considered in recent publications to present great challenges for science, technology and innovation (ST&I) policies and to be one of the sources of discussion about RI [4, 6, 17].

4.2 Approaches to Innovation

It is worth highlighting the conceptual approaches to "innovation" discussed. With regard to typologies, Meissner, Polt and Vonortas [14] discuss traditional types of innovation as being product innovation, process innovation, marketing innovation and organizational innovation. According to Wodzisz [32], one should consider innovations as being "already existing," "undergoing implementation" and "to be implemented in the future."

According to Legault, Verchère and Patenaude [12], innovation is the result of supply and demand, is not limited to production components and needs to be analyzed based on its impacts on cultures and societies. Thus, innovation can be seen as a complex, collective and dynamic process [4, 15, 24]. Owen, Macnaghten and Stilgoe [15] add that based on its collective character, innovation can shape the future.

This collective feature of innovation can be explained by considering that innovation is linked to socioeconomic, environmental, health and safety factors and that to provide benefits, these factors should be seen as interrelated integrating factors [14]. Along similar lines, Arentshorst et al. [1] emphasize that innovation depends on interrelated dynamics and mechanisms such as demand, networks and technologies.

Robinson [20] suggests a metaphor for innovation as a journey involving actors, artifacts and infrastructure in a dynamic process of co-development. Underscoring that innovation is much more than technology and that the value chain of innovation is marked by nonlinear dynamics, Meissner, Polt and Vonortas [14] emphasize that other resources are essential to determining an innovation's adoption and survival in the marketplace, indicating a new direction for the mission.

In this sense, Shortall, Raman and Millar [23] highlight that innovation can take forms other than an industrial focus, but it is important to keep in mind that quality must be maintained. Wodzisz [32] discuss the importance of developing innovations to improve conditions without affecting people and the planet, thus following a logic of "doing good."

Foley and Wiek [6] believe that innovations can have long-range impacts and become global phenomena. Along similar lines, Owen, Macnaghten and Stilgoe [15] emphasize that being responsible in terms of innovation is itself innovative and has a collective aspect.

4.3 Concepts and Approaches of Responsible Innovation

Analysis of the articles showed that four authors are key to shaping the concept of RI: Von Schomberg, Stilgoe, Macnaghten and Owen. Of the 18 articles selected, 10 cite or refer to these authors.

Von Schomberg is generally associated with the initial concept of RRI, as he was a member of the European Commission [21, 32]. The articles that cite the works of Stilgoe, Macnaghten and Owen discuss a conceptual broadening that extends the focus of RRI, presenting RI as concept that goes beyond science and the political environment of the European Union. It is worth noting that these authors sought to complement and broaden von Schomberg's initial concept, proposing a definition based on a prospective notion of responsibility based on four dimensions: anticipation, reflexivity, inclusion and responsiveness [24].

Due to its emerging nature, the concept of RI has been criticized for its close association with the European Union and the Global North in general [8, 24], as well as for the vague nature of the concept [21] and its lack of practical orientation [21], all of which makes it difficult to institutionalize [4].

The point about the concept's geographically limited scope can be seen in the articles chosen for analysis, which considered only the context of developed countries, or, as they are known in the literature, countries of the Global North [8]. The selected articles addressed regions in different ways: two about the European Union, five about the United Kingdom, two about the United States, one about Norway, Holland, and Canada, and one about OECD member countries.

A variety of theories and practical approaches were related to RI, as displayed in Table 1.

Table 1. Practical approaches related to Responsible Innovation

Approach related to RI	Authors cited
Value-sensitive design (VSD)	[5, 12]
Corporate social responsibility	[12, 27]
Constructive technology assessment (CTA)	[12, 15, 20]
Technology assessment (TA)	[5, 8, 20, 24, 31]
Scenarios	[6, 24]
Sociotechnical integration research (STIR)	[5, 24, 31]

It is worth noting that [24] suggest techniques and approaches to each dimension of the framework they propose (anticipation, reflexivity, inclusion and responsiveness).

4.4 Integrative Review and Theoretical Framework

Analysis of the articles showed that four authors are key to shaping the concept of RI: Von Schomberg, Stilgoe, Macnaghten and Owen. Of the 18 articles selected, 10 cite or refer to these authors.

According to Von Schomberg [29], Irresponsible Innovation is characterized by the intentions and actions of innovation that focus on technology push and policy pull, neglecting ethical aspects, foresight and caution. To fend off criticism about a classification that might be seen as pejorative, based on Von Schomberg [29], Traditional Innovation will be treated here as a type of innovation that has not yet subscribed to the premises of RI.

Based on the concepts and treatment highlighted by the articles selected for review, Responsible Innovation, as opposed to traditional innovation, is related to ethics: the lack of separation between technical and nontechnical aspects; the relationship between economic, social and environmental goals; collective values; integrative propositions; intentions for the right intergenerational impacts; innovation based on quality, security and well-being; development based on constructive dialogue with stakeholders; and attention to the country/context/domain as part of the innovative process.

A theoretical framework was therefore developed (Fig. 4) to detail the concept of RI based on the constitutive elements found in the integrative review of the literature. It is emphasized that this framework is also based on the treatment of Irresponsible Innovation highlighted by Von Schomberg [29], which is treated here as Traditional Innovation.

First, it is emphasized that innovations are distinguished by management. Responsible Innovation is considered the management of innovation, dealing with anticipation, reflexivity, inclusion and responsiveness; traditional innovation focuses on risk management in economic terms.

Responsible innovation is distinguished from traditional innovation by its premises, development interests and impacts. It starts with a project that is developed by a dynamic and nonlinear process of innovation until it reaches the market, society and

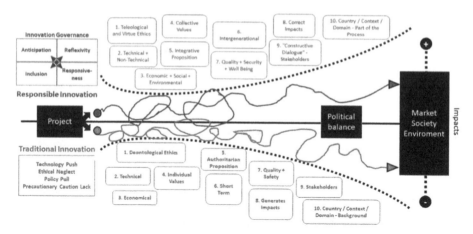

Fig. 4. Theoretical framework

the environment. It is argued that traditional innovation has a greater tendency to produce negative impacts. Responsible innovation, on the other hand, leads to more positive impacts because of its more social, ethical, sustainable and forward-looking management. However, it is not argued here that RI produces only positive impacts.

Depending on the innovation project, the path taken differs as to the premises. The nonlinearity of the innovation journey is shown using red and blue lines. It cannot be said that responsible premises facilitate the development of a project, but we state that the inclusion of elements of responsibility from the very beginning of the conception reduces the potential for problems. This is mainly due to the multidisciplinary nature of the stakeholders (inclusion), who provide a variety of perspectives on the same topic, and because they focus on reducing future uncertainties (anticipation), considering limits, barriers and conceptions (reflexivity), and paying attention to public values to improve their ability to respond to potential impacts (responsiveness).

The literature has noted the importance of political action to promote a balance between traditional and responsible innovation. This political balance can be seen as an action that values reflection, deliberation and democracy, seeking to guide responsible actions and programs without limiting the range of innovation [4, 8, 14, 23]. Policymakers take on the role of orchestrating relationships among stakeholders, focusing on a common language, promoting new initiatives and regulating the existing initiatives without taking a heavy-handed approach [14, 27].

Responsible Innovation is a meta-responsibility [21]. There is a focus on specific issues of responsibility, such as ethics [12, 21], social acceptance [5] or sustainability [6, 23, 26, 27, 31, 32]. The question thus arises: To be considered responsible, can an innovation develop aspects separately, or must it be a complete conceptual package?

We will use the term Pure Responsible Innovation to refer to an innovation that contains all the premises of RI, without any aspect or feature of Traditional Innovation. However, we argue that an innovation does not need to be pure to be responsible. The purpose of this premise is that it is necessary to avoid the utopia of a Pure RI, as a variety of contextual obstacles can interfere with a smooth journey for RI. Considering the circumstances of the Global South (underdeveloped or emerging countries), some innovations may have more 'impurities'. However, recognizing barriers is already a responsible action, and it is imperative to make an effort to develop an innovation that does good and seeks to minimize negative impacts and maximize positive ones, discussing uncertainties to clarify them and benefit the environment, the market and society. An innovation can therefore be considered responsible even if it contains aspects of traditional innovation, and vice versa.

It is therefore argued that a project can overcome the dichotomy between responsible and traditional innovation along the road to innovation. As innovation is a process that takes place under specific circumstances, a responsible project can show traces of traditional innovation, such as focusing on technology push, being highly dependent on policy pull or focusing on economic and commercial goals.

RI goes beyond regulation and institutionalization by considering contextual and disciplinary differences, focusing its action on public values [5, 15, 24, 32]. Working with transparency, openness, inclusion and dialogue, an interdisciplinary effort focuses on processes rather than solely on results and looks at risks from a variety of perspectives, building a future of co-development. It is therefore necessary to pay attention to flows, links, political environments, infrastructure, markets, diversity, culture, barriers and limitations, making constructive interventions and taking into account the logic of cause and effect and the uncertain scale of an innovation's impact.

Pandza and Ellwood [17] emphasize that RI is predominantly tied to deontological and teleological ethics, often paying less attention to ethics as a virtue. Deontological ethics relates innovation to rules, norms and principles, making it easier to ensure responsibility. From a teleological perspective, innovation based on the understanding of its agents concentrates only on consequences. However, given the intrinsic uncertainty of an innovation's journey and the limitations of regulatory structures and risk management techniques, it is necessary to take a further step toward ethics based on virtuous actors. Thus, the ethics of virtue emphasize that motivation must be based on contributing to the world through innovation. This treatment highlights the importance of including stakeholders in every step of the project. Based on these considerations, it is suggested that we need to consider the consequences and rely on virtuous agents so that RI will therefore be responsible based on teleological and virtuous ethics.

In short, it is argued that we must create a responsible ecosystem. This argument is based on contextual specifics, the particulars of the practical fields, and a recognition of the importance of ethics in a scenario of coexisting factors.

5 Conclusions

According to Koops [11], responsibility in the concept of Responsible Innovation refers to ethical acceptance with regard to sustainability and suitability with regard to social questions so that the innovation's objectives are careful about the future, considering and balancing economic, sociocultural and environmental factors. In short, the emphasis is on including ethical and social values in the innovation process.

To understand the concept of Responsible Innovation (RI), we extend an invitation to reflection, as we believe it is necessary to structure the innovation journey around central questions: What will be created? What will be the results and implications of this innovation? [6]. What future do we want for ourselves and for future generations? [15]. These questions indicate the main premises of RI.

To understand how the concept of Responsible Innovation may prevail over the Traditional Innovation approach, a theoretical framework was developed based on the analyses derived from the integrative review of the literature on RI, Irresponsible Innovation [29], and the criticism raised about the concept of RI.

Based on this framework, it is suggested that the standard for innovation be reflection and ethics based on teleology and virtues. In this way, recognizing that the future is built in the present, the focus turns to impacts, and it is possible to develop innovation that serves as the engine of growth and adds socioeconomic and environmental value to society, the market and the environment.

The following reflective question was thus posed: To be considered responsible, can an innovation develop aspects separately, or must it be a complete conceptual package? It is argued that the framework is not a model, but a recommendation for the best use of the Responsible Innovation approach. This is done by proposing the concept of Pure Responsible Innovation (Pure RI), which is an innovation characterized exclusively by the incorporation of all the premises of RI. However, considering the contextual factors and other characteristics of a country, it is understood that an innovation does not necessarily need to be pure to be responsible. It is argued that the very recognition of barriers is a responsible act, which maximizes the innovation's responsibility by aligning it with the effort to do good and seeking to minimize negative effects.

This study presents important contributions in that it develops a concept that includes not only the "p's" of technological innovation (product, patent, production, profit, pioneering) but also the "p's" of Responsible Innovation: people and planet. It is hoped that this article will contribute to academic progress, a general overview of the state of the art on the topic and practical treatments, as the theoretical field around RI is still being developed.

It is noted that the use of the impact factor as a filter in the selection of articles may have limited this study. However, this is a limitation designed to ensure that the study works with the most influential articles in the literature [25].

It is suggested that future research include a deeper analysis of each of the characteristics of Traditional and Pure Responsible Innovation, as well as the application of the theoretical framework in a practical context, thus proposing the applicability of Responsible Innovation with nonpure characteristics. Moreover, future studies can highlight the roles of the stakeholders involved in RI in a manner that addresses the identified gaps, such as criticism of the lack of practical approaches to the concept.

Acknowledgments. This work is supported by the "ADI 2019" project funded by the IDEX Paris-Saclay, ANR-11-IDEX-0003-02.

References

1. Arentshorst, M.E., Buning, T.C., Boon, W.P., Broerse, J.E.: Prospecting responsible technology paths: management options for an appropriate societal embedding of medical neuroimaging. Sci. Public Policy **42**(6), 775–788 (2015). https://doi.org/10.1093/scipol/scv004
2. Bessant, J.: Innovation in the twenty-first century. In: Owen, R., Bessant, J., Heintz, M. (eds.) Responsible Innovation: Managing the Responsible Emergence of Science and Innovation in Society, pp. 01-26. Wiley, New York (2013). https://doi.org/10.1002/9781118551424
3. Blok, V., Lemmens, P.: The emerging concept of responsible innovation. three reasons why it is questionable and calls for a radical transformation of the concept of innovation. In: Koops, B.-J., Oosterlaken, I., Romijn, H., Swierstra, T., van den Hoven, J. (eds.) Responsible Innovation 2, pp. 19–35. Springer, Cham (2015). https://doi.org/10.1007/978-3-319-17308-5_2
4. Flink, T., Kaldewey, D.: The new production of legitimacy: STI policy discourses beyond the contract metaphor. Res. Policy **47**(1), 14–22 (2018). https://doi.org/10.1016/j.respol.2017.09.008
5. Flipse, S.M., Puylaert, S.: Organizing a collaborative development of technological design requirements using a constructive dialogue on value profiles: a case in automated vehicle development. Sci. Eng. Ethics **24**(1), 49–72 (2018). https://doi.org/10.1007/s11948-017-9877-3
6. Foley, R.W., Wiek, A.: Scenarios of nanotechnology innovation vis-à-vis sustainability challenges. Futures **64**, 1–14 (2014). https://doi.org/10.1016/j.futures.2014.09.005
7. Francis, D., Bessant, J.: Targeting innovation and implications for capability development. Technovation **25**(3), 171–183 (2005). https://doi.org/10.1016/j.technovation.2004.03.004
8. Genus, A., Iskandarova, M.: Responsible innovation: its institutionalisation and a critique. Technol. Forecast. Soc. Chang. **128**, 1–9 (2018). https://doi.org/10.1016/j.techfore.2017.09.029
9. Grinbaum, A., Groves, C.: What is "responsible" about responsible innovation? Understanding the ethical issues In: Owen, R., J. Bessant and M. Heintz (eds.): Responsible Innovation: Managing the Responsible Emergence of Science and Innovation in Society, pp. 119–142. Wiley, New York (2013). https://doi.org/10.1002/9781118551424
10. Jonas, H.: Toward a philosophy of technology. Hastings Cent. Rep. **9**(1), 34–43 (1979). https://doi.org/10.2307/3561700
11. Koops, B.-J.: The concepts, approaches, and applications of responsible innovation. In: Koops, B.-J., Oosterlaken, I., Romijn, H., Swierstra, T., van den Hoven, J. (eds.) Responsible Innovation 2, pp. 1–15. Springer, Cham (2015). https://doi.org/10.1007/978-3-319-17308-5_1
12. Legault, G.A., Verchère, C., Patenaude, J.: Support for the development of technological innovations: promoting responsible social uses. Sci. Eng. Ethics **24**(2), 529–549 (2018). https://doi.org/10.1007/s11948-017-9911-5
13. Macnaghten, P., et al.: Inovação responsável através de fronteiras: tensões, paradoxos e possibilidades. Teoria & Pesquisa: Revista de Ciência Política **24**(2), 18–24 (2015). https://doi.org/10.4322/tp.24210
14. Meissner, D., Polt, W., Vonortas, N.S.: Towards a broad understanding of innovation and its importance for innovation policy. J. Technol. Transf. **42**(5), 1184–1211 (2017). https://doi.org/10.1007/s10961-016-9485-4
15. Owen, R., Macnaghten, P., Stilgoe, J.: Responsible research and innovation: from science in society to science for society, with society. Sci. Public Policy **39**(6), 751–760 (2012). https://doi.org/10.1093/scipol/scs093

16. Owen, R., Stilgoe, J., Macnaghten, P., Gorman, M., Fisher, E., Guston, D.: A framework for responsible innovation. In: Owen, R., Bessant, J., Heintz, M. (eds.) Responsible Innovation: Managing the Responsible Emergence of Science and Innovation in Society, pp. 27–50. Wiley, New York (2013). https://doi.org/10.1002/9781118551424

17. Pandza, K., Ellwood, P.: Strategic and ethical foundations for responsible innovation. Res. Policy 42(5), 1112–1125 (2013). https://doi.org/10.1016/j.respol.2013.02.007

18. Paredes-Frigolett, H., Gomes, L.F.A.M., Pereira, J.: Governance of responsible research and innovation: an agent-based model approach. Procedia Comput. Sci. 55, 912–921 (2015). https://doi.org/10.1016/j.procs.2015.07.113

19. Pavie, X., Carthy, D.: Leveraging uncertainty: a practical approach to the integration of responsible innovation through design thinking. Procedia Soc. Behav. Sci. 213, 1040–1049 (2015). https://doi.org/10.1016/j.sbspro.2015.11.523

20. Robinson, D.K.R.: Co-evolutionary scenarios: an application to prospecting futures of the responsible development of nanotechnology. Technol. Forecast. Soc. Chang. 76(9), 1222–1239 (2009). https://doi.org/10.1016/j.techfore.2009.07.015

21. Stahl, B.C., McBride, N., Wakunuma, K., Flick, C.: The empathic care robot: a prototype of responsible research and innovation. Technol. Forecast. Soc. Chang. 84, 74–85 (2014). https://doi.org/10.1016/j.techfore.2013.08.001

22. Stahl, B.C., Eden, G., Flick, C., Jirotka, M., Nguyen, Quang A., Timmermans, J.: The observatory for responsible research and innovation in ICT: identifying problems and sharing good practice. In: Koops, B.-J., Oosterlaken, I., Romijn, H., Swierstra, T., van den Hoven, J. (eds.) Responsible Innovation 2, pp. 105–120. Springer, Cham (2015). https://doi.org/10.1007/978-3-319-17308-5_6

23. Shortall, O.K., Raman, S., Millar, K.: Are plants the new oil? Responsible innovation, biorefining and multipurpose agriculture. Energy Policy 86, 360–368 (2015). https://doi.org/10.1016/j.enpol.2015.07.011

24. Stilgoe, J., Owen, R., Macnaghten, P.: Developing a framework for responsible innovation. Res. Policy 42(9), 1568–1580 (2013). https://doi.org/10.1016/j.respol.2013.05.008

25. Tsujimoto, M., Kajikawa, Y., Tomita, J., Matsumoto, Y.: A review of the ecosystem concept - towards coherent ecosystem. Technol. Forecast. Soc. Chang. 136, 49–58 (2018). https://doi.org/10.1016/j.techfore.2017.06.032

26. van Geenhuizen, M., Ye, Q.: Responsible innovators: open networks on the way to sustainability transitions. Technol. Forecast. Soc. Chang. 87, 28–40 (2014). https://doi.org/10.1016/j.techfore.2014.06.001

27. Voegtlin, C., Scherer, A.G.: Responsible innovation and the innovation of responsibility: governing sustainable development in a globalized world. J. Bus. Ethics 143(2), 227–243 (2017). https://doi.org/10.1007/s10551-015-2769-z

28. Von Schomberg, R.: Towards responsible research and innovation in the information and communication technologies and security technologies fields. European Commission-DG Research and Innovation, Luxemburgo (2011). https://doi.org/10.2777/58723

29. Von Schomberg, R.: A vision of responsible innovation. In: Owen, R., J. Bessant and M. Heintz (eds.) Responsible Innovation: Managing the Responsible Emergence of Science and Innovation in Society, pp. 01–26. Wiley, New York (2013). https://doi.org/10.1002/9781118551424

30. Whittemore, R., Knafl, K.: The integrative review: updated methodology. J. Adv. Nurs. 52(5), 546–553 (2005). https://doi.org/10.1111/j.1365-2648.2005.03621.x

31. Wiek, A., Foley, R.W., Guston, D.H., Bernstein, M.J.: Broken promises and breaking ground for responsible innovation–intervention research to transform business-as-usual in nanotechnology innovation. Technol. Anal. Strateg. Manag. **28**(6), 639–650 (2016). https://doi.org/10.1080/09537325.2015.1129399

32. Wodzisz, R.: Case Study of R-1234yf refrigerant: implications for the framework for responsible innovation. Sci. Eng. Ethics **21**(6), 1413–1433 (2015). https://doi.org/10.1007/s11948-014-9612-2

Towards a Process Based Approach to Address Investment Inefficiencies in Digitalization

Domonkos Gaspar[⊠] ⓘ and Katalin Ternai ⓘ

Corvinus University of Budapest, Fővám tér 8., Budapest 1093, Hungary
domonkos.gaspar@stud-uni.corvinus.hu,
katalin.ternai@uni-corvinus.hu

Abstract. Recent research show that 70% of the digitalization initiatives do not reach their goal [1, 2], posing an obvious challenge to digitalization leaders. Enterprises reconsidering their investments into digitalization, while technology push stays high: current epidemy-forced home office based working proves value add of digitalization, while the second wave of digitalization is already on the doorsteps [3–5]. Digitalization is demanding major changes in the organizations with the promise to conduct business still (or more) profitably. As markets keep evolving, competitive enterprises have to adapt core value-added processes with unprecedented speed, to act appropriately regardless of the situation [6]. For this, well designed and continuously improved process models must be implemented in the real world with real employees interacting with real software applications and physical automation devices which must be integrated with real integration platforms to achieve and sustain the intended change results. Modern BPM suites are evolving to automate the modeling, monitoring and redesign of complex, collaborative processes to achieve these goals [7]. In this paper we reason for utilizing research made into business process management, to address investment efficiency challenges in digitalization. We will also share the first results of our case study based research that is conducted to verify our hypothesis.

Keywords: Digitalization · Business process modelling · Process Management · Integrated Change Management · Efficiency · Sustainability

1 Introduction and Problem Statement

Digitalization has been a key factor in recent business considerations. Although focus seems to be shifting year-to-year, the subject at large has not lost on importance. It has significantly matured in the past years, which is reflected by the amounts invested, the number of success stories published. Almost every offering on the market today has a "digital" component and legislation is actively supporting the adaption of digital business. One can obtain the impression that digitalization is well under way.

Increasing maturity brings forward research suggesting that behind the scenes digitalization has a major efficiency problem: "of 1.3 Trillion USD invested into Digital Transformation in 2018, an estimated 900 Billion went to waste. 70% of the digital

© Springer Nature Switzerland AG 2020
A. Kő et al. (Eds.): EGOVIS 2020, LNCS 12394, pp. 64–77, 2020.
https://doi.org/10.1007/978-3-030-58957-8_5

initiatives do not reach their goal." [1] and despite digitalization is key for industry players, only 30% of them is happy with what they achieved in this area [2]. Despite promising concept studies (PoCs) and ambitious business cases, practitioners find that organizational integration of the new technologies is difficult, hindering the needed scale up. Furthermore, lack of clear focus of the organizations result in a broader-than-needed scope. The widely spread digitalization investments establish an unfortunate position for ROI calculations.

Retrospective into the past decades of advanced information technology causes a deja'vu with many practitioners: in the end of the 1990's early 2000 reports revealed very similar figures on the success rate of ERP implementations [8, 9]. In response, scholars and practitioners conducted extensive research to find the root causes of the inefficiency and appealing solutions to address them. Efforts were not without results: recent surveys show significant improvement in the IT project success [10, 11].

In this article we argue that there are sufficient similarities to consider solutions developed for efficiency increase in ERP implementations (specifically the business process based implementation approach) to shortcut the learning curve for digitalization. In the second part of this work we will introduce the intermediary results of our research intended to examine our assumption.

2   History Repeats Itself?

Based on the initial impressions it is worth taking a deeper look into the context of the situation 20–25 years ago – "ERP age", and now – "Digitalization".

Although a comprehensive study of the two "ages" would exceed the context of this article, there are noteworthy similarities. In the below table we highlight some characteristics of the ERP age and Digitalization (Table 1).

Table 1. Characteristics of the ERP-era and digitalization (Source: own work)

	ERP	Digitalization
Initial success rate of goal achievement	<70%	
Push from…	Technology	
Organizational impact	Large	
Initiative led by typically by	IT	IT/Digitalisation Leader
Visible improvements in implementation efficiency?	Yes	No
Technology	Semi-mature	New/Innovative

There are similarities and differences in the circumstances which can be described as below:

- Similarity: Besides the mentioned low level of investment efficiency it is visible that both "ages" were driven by a technology push, in other words fast spreading of technologies becoming accessible to a wide range of companies, with the promise of economic benefits when implementation completed. The core of the matter is, that in order to achieve the economic benefits with technology, a "new way of working" needs to be implemented: facilitation of technology must be assured, thus, besides the obvious technology integration and data management aspects, changes need to take place in business processes, organizational structure and capabilities.

- Biggest differences between the cases lay in the maturity of the technology and the type of organizational change in the respective time. In the "ERP age" existing processes were covered by digital means, while in digitalization new and improved processes are the objective.

In summary, both ages, ERP and Digitalization facing the same challenge: without proper embedment of technology into the organizational setting, technology cannot facilitate the expected economic improvements. The referred surveys results that the most important challenges of in implementing digitalization initiatives relate to operational aspects. Therefore technology embedment needs thorough review of the company's operations: procedural, organizational and cultural changes to be implemented.

At this point we would like to highlight that the development of technologies is not subject to our research, nevertheless we argue that utilization of any kind of technology in business context needs a proper embedment into the company's business model and capabilities. All aspects need review and bound to be affected, the extent of change will vary.

Beyond the range business model and capability aspects affected and needed to be changed in the implementation, the business process and technology integrity needs to be maintained on an ongoing basis.

'Ignore history - condemned to repeat it' [12]. Even if no one can step into the same river twice, similarities between the ages grant the opportunity to consider applying improvement measures on investment efficiency from the ERP "age" to current Digitalization.

3   Approach Selection and Contribution

Multiple approaches have been drawn up by scholars to capture the complexities and problems in ERP implementations [8, 20] which have made inroads and further diversified in the commercial ERP implementation approaches. Among the approaches Business Process Management (BPM) stands out. We selected BPM as a basis for our research for the following reasons:

- Due to its origins in TQM, BPM provides an adequate bridge to industrial Operations management [39]
- BPM through its dynamic (process flow) and static (organization, data, systems) models provide an organization-wide coverage for change implementation [13]
- BPM has been developed into a comprehensive system of BPM Lifecycle that supports ongoing optimization of processes – another bridge linking through Continuous Improvement to Operation Management [36, 40, 41]
- BPM is the underlying approach for ARIS, the implementation support tool of one of the most recognized ERP system: SAP.

Contribution of our Research is the adaption and validation of a BPM based implementation architecture that provides basis for analysis of difference between existing and intended state, to be used with digitalization initiatives in industrial context. Our research is ongoing. Partial results are published as research progresses.

4 Literature Review

Process based approach to Change Management is deeply rooted in the knowledge based theory of the firm. Corporate scholars agree that a dynamic co-creation among the aspects of the individual, corporate culture and organizational structures are indispensable for the value creation of an organization, especially in current developments, where "machine" organizations are being taken over by quickly mobilizing, nimble and empowered (in short: agile) organizations [14–16].

An organization in an ever changing, vibrant environment require effective, continuous improvement so to remain existent and propagate. Manufacturing organizational methodologies, such as LEAN, developed in the midst of the 3rd industrial revolution in the 1950s and 1960s retain their strong structuring position and through their Continuous Improvement approach enable organizational agility [13, 17–20].

Since its inception, Information Technology (IT) has been the enabler of the business and became inevitable for the existence of organizations while it has been a scientific and organizational domain on its own merit. IT is necessary contributor and has the potential to be the carrier of digital transformations, while it still often find itself in translation problems with the business. During its commoditization process throughout the decades own methodologies and standards were developed and succeeded to cross-fertilize business approaches [21–27].

Scholars argue, and we have in our earlier paper outlined a practical approach, that Business Process Management through its tool of BPMN can provide a common denominator that can solve imminent translation problems between business and IT and can limit instinctive reactions (rejection) to change while promoting a contemporary individual (employee) focused change management approach to build agile organizations [13, 28–31].

4.1 Business Process Modelling (BPM) Languages

Modeling languages are beneficial for process description, simulation and execution purposes as prose descriptions of complex processes is challenging to understand and thus a source of error whereas a picture of "a workflow of a business process is in most cases self-explaining" [32] Additionally, a visual description of a process reveals inconsistencies, infinite loops or non-terminating conditions. All modeling languages define a consistent set of rules with different strengths and weaknesses with the ambition to allow improved readability.

BPMN is the dominating notation for business process modeling with a market share of about 85% (BPMN 1.2 & BPMN 2.0 combined) [32]. Nevertheless, Event Driven Process Chain (EPC), Unified Modeling Language (UML), Case Management Model and Notation (CMMN) and Decision Model and Notation [DMN] are alternatives worth mentioning. While multiple notations seem to be worth noticing alternatives to BPMN, the wider dissemination and thus knowledge of BPMN is a clear advantage. As in our research we use BPMN this is in the center point of our paper.

4.2 BPM Tools

Modern BPM suites are evolving to automate the modeling, monitoring and redesign of complex, collaborative processes to achieve these goals [7]. At the core of their purpose BPM tools are developed to facilitate BPM related work and provide a "single source of truth" in the organization, related to BPM. They promise a comprehensive set of functionality that support process description, feature process related attributes, allows (capacity-, workload-, path-, etc.) simulations, analysis, reporting and documentation. Due to the increasing popularity of the BPMN standard, the numbers of tools for modeling processes with BPMN are available ten a penny. Available tools are of very different nature (e.g. industrial vs. academic, open source vs. commercial, few functions vs. software suites, BPMN 1.2 vs. BPMN2.0…) which can derive from an open source project to an intelligent business suite, all serving similar but different purposes. Extensive research has been conducted on the capabilities, dissemination and specifics of tools available on the market. A review of that literature would exceed the capacities of this paper [32–35].

4.3 Process Analysis Framework

Business Process Redesign and Transformations in their execution on business processes and information systems can in their essence be regarded as larger scale Change Requests. We argue that, with certain enhancements, our integrated Change Management approach can serve as basis for those large-scale re-design and transformation approaches [31, 36].

In order to handle to the dynamics that business process changes present, extensions are made to the earlier version of our model: "Process & Organization" category is split. The logic of the five categories is as follows: (i) Business Processes are executed by (ii) People in a defined (iii) Organization(al structure), while doing this (iv) Data is generated, handled or adjusted which is (v) supported by Technology (Fig. 1).

Main Process
Trigger
Results
Sub-process A
Sub-process B
Sub-process C
Sub-process X
Business Process
People
Organization
Data
Technology
Change Categories
Business function 1
Business function 2
Business function n

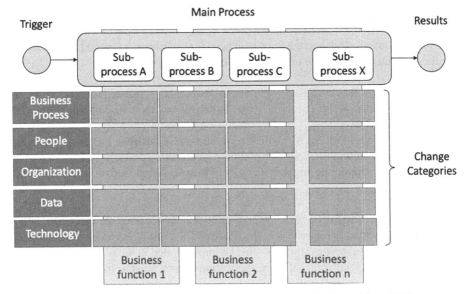

Fig. 1. Process analysis framework (Source: own work adapted from [30])

The five categories cover all aspects of a comprehensive change which, by intention, needs to be made in a sustainable manner (Fig. 2).

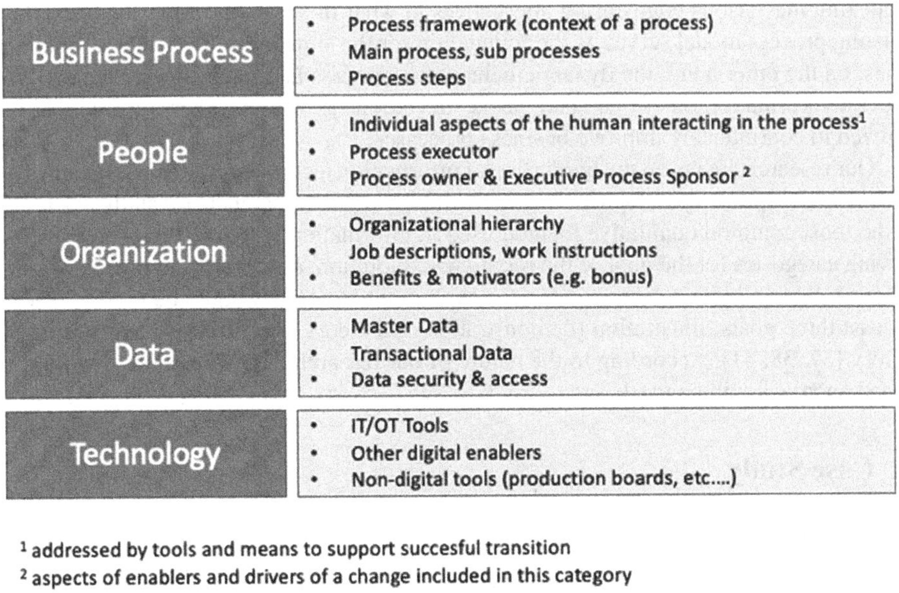

Business Process
• Process framework (context of a process)
• Main process, sub processes
• Process steps
People
• Individual aspects of the human interacting in the process1
• Process executor
• Process owner & Executive Process Sponsor 2
Organization
• Organizational hierarchy
• Job descriptions, work instructions
• Benefits & motivators (e.g. bonus)
Data
• Master Data
• Transactional Data
• Data security & access
Technology
• IT/OT Tools
• Other digital enablers
• Non-digital tools (production boards, etc....)
1 addressed by tools and means to support succesful transition
2 aspects of enablers and drivers of a change included in this category

Fig. 2. Change categories (Source: own work)

5 Research Questions and Approach

Based on previous research and the imminent need for improvement in the Digitalization projects, we focus our research on answering the following questions

1. Can the Business Process based implementation method, suggested for more efficient ERP implementations [41] be utilized for Digitalization Initiatives? Should the model be adjusted and how?
2. How can Business Process Modelling tools support a Business Process Modelling based implementation method? What should be considered when selecting a tool?
3. How can BPM support the ongoing integrity of Business needs and fitting IT solutions and services?

A competitive enterprise has to adapt core value-added processes with unprecedented speed, to act appropriately regardless of the situation [6]. For this perfectly designed and continuously improved process models must be implemented in the real world with real employees interacting with real software applications which must be integrated with real integration platforms.

A general business process architecture encompasses the whole life-cycle: from business process design to information technology deployment, leading to a process-oriented software concept, from Business Process Reengineering to Continuous Process Improvement. When engineering optimal business processes, it is possible to compare alternative procedures (benchmarking) or carry out simulation studies or quality evaluations. No methodical enhancements of the business process model are necessary for defining and analyzing the various engineering alternatives in what-if-situations. After analysis, the existing process model serves as the foundation for the simulation. In dynamic simulations, on the other hand, the dynamic behavior of process alternatives is studied. BPM provide information on "to-be" and "as-is" deviations as well as other information, is utilized to continuously improve business processes.

Our research area is on the borderline of information technology and social sciences. This interdisciplinarity influences the methodology of the research. Case study research is the most common qualitative method used in information systems. Yin used the following categories for the goal of the research: exploration, description and explanation. Case studies could be used not only in an explorative way. They could be used to reach at least three goals: illustration (demonstration of a theory), constructing and testing a theory [37, 38, 41]. According to the nature of our research only a detailed, case study based approach will be used.

6 Case Study

6.1 Background

A medical devices company launched an initiative to investigate relevant digital tools which could be useful for its future Research and Development approaches and processes. Following analysis of current needs and future opportunities, the correlation between benefits and ability to execute has been particularly attractive in the case of

"Augmented and Virtual Reality in the Research and Development process". Following a Proof of Concept (PoC) and a number of technology clarifications, a subsequent business case had proven a positive Return on Investment (RoI) scenario when introducing this technology in their business.

As user related benefits outweighed other areas, decision has been made to focus implementation efforts in that area. In order to assure integrity, the wider context of the product development project as well as regulatory compliance constraints had to be considered. Due to the high degree of procedural changes imposed by the technology to Product Development, especially in the area of User Experience related conceptualization and testing, a Business Process focused implementation method was decided focusing on the User Experience Engineering process.

6.2 Project Approach – Research Phases

For our research project, a distinct three phases approach was built with the content in each step as described in the below table (Table 2).

Table 2. Phases of the research project (Source: own work)

Phases	Phase 1	Phase 2	Phase 3
Title	**AS-IS**	**TO-BE**	**GAP & ACTIONS**
Main content	• Stakeholder definition and engagement • Agreement on process notation • As-Is process documentation	• Establishment of the To-Be process • Evaluation of available BPM tools to be used in Phase 3	• Analysis of the difference between "as-is" and "to-be" • Determining areas of change, handling recommendations • Conclusions, recommendation, further research

6.3 Phase 1: Mapping of the as-is Situation

6.3.1 Launch of the Assessment

Assessment of the as is situation required the identification and engagement of the stakeholders with a variety of affiliated roles within the User Experience (UX) Engineering process. Key activity areas and relevant contribution was mapped

- Project Manager: overall development project responsibility. Coordinates project activities, disposes over budget and scope.
- Development Engineer: responsible for the development of the device. Design is developed in CAD tool. Due to the complexity, multiple teams of Development Engineers work on the same device, coordinated by System Engineer(s).

- UX Engineer: develops and verifies the device for user friendliness and use safety during the development process.
- Process Owner: owns the respective process, assures compliance and integration related criteria, provides training for the organization and for customers, contact person for audit related subjects.
- Suppliers: suppliers of sub-assemblies and special deliverables during the development project.
- Test Persons: testers who validate the device during the development phase for various features and aspects. Testers can be internal persons as well as representatives of selected customers.
- Configuration Manager, Risk Manager,…: multiple associated roles enabling and/or facilitating the activities of the stakeholders.

In order to advance common understanding, a codification language has been agreed with the stakeholders. This project came "on-top of" existing obligation of key data sources (stakeholders), which made reduction of training need important, while necessary levels of common language between domains had to be maintained. As a basis Business Process Modelling Notation (BPMN) 1.2 was selected and a reduced number of elements were selected for use as required.

- Swim lanes in order to distinguish between executing roles
- Activities: Tasks, Sub-Tasks and Recurring Tasks
- Artifacts: Data Objects and Text Annotation
- Connecting Objects: Sequence Flow
- Events: Start and End

6.3.2 Data Analysis and Findings

Intended data source for the as-is situation was the relevant Business Process repository, through the Process Owner. Business Process Repository is a higher ordained Documentation system assuring comprehensiveness and integration between overall approach and individual Business Processes. Content of the Business Process repository have a comprehensive standardized structure and content:

- Version Control and Document History
- Classification
- Purpose and Scope
- Process – detailed description including:

  - Tasks and Gateways in flow diagram and for each task in free text Annotation
  - Activity
  - Responsibility
  - Output (type of artifact indicated with text, not with notation)

- Roles and Responsibility in Table format
- Application

The Business Process Description is detailed to the level that has historically proven to be necessary for implementing the process among various stakeholders. It has been observed, however claimed intentional, that the Business Process description is not referring to process related data structures and processing Information Technology tools.

Clarification on details with the Process Owner revealed, that the documented process is not in line with the process being practically followed. The Process Owner provided adjustments to the process based own experience and practice. In order to verify deviations we have used triangulation in form of targeted interviews in addition with the Project Manager and the UX Engineer – the two other practical users of the process.

The triangulation interviews revealed that data integrity is at the heart of the problem: key stakeholders have different understanding and information levels on the Business Process. A summary of the deviations is listed in the table below (Table 3).

Table 3. Major differences in data between sources (Source: own work)

	Documented Process	Process Owner view	Project Manager view	UX Engineer view
Description level	**Activities**	Activities	High level no activities	High level major steps
Output/Artifacts	**Defined without notation**	Incoherent handling in projects	Conceptually considered	Conceptually considered
Roles and responsibilities	**Defined**	Defined, partially different	Not defined	High level defined
Data handling in the process	**Not included**	Partially included, not integrated	Not included	Included, integrated
Tool use in the process	**High level, fragmented**	High level, fragmented	Not included	Included, integrated
Contextual fit	**Defined**	Not defined	Defined, not in detail	Indirect
Major deviation from documented process		• Process steps added/modified • Artifacts modified	• Project level view, no details • Responsibilities not clear	• Conceptual view • Integrated view on data, tools and artifacts

Data cleansing became necessary in the form of defining a common basis for as-is process. Four major cause of the differences to the documented process have been identified and addressed:

- Documentation not covering process in practice. In a dynamically changing process environment, regular revision on the Business Processes is necessary. Furthermore Process Management is intended to drive change as opposed to following change. The mandatory period of 36 months for reviews is suspect to be too long to follow changes in practice. Furthermore change leadership in Process Management shall be event driven as opposed to time period driven.
- Deviating needs and requirements towards the process by stakeholders. Depending on the engagement levels the need and expectations deviate by stakeholders. In order to service needs of conceptual and project management aspects as well as Process Owner and compliance-requested documentation need, different layers had to be defined for the process.

- Level of knowledge of the Process by the stakeholders. If stakeholders are not aware of the process in detail, compliance and consideration of the specifics on higher aggregated level cannot be expected. In relation with point one above, training of processes that are not covering practice and vice versa cannot be expected efficiently.
- Handling of artifacts and deviation among various projects is due to (i) missing contextual considerations such as data life cycle along the project, (ii) incomplete description and outdated templates (iii) island-like tool architecture forcing stakeholders to multiple entry with a risk of manual error.

6.3.3   Establishment of the as-is Process

As a response to the discovered status and in response to point two above, a new version of the process was drawn to depict status as-is. The new as-is process was defined on two layers, with the following focus points (Fig. 3).

Conceptual level	Detail level
1. Contextual fit (i.e. Project Management) 2. Integrated data lifecycle view 3. Integrated tool collaboration and use	1. Tasks and Gateways 2. Activities 3. Responsibilities 4. Artifacts

Fig. 3. Focus areas of the process layers (Source: own work)

The actual as-is process established as above, was recognized and accepted by all stakeholders. Further, it has been agreed, that to-be process documentation will include both layers of the process as well as reference to a form of pro-active process management discipline.

7   Intermediary Findings and Further Research

Although majority of digitalization initiatives do not reach their goal, and significant amount invested into digitalization is wasted, retrospective on past experience can help finding responses. One of these are the Process Modelling Based implementation method. Our preliminary research into literature as well as into the practice indicates that business processes can eliminate the translation problem between stakeholders, thus become a beneficial starting point.

In order to elaborate on our hypothesis we have started a case study based research, where a new technology solution will be introduced in the industrial environment to a specific business area using a process based approach. During the implementation, the use of a business process modelling tool will be propagated. Currently the first of a three steps approach is completed and intermediary findings recorded:

- Documentation of an existing process is not necessarily complete, adherence to the (documented) process may not be sufficient. Research methodologies (e.g. Triangulation) are needed to establish a common starting point.
- Continuous Improvement is a necessity in Process Management to assure that practice and standards are aligned and changes are proactively introduced and/or documented as well as to assure consistent level of knowledge about the process.
- Data life cycle and tool architecture must be considered at the establishment and further development of a process. The respective details need to be documented on the relevant level of the process.
- Current format of Business Process documentation extended will be the orientation for the "to-be" process extended with currently missing components and changes as worked out in phase 2 and 3.
- A large variety of BPMN tools are available on the market. A complete overview is impossible. Critical factors need to be defined to select a sufficiently supporting tool.

Our research will continue for a planned conclusion by the end of 2020 with the further steps which includes:

- Phase 2 will see two parallel actions:

  - the to-be processes will be worked out including all categories
  - market survey will be conducted and appropriate BPMN tool will be selected to support Phase 3

- In Phase 3 gap analysis will be made in order to determine necessary activities for the implementation of the change, in all five categories. Support of the BPMN tool during the analysis will be critically observed in order to gain supporting data for the elaboration on our research question 2. As Phase 3 will conclude our research, this section will see our conclusions, recommendations and directions of further research.

Conclusively, the Business Process Modelling based approach to the embedment of digital technologies in business, supported by current BPM based technology, is so far proving to be suitable to address efficiency challenges in digitalization. The research continues, where Phase 2 and 3 will provide more evidence for forming a final conclusion.

Acknowledgements. This research was supported by the project "Aspects on the development of intelligent, sustainable and inclusive society: social, technological, innovation networks in employment and digital economy" (EFOP-3.6.2-16-2017-00007). The project has been supported by the EU, co-financed by the European Social Fund and the budget of Hungary.

References

1. Tabrizi, B., et. al.: Digital transformation is not about technology. Harward Bus. Rev. (2019). Online edition, 13 March 2019, downloaded: 20 August 2019

2. Peter, M.K.: KMU-transformation: Als KMU die digitale transformation erfolgreich umsetzen. Forschungsresultate und Praxisleitfaden. 1st edn., Olten, p. 54 (2017)
3. Wahlster, W.: Künstliche Intelligenz als Treiber der zweiten Digitalisierungswelle. In: IM+io Das Magazin für Innovation, Organisation und Management, June 2017, no. 2, pp. 10–13 (2017)
4. Schäffer, U.: KI sehe ich als zweite Welle der Digitalisierung. Control. Manage. Rev. **63**(4), 18–23 (2019). https://doi.org/10.1007/s12176-019-0019-4
5. Altmaier, P.: Die zweite Welle der Digitalisierung ist Europas Chance. On-line portal of the German Ministry of Economy and Energy (2019). https://www.bmwi.de/Redaktion/DE/Artikel/Digitale-Welt/20191028-die-zweite-welle-der-digitalisierung-handelsblatt.html. Accessed 12 Dec 2019
6. Sprott, D.: Service Oriented Architecture: An introduction for managers, CBDI Report (2004). www.cbdiforum.com
7. Carter, S.: The New Language of Business, The: SOA & Web 2.0, IBM Press (2007)
8. Sammon, D., Adam, F.: Decision making in the ERP community. In: ECIS 2002 Proceedings, vol. 8 (2002)
9. Donovan, M.: There is no magic in ERP software: it's in preparation of the process and people. Midrange ERP, September, p. 8 (1998)
10. Fruhlinger, J., et al.: 16 famous ERP disasters, dustups and disappointments. CIO.COM 20 Mar 2020 (2020). https://www.cio.com. Accessed 25 Mar 2020
11. Pulse of the profession 2020. Project Management Institute, Philadelphia (2020)
12. Judge, A.: The Art of Non-Decision Making and the manipulation of categories (1997). www.uia.org/uiadocs/nondec.htm. Accessed 24 Oct 2001
13. Scheer, A.-W., et al. (eds.): Business Process Excellence - ARIS in Practice. Springer, Heidelberg (2002). https://doi.org/10.1007/978-3-540-24705-0
14. Wien, A., Franzke, N.: Unternehmenskultur – Zielorientierte Unternehmensethik als entscheidender Erfolgsfaktor; Springer Gabler, Wiesbaden; pp. 29–45 (2014). https://doi.org/10.1007/978-3-658-05993-4. ISBN: 978-3-658-05992-7
15. Aghina, W.: The 5 Trademarks of Agile Organisations, pp. 2–5. McKinsey & Company, New York (2017)
16. Schein, E.: Organisational Culture and Leadership: A Dynamic View. Jossey-Bass, San Francisco, p. 417 (1992)
17. Black, J.A.: Fermenting change, capitalising on the inherent change found in dynamic non-linear systems. J. Organ. Change Manage. **13**(6), 520–525 (2000)
18. Shewhart, W.A.: Statistical Method from the Viewpoint of Quality Control, p. 45. Dover Publications, New York (1986). ISBN 0-486-65232-7
19. Tennant, G.: SIX SIGMA: SPC and TQM in Manufacturing and Services, pp. 3–4. Gower Publishing, Ltd., Farnham (2001). ISBN 0-566-08374-4
20. Moen, R., Norman, C.: Evolution of the PDCA Cycle, 12 February 2017
21. Berry, D., et al.: Managing Successful Projects, pp. 251–291. TSO Publishing, London (1996)
22. SMME: ITIL V3 Foundation – Student Manual; Ver 5; pp. 234–272. Leuven (2009)
23. Laudon, K., Laudon, P.: Managing Information Systems, pp. 109–143. Pearson, Essex (2012)
24. Kroenke, D.M.: Using MIS, pp. 29–35. Pearson, Essex (2012)
25. Sowden, R., et al.: Managing Successful Programmes, pp. 47–75. TSO Publishing, London (2007)
26. Alonso, I.A.; Verdún, J.C; Caro, E.T.: Description of the structure of the IT demand management process framework. Int. J. Inf. Manage. **37**(1), Part A, pp. 1461–1473 (2017)
27. Rahimi, F., Møller, C., Hvam, L.: Business process management and IT management: the missing integration. Int. J. Inf. Manage. **36**(1), 142–154 (2016)
28. Morton, S.: The Corporation of the 1990's: Information Technology and Organisational Transformation. Sloan School of Management, Oxford University Press, New York (1991)

29. Kazmi, S.A.Z., Naarananoja, M.: Collection of change management tools – an opportunity to make the best choice from the various organizational transformational techniques. GSTF Int. J. Bus. Rev. **3**(3) (2014)

30. PROSCI: Best Practices in Business Process Reengineering Report (2002). http://www.pro sci.com/bprbestpractices.htm

31. Gaspar, D., Ternai, K.: Toward value creation in e-governance through digitalization – an industry-based approach. In: Kő, A., Francesconi, E., Anderst-Kotsis, G., Tjoa, A.M., Khalil, I. (eds.) EGOVIS 2019. LNCS, vol. 11709, pp. 235–246. Springer, Cham (2019). https://doi. org/10.1007/978-3-030-27523-5_17

32. Delgado, A., Calegari, D., Milanese, P., Falcon, R., García, E.: A systematic approach for evaluating BPM systems: case studies on open source and proprietary tools. In: Damiani, E., Frati, F., Riehle, D., Wasserman, Anthony I. (eds.) OSS 2015. IAICT, vol. 451, pp. 81–90. Springer, Cham (2015). https://doi.org/10.1007/978-3-319-17837-0_8

33. Delgado, A., Calegari, D., Arrigoni, A.: Towards a generic BPMS user portal definition for the execution of business processes. Electron. Notes Theoret. Comput. Sci. **329**, 39–59 (2016)

34. Snoeck, M., Moreno-Montes de Oca, I., Haegemans, T., Scheldeman, B., Hoste, T.: Testing a selection of BPMN tools for their support of modelling guidelines. In: Ralyté, J., España, S., Pastor, Ó. (eds.) PoEM 2015. LNBIP, vol. 235, pp. 111–125. Springer, Cham (2015). https:// doi.org/10.1007/978-3-319-25897-3_8

35. Wiechetek, Ł., Mędrek, M., Banaś, J.: Business process management in higher education. The case of students of logistics. Problemy Zarządzania **4**(71), 146–164 (2017)

36. Gaspar, D.: Organizational value creation by IT in Industry 4.0. In: Buchmann, R.A., Karagiannis, D., Kirikova, M. (eds.) PoEM 2018. LNBIP, vol. 335, pp. 274–287. Springer, Cham (2018). https://doi.org/10.1007/978-3-030-02302-7_17

37. Ternai, K.: The metamorphosis of ERP systems. Ph.D. dissertation, Corvinus University of Budapest, Budapest (2008)

38. Yin, R.K.: Case Study Research, 2nd edn. Sage Publications, London (1994)

39. Eisenhardt, K.M.: Building theories from case study research. Acad. Manage. Rev. **14**, 532–550 (1989)

40. Dumas, M.: Fundamentals of Business Process Management. Springer, Heidelberg (2018). https://doi.org/10.1007/978-3-662-56509-4

41. Gábor, A., Kő, A. (eds.): Corporate Knowledge Discovery and Organizational Learning. KMOL, vol. 2. Springer, Cham (2016). https://doi.org/10.1007/978-3-319-28917-5

Event-Centric Microservices for E-states

Dimitrios Tourgaidis and Alexandros Karakasidis(⊠)

Department of Applied Informatics, University of Macedonia, Thessaloniki, Greece
{dai16057,a.karakasidis}@uom.edu.gr

Abstract. Technology evolution may be used by countries' administrations in order to offer better and more effective citizen services. In this paper, we present our vision for e-states, a notion beyond the urban boundaries of smart cities, by introducing a concept for an event-centric, e-governance system, based on the microservices architecture. We discuss the benefits of such an approach and show how such services may be designed for the e-states we envision.

Keywords: Information systems · E-governance · Microservices

1 Introduction

In the era of Big Data and Internet of Things (IoT), organizations, businesses and governments move toward taking advantage both of existing and every-day growing amounts of data, leading us to discuss about smart cities in the field of e-governance [5,10]. There have been many definitions to describe the notion of a smart city in the literature [1]. Their common ground is the improvement of urban life through the use of Information and Communication Technologies.

In this paper, we move ahead, discussing the concept of an e-state which goes beyond the urban boundaries of a city. We consider the case of an entire state and operations tailored for central administration services. In the e-state paradigm, there are complex procedures involving heterogeneous systems for data storage and processing due to the diversity of underlying organizations. The situation becomes more complicated considering the desired capacity for scalability, so as to provide efficient interactions with the large amounts of civilian requests for these complex services. Moreover, the mechanisms of an e-state should be extendable and adaptable so as to comply with policy changes and new challenges.

To this end, we consider a high abstraction level in order to capture these characteristics of entire states, which is based on the use of a microservices-based architecture as the most prominent way to develop and deploy e-governance operations. A microservice may be briefly described as a small application that can be deployed, scaled and tested independently and that has a single responsibility [16]. These properties make them ideal for rapid deployment in cases of emergency, as in the current CoViD-19 situation with the new SARS-CoV-2 virus. In this paper, we take previous work on microservices for e-governance [10,12] a step further, by considering an event-centric system.

© Springer Nature Switzerland AG 2020
A. Kő et al. (Eds.): EGOVIS 2020, LNCS 12394, pp. 78–88, 2020.
https://doi.org/10.1007/978-3-030-58957-8_6

An event-centric system considers and records real world events, an app-roach which is ideal for e-governance. For example, a person's current state can be described as a sequence of events that have occurred up to the current time point; their birth, their graduation from school, their hiring, or being fired, their marriage, their children birth, and so on. To achieve this functionality, we pro-pose the use of *Event Sourcing* [9] for recording, storing and processing all these events. This allows state services not only maintaining persistent archives of all previous events, but also facilitating automation of processes and gaining added value by having the capacity to easily calculate analytics over periods of time.

To this end, in our work, we consider an e-governance system as event-centric, design its architecture and show how microservices can be coupled with the event sourcing pattern for storing data. Also, we argue for the benefits of our approach and provide an example for designing an event-centric service.

The rest of this paper is organized as follows. Sect. 2 describes works related to ours. In Sect. 3, we provide the building blocks of our approach. We present the proposed architecture in Sect. 4 and we argue for its benefits in Sect. 5. Our paper concludes in Sect. 6 with some plans for future work.

2   Related Work

Let us now examine works related to ours. Fang et al. [8], define and discuss the concept of e-government, presenting related challenges and problems, proposing eight different models for an e-government system. In [12], benefits and challenges of migration from a monolithic system to a system based on the microservices architecture are discussed. Benefits include continuous delivery, more flexible deployment, innovation leverage, reduced time-to-market, DevOps adoption, and increased software availability. The most important of the challengers are related to the decomposition of a monolithic system into microservices and the lack of decision makers involvement.

Next, we present works focusing on smart cities. Although our work focuses in the broader notion of e-states, our methodology can be applicable to smart cities as well. In [3], Chamoso et al. discuss the concept of smart cities and an architecture for a smart city development is proposed. In the same context, Hidayat et al. [10] present a case study of how to develop a system for a smart city using microservices, describing four stages; business logic identification, service architecture design, development, and deployment. However they analyze only the first three stages. Esposte et al. introduce the InterSCity platform [5], also based on the microservices architecture, consisting of six 'master' services, each having a crucial role for the entire system. However, each of these master services may act as a single point of total system failure and each of them encapsulates a large volume of business logic making them more difficult to scale. In our approach, we offer a distributed design, to avoid such bottlenecks, coupled with the event-centric concept so as to better capture real-world events.

We envision the event-centric nature of our system to be implemented using Event Sourcing [9] and Command Query Responsibility Segregation (CQRS)

[4,18,19]. So far, event sourcing has been primarily used for e-commerce systems [2,15]. In this work, we present how event sourcing can be used in the domain of e-governance, so that states can persist real-life events.

3 Background

In this section, we provide the necessary background of our vision, presenting the notions for our basic architectural elements and approaches, namely, Microservices, Event Sourcing and Domain Driven Design.

3.1 Microservices

A *microservice* is an independent and autonomous software interacting through message passing [6]. Independent, since its features have been developed, and the technologies that have been used for its development do not depend on other services. Autonomous, due to its deployment, which is independent related to the other services. A *Microservices Architecture* regards the development of a system in a distributed manner. System features are decomposed in a number of autonomous services, implementing the entire business logic.

Microservices may be deployed in a variety of architectures depending on the needs of the problem to be addressed. One such pattern is called API Gateways [13]. An API Gateway is also a service, comprising a single entry point for a microservices architecture. It is used when a microservice may need to serve different kinds of clients and user interfaces, also allowing for deploying new services, at runtime, for the lifecycle of a microservices architecture.

3.2 Event Sourcing

Event Sourcing is a pattern for storing data [7]. A system persists each of its *entities* as a sequence of events, indicating that, in event sourcing, data are stored as sequences of events. For a system, any creation of an entity is a separate event as also any change of their state. All events are stored in an *Events* table, where each event is a distinct record. Furthermore, events are not deleted from the Events table. To retrieve the current state of an entity, the entire history of the event has to be replayed. To avoid replaying history each time the state of an event is required, *Checkpointing* is used. To achieve this functionality, two types of objects are assumed in this design; event objects which refer to real world events and domain objects which refer to real-world entities. Event sourcing has the following benefits:

- Complete Rebuild: We can discard the application state completely and rebuild it by re-running the events from the event log on an empty application.
- Temporal Query: We can determine the application state at any point in time, by starting with a blank state and rerunning the events up to a particular time or event.

- Event Replay: In the case where a past event found to be incorrectly recorded, or recorded in incorrect order, we may replace the problematic event and current state and replaying consequent events in order to reach a correct state.
- Maintain history of states for entities and aggregates: This allows retrieving any past state of any entity by querying all events occurred until the required timestamp, and replay them. Such a function is a temporal query.

Event Sourcing is often combined with *Command Query Responsibility Segregation* (CQRS) [18,19]. CQRS separates actions into those that change data, called commands, and to those that ask for data, called queries. As such, distinct data stores are used for the action side and for the command side. This separation results in optimizing each side based on demands and circumstances.

3.3 Domain Driven Design

In order to design an e-governance system with microservices, we are going to employ *Domain-Driven Design* [7]. A *Domain* refers to the entire problem space we are addressing, including its entities and rules. Domains may further be decomposed into *Subdomains*, each of them focusing on a particular aspect of the problem. In our case, we consider an *e-state* having as distinct Domains each of its core operational agencies and services, which, then, may be decomposed into a number of subdomains, e.g., the Domain of a Tax Agency, has Subdomains related to citizen income, business income, and so on, each of them being independent from others and related to a particular microservice.

A microservice, now, strictly, implements the features of a single Subdomain [14]. However, this microservice's features and components may be accessible by other services as well. To this end, a microservice may either be consumed by external clients, by other microservices, or both. This complies with the design we want to apply for state services. These may either be totally independent or correlated with others. As such, they can be modeled by a microservices-based architecture, which has the capacity of modeling such relations. The most important advantage of this pattern is that for a subdomain, each of its entities is reflected into the design and the implementation is self-contained and independent, not sharing redundant information with other entities. An entity in such a system is designated by a global unique identifier, which is common for all the system's microservices, regardless of the data model used in each of them.

4 An Event-Centric System for E-governance

Let us, now, describe how we envision an event-centric system for e-governance.

4.1 A Conceptual Architecture for Event-Centric E-states

First, we will describe the types of entities we consider in the architecture we propose for an event-driven e-governance system based on microservices. These

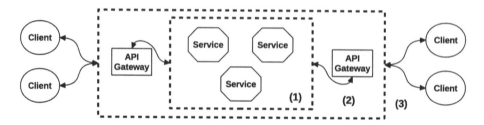

Fig. 1. Concept of domain architecture.

are illustrated in Fig. 1. First, there are the system's clients. We basically consider two types of clients for our system; citizens and government officials. Both types of clients may insert or query data to the system, but with different levels of access, since citizens may only have access to their personal data, but officials may handle data of numerous citizens. As such, each of them may have different access to the system's services.

To this end, API Gateways come into place. As discussed earlier, API Gateways are microservices themselves, however, they have the capacity of providing different communication APIs depending on the nature of the system's clients. Distinct kinds of clients will require distinct types of user access having different user interfaces, such as those found in web browsers and various smart devices (e.g., smartphones). Every client may have different needs, depending on its target usage, form factor, and processing power [13]. This design also caters for extendability, since more types of clients with different needs may be considered in the future. API Gateways are illustrated in Fig. 1 as solid line rectangles.

Next, there are the system's services, each implemented using the Microservices Architecture. The first step toward utilizing such an architecture is to decompose the entire business logic of state services, thus defining the system's services and the part of the overall business logic, each will implement. As we discussed earlier, using Domain Driven Design, the complete Domain is decomposed into Subdomains and each leads to a distinct microservice that has its own separate data-model, compared to the data-models of the other services. In Fig. 1, microservices are illustrated as hexagons.

We will, now, examine how these aforementioned components interact with each other. In our envisioned architecture, we consider three distinct layers, designated by the dotted rectangles in Fig. 1. Layer (1), which is the inner one, comprises all system services, implemented by microservices, except those implementing the API gateway pattern. Then, Layer (2) includes all services implementing the API gateway pattern. To this end, Layers (1) and (2) constitute the system's back-end. Layer (3), now, represents the external clients of the system, which, as we discussed earlier, are represented by ellipses. Arrows from these clients are directed to layer (2), meaning that all client requests are directed to the services implementing the API gateway pattern. The fact that arrows

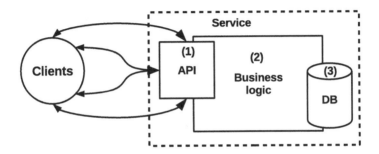

Fig. 2. Conceptual microservice architecture for a service.

from API gateway services are directed to layer (1), indicates that API gateway services are routing the request of clients to system services. Therefore, the role of layer (2) is to route each request of an external client to the corresponding service, and, if needed, system services respond back to clients through layer (2). Overall, communication between clients and services is implemented indirectly.

All services have common functionalities regardless of the subdomain each implements; authentication, authorization, monitoring, metric collection, caching, protocol translation etc. Using the API gateway pattern, all these functions are implemented by the gateways leading to the capacity of independently developing each core system service. The number of gateways to be employed depends on the number of expected requests to the system. This may be related to the state's population, or other administrative factors. For instance, depending on population we may use one or more gateways per region, or per city.

4.2 Designing a Microservice for E-governance

Let us now see how we may implement such a service using the microservices concept. Figure 2 shows the conceptual architecture of such a microservice, designated by the dotted rectangle, which consists of three parts. First of all, there is an API (1) which carries out communication with its client applications. Component (2) is the service's business logic implementation. Component (3) is a database, in which it stores and persists its entities. It is evident that such a design is applicable to any microservice case. Considering the system's architecture in Fig.1, each Layer (1) service consists of these three aforementioned components. Finally, the circle on the left represents the service's clients which may either be other Layer (1) services, or external clients, routed through Layer (2).

A microservice may expose a synchronous, asynchronous or both API's, depending on the model required by the other microservices it communicates. As for the database of the service, the most suitable type of data store may be selected, independently from other services, a fact that exploits heterogeneity [14], one of the major benefits of the microservices architecture, where each feature of the business logic can be developed using the most appropriate technology.

To better illustrate how such a service may be implemented and the related benefits of using this architecture, we are going to use an example, motivated by the current situation triggered by the new SARS–CoV-2 virus. Certainly our concept is not limited to emergency situations like the one we are currently experiencing, but also to traditional governmental operations. However, by choosing this kind of example we exhibit how event-centric architectural elements may be deployed without disrupting existing governmental services and operations. To this end, let us consider a state's Public Healthcare System (PHS). The PHS should be considered as a separate Domain and data should be stored related to the status of patients, thus making it an ideal field for applying our methodology.

Given the emergency and the particularities of current circumstances, a SARS–CoV-2 Subdomain is formed for interactions regarding the new virus. These interactions will be handled by a microservice named *CovidService*. This service persists two distinct things; patients' states and an event log. As the service implements CoViD-19 oriented operations, its domain entity is the *Covid-Case* entity, having the following fields: ID, status. Since this is an e-governance system, ID is going to refer to the unique ID referring to a single person, used throughout the system. Apart from gaining a log with all previous events, the key point of using event sourcing is the fact that all changes to the domain object *CovidCase* are initiated by the event objects.

It is not necessary to provide a new microservice for each certain disease. However, in this case, launching a new service may offer many benefits. First of all, given the global alarm, special handling is required for such incidents, a fact that will also be illustrated next, where we describe how e-governance automation might be achieved using microservices. Second, by deploying a new dedicated microservice, the system is extended in a modular way, since there is no intrusion to the current PHS and the established services that continue to run for all other diseases and cases. Finally, using an API Gateway many types of clients may be supported with different interfaces; from mobile devices for mobile test units to web based applications for hospitals and health centers.

CovidService uses Event Sourcing, consequently persisting its entities as a sequence of events. In Table 1, column *Event Object* shows event objects stored by the service in its Events Table. The second column shows their real life coun-

Table 1. Events stored in the Events Table.

Event object	Real - life event	Status
TestCovidCase	Person tested for SARS–CoV-2	Unconfirmed
PositiveCovidCase	Tested-Positive for SARS–CoV-2	Tested-positive
NegativeCovidCase	Tested-Negative for SARS–CoV-2	Tested-negative
RecoveredCovidCase	Recoverd from SARS–CoV-2	Recovered
DeceasedCovidCase	Deceased due to CoViD-19 disease	Deceased

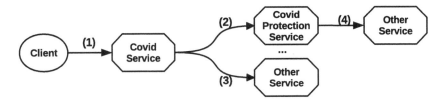

Fig. 3. CoViD-19 case workflow between related services.

terparts. A patient's status, might be *unconfirmed*, when being checked, *tested-negative*, if the results of the test are negative, *tested-positive*, in the opposite case, *recovered*, or, as we unfortunately see quite often, *deceased*.

To continue with our running example, let us consider a simplistic scenario with a single CoViD-19 patient, named Eva, who is infected, exhibiting flu-like symptoms and signs in with the PHS. There, she takes a SARS–CoV-2 test. In this case, the *TestCovidCase* object is stored in the events database. Until the results come out, she is a suspicious case and her status is *unconfirmed*. After the results come out, a *PositiveCovidCase* object is stored in the Events Table and Eva's status switches to *tested-positive*. Eva finally recovers and a *RecoveredCovidCase* object is eventually persisted changing her status to *recovered*.

Eva's state is the result of a series of events, an approach that also covers cases of recurring CoViD-19 patients. This sequence of events may be very easily stored using the Event Sourcing pattern. One might argue that, for such an application, only the last state should be stored. However this is not the case, since this is a new disease and we would like historical data both for gaining new knowledge over this new health threat and assessing the responsiveness of PHS.

4.3 Event-Centric Systems for E-governance Automation

A key benefit of event sourcing is process automation. Let us add in our example a Civil Protection Agency (CPA), forming a separate Domain. This agency decides, among others, for lockdowns to prevent virus spread. Similarly to PHS, a new microservice is launched called *CovidProtectionService*. Its goal is to provide aggregate information for CoViD-19 related cases throughout the state so as to assist decisions for preventing further infections. To preserve patients' privacy, CPA only handles aggregate and location data from the reporting PHS centers.

Figure 3 illustrates the connection between the two services. The operation in this case is quite straightforward. Each time an Event Object is stored by a *CovidService* client (1), e.g. hospital, the delivery of a newmessage from PHS to CPA is triggered (2), while the patient's privacy is preserved, as only an increment and the location of the hospital or health center that manages the case is delivered. *CovidProtectionService* also persists in a similar manner every event it receives, so as to be able to extract time-based analytics. To this end, decisions over measures to prevent virus widespread might be taken. This architecture is easily extendable so as to provide the capacity for *CovidService* and *CovidProtectionService* to communicate with other services as well (3), (4).

In the same manner, any state service may be automated. An event stored by a service may trigger a workflow, able to accomplish a process of validations and decisions automatically. This procedure will be accomplished, if the involved services are not out of order, within a minimal amount of time.

5   Benefits

Let us now discuss how an event-centric microservices architecture benefits e-governance. Occurring benefits augment those provided by cloud computing in e-governance, as described in [17].

Independent Data Scaling. Databases should be scalable, to deal with large data over the years for e-governance applications [17]. The fact that each microservice may use its own datastore solution, not only allows it to scale, but to also do this independently from the rest of the system. As such, a microservice, depending on the amount of events it handles may be coupled with a range of storage solutions, from a single RDBMS to a distributed NoSQL database.

Auditing and Logging. Traceability to any changes to information content in e-governance services is required to ensure transparency in public administration and fight corruption. To this end, Event Sourcing, which persists all actions for a domain object, is the ideal way to go, since replaying events from Events tables may reveal illegal actions, and, second, it is much more difficult to erase traces of illegal activities, since all actions on an object are recorded in the Events table.

Performance and Scalability. Having the capacity to deploy each service independently, depending on its usage, a separate deployment approach may be employed. Either in-house, or cloud-based, a service based on microservices may scale-out or scale-up, depending on the case. Exploiting the capacity for independent development, a state may rapidly introduce new services or remove unnecessary ones, without disrupting the operation of the system. Furthermore, using API gateways can support increased traffic and future needs of multiple types of clients.

Reporting and Intelligence. Persisting all actions through event sourcing may be beneficiary both for discovering knowledge not only for the actual domain objects a microservice handles, but also for the system per se. As such, statistics may be gathered regarding e-governance performance so as to overcome possible bottlenecks and offer better services to the citizens.

Policy Management. E-governance applications have to adhere and implement policies of the governments in terms of dealing with citizens. However, as situations change rapidly in the modern world, so do policies. In the paradigm we propose, using distinct microservices allows for altering only those microservices involved in a policy change. Thus adapting to new circumstances is quick, saving both time and resources.

Legacy Software and Maintainability. Microservices may promise high maintainability due to smaller code bases, strong component separation and independent life cycle, making them an interesting option for software modernization [11]. The fact that each microsevice is also independently deployed, communicating through messages makes them suitable for legacy software integration.

6   Conclusions and Future Work

In this paper, we layed out our vision of a microservices architecture for e-states and the advantages of this approach. Also, we provided a detailed example of how we conceive the operation of a service based on our design. Considering the difficulty of decomposing and reorganizing state procedures, our ambition is to further evolve our design. To this end, we aim at performing detailed case studies of governmental layers and their competencies and bodies, so as to result in guidelines for efficiently adapting them into the event-centric microservices paradigm. Then we consider the implementation of prototypes, based on these guidelines.

References

1. Albino, V., Berardi, U., Dangelico, R.M.: Smart cities: definitions, dimensions, performance, and initiatives. J. Urban Technol. **22**(1), 3–21 (2015)
2. Betts, D., Dominguez, J., Melnik, G., Simonazzi, F., Subramanian, M.: Exploring CQRS and Event Sourcing: A Journey into High Scalability, Availability, and Maintainability with Windows Azure. Microsoft Patterns & Practices (2013)
3. Chamoso, P., González-Briones, A., Rodríguez, S., Corchado, J.M.: Tendencies of technologies and platforms in smart cities: a state-of-the-art review. Wirel. Commun. Mob. Comput. **2018** (2018). http://downloads.hindawi.com/journals/wcmc/2018/3086854.pdf
4. Dahan, U.: Clarified CQRS (2009). http://www.udidahan.com/2009/12/0. Accessed 10 Mar 2020
5. Del Esposte, A.M., Kon, F., Costa, F.M., Lago, N.: InterSCity: a scalable microservice-based open source platform for smart cities. In: Proceedings of the 6th International Conference on Smart Cities and Green ICT Systems, pp. 35–46 (2017)
6. Dragoni, N., et al.: Microservices: yesterday, today, and tomorrow. In: Mazzara, M., Meyer, B. (eds.) Present and Ulterior Software Engineering, pp. 195–216. Springer, Cham (2017). https://doi.org/10.1007/978-3-319-67425-4_12
7. Evans, E.: Domain-Driven Design: Tackling Complexity in the Heart of Software. Addison-Wesley Professional, Boston (2004)

8. Fang, Z.: E-government in digital era: concept, practice, and development. Int. J. Comput. Internet Manag. **10**(2), 1–22 (2002)
9. Fowler, M.: Event sourcing. https://martinfowler.com/eaaDev/ (2005). Accessed 10 Mar 2020
10. Hidayat, T., Kurniawan, N.B., et al.: Smart city service system engineering based on microservices architecture: case study: government of Tangerang city. In: 2017 International Conference on ICT For Smart Society (ICISS), pp. 1–7. IEEE (2017)
11. Knoche, H., Hasselbring, W.: Using microservices for legacy software modernization. IEEE Softw. **35**(3), 44–49 (2018)
12. Luz, W., Agilar, E., de Oliveira, M.C., de Melo, C.E.R., Pinto, G., Bonifácio, R.: An experience report on the adoption of microservices in three Brazilian government institutions. In: Proceedings of the XXXII Brazilian Symposium on Software Engineering, pp. 32–41 (2018)
13. Montesi, F., Weber, J.: Circuit breakers, discovery, and API gateways in microservices. arXiv preprint arXiv:1609.05830 (2016)
14. Newman, S.: Building Microservices: Designing Fine-Grained Systems. O'Reilly Media Inc., Sebastopol (2015)
15. Richardson, C.: Microservices Patterns: With Examples in Java. Manning Publications, New York (2019)
16. Thönes, J.: Microservices. IEEE Softw. **32**(1), 116 (2015)
17. Tripathi, A., Parihar, B.: E-governance challenges and cloud benefits. In: 2011 IEEE International Conference on Computer Science and Automation Engineering, vol. 1, pp. 351–354. IEEE (2011)
18. Young, G.: CQRS and Event Sourcing (2010). http://codebetter.com/gregyoung/2010/02/13/cqrs-and-event-sourcing. Accessed 10 Mar 2020
19. Young, G.: A Decade of DDD, CQRS, Event Sourcing - Domain-Driven Design Europe (2016). https://www.youtube.com/watch?v=LDW0QWie21s. Accessed 10 Mar 2020

E-Government Cases - Data and Knowledge Management

Data Acquisition for Integrated Coastal Zone Management and Planning in a Climate Change Perspective

Lone S. Hendriksen[✉], Henning Sten Hansen, and Lars Stenseng

Aalborg University Copenhagen, A.C. Meyers Vænge 15, 2450 Copenhagen, Denmark
lonesh@plan.aau.dk

Abstract. The coastal zones are characterised with high populations densities and sensitive ecosystems which requires efficient planning and management. The ongoing climate change will make this task more challenging with sea level rise and increased storminess. Digital governance is an efficient instrument to cope with climate change in the coastal zone but requires up-to-date and high-quality information. The current research has aimed at providing an overview of the currently available data sources, gaps in data availability, and new approaches to data collection in a very dynamic coastal zone.

Keywords: Coastal zone planning · Spatial data infrastructure · Climate change · UAV · Remote sensing · LiDAR · Mobile mapping

1 Introduction

Coasts are attractive places to live with average population densities three times the global average, and approximately 40% of the EU population lives within 50 km of the sea [1]. The European coastal areas are very important for Europe's economy, and to emphasize the importance of the coastal areas, nearly 40% of the EU's GDP is generated in these maritime regions.

The coastal zone is already characterised as being a very dynamic zone representing the interface between the terrestrial and marine environments, and where different weather conditions continuously changes the course of the coastline. This dynamic is currently being enhanced by climate change bringing more frequent heavy storms to North-western Europe [2]. The heavy storms surges can create flooding along the coasts and contribute to increased erosion along some parts of the coasts and accretion along other parts and thus taking and giving land. Clearly, erosion is the most challenging part from a coastal planning point of view and for example some parts of Danish coasts suffer from heavy erosion, where some beach is retreating up to 6 m per year 3 under current climate conditions [3] generating large damage to properties near to the coast (Fig. 1).

Thus, climate change may have severe consequences for coastal cities and settlements, requires adaptation actions in order to protect people and goods, and an *efficient digital governance* from local over regional to national levels. This requires up-to-date

© Springer Nature Switzerland AG 2020
A. Kő et al. (Eds.): EGOVIS 2020, LNCS 12394, pp. 91–105, 2020.
https://doi.org/10.1007/978-3-030-58957-8_7

Fig. 1. Coastal erosion in Kjul Beach Northern Jutland (photo by authors).

information, which is a particular challenge in a dynamic coastal zone in a changing climate.

The aim of the current research has been to analyse 1) the data required for integrated coastal zone management in a climate change perspective; 2) existing data collections and their appropriateness and identifying gabs between the existing data and the needs; 3) suggesting new innovative techniques for data collection.

After this introduction follows a chapter describing the background and theoretical foundation for the data needs for coastal zone planning in a climate change perspective. The third chapter describes existing data infrastructures to support coastal zone planning and identifies the gaps in data. The fourth chapter describes how modern data acquisition methods can contribute to fill these gabs. The paper ends with a discussion and some concluding remarks including perspectives for subsequent research.

2   Background and Theory

In 1992, at the Earth Summit in Rio de Janeiro, the need for environmental action for oceans and coastlines was recognised in chapter 17 of Agenda 21 [4]. Coastal States committed themselves to integrated management and sustainable development of coastal areas and the marine environment under their national jurisdiction. This should be achieved by: a) Providing for an integrated policy and decision-making process, including all involved sectors; b) Identifying existing and projected uses of coastal areas and their interactions; c) Concentrating on well-defined issues concerning coastal management; d) Applying preventive and precautionary approaches in project planning and implementation, including prior assessment and systematic observation of the impacts of major projects; e) Promoting the development and application of methods, such as national resource and environmental accounting, that reflect changes in value resulting from uses of coastal and marine areas, including pollution, marine erosion, loss of resources and habitat destruction; f) Provide access for concerned individuals, groups and organisations to relevant information and opportunities for consultation and participation in planning and decision-making at appropriate levels.

On 30 May 2002 the Recommendation concerning the implementation of an Integrated Coastal Zone Management (ICZM) in Europe was approved by the European Parliament and the European Council [5]. This article provided the European Council with the possibility of elaborating measures for protection of the environment. In this Recommendation, the European Member States were requested to develop one or more national strategies for their coastal policies, taking account of the strategy for sustainable development.

Later on, climate change has added further challenges to managing and planning the coastal zone.

2.1 Data Needs

Access to data and information is fundamental to all spatial planning and management to perform knowledge-based decision-making. This has been facilitated by several efforts during the last 20 years aiming at building up spatial data infrastructures at supranational (e.g. EU), national, regional and local levels.

However, coastal zone management is more complicated than traditional terrestrial planning by the fact that the process comprises two domains – the terrestrial and the marine. Generally, it is easier to collect data on land than in the sea, and the need for planning and regulation has also until recently been more or less absent for the marine space.

2.2 Spatial Data Infrastructures

A Spatial Data Infrastructure is about facilitation and coordination of the exchange and sharing of spatial data. It is described as the underlying infrastructure, often in the form of policies, standards and access networks that allows data to be shared between people within organisations, states or countries. The fundamental interaction between people and data is governed by the technological components of SDI represented by the access network, policies and standards [6]. The dynamic nature of the spatial data infrastructure is attributed to the rate of technological advancement and changing user needs. People and data are the key elements in SDI, and a spatial data infrastructure at any level whether local, regional, national or even global involves an array of stakeholders both within and across organisations including different levels of government, the private sector and a multitude of users. In order to design and implement a spatial data infrastructure, the stakeholders need to be identified together with the business processes and functions of the organisations involved. Besides you must know the data required or provided by the functions – and the flow of data between various functions. In this respect data sharing, exchange, security, accuracy and access as well as rights, restrictions and responsibilities must be managed.

2.3   The EU INSPIRE Directive

Directive 2003/4/EC (Commission of the European Communities [7] on public access to environmental information was implemented in February 2005, and although this Directive addresses specifically environmental information, it has nevertheless contributed significantly to the notion of easier access and sharing of public sector information. The PSI Directive [8] was implemented in July 2005 aiming at regulating and stimulating the reuse of public sector information (PSI). An updated and modernised version of the PSI Directive has been adopted in 2019 [9]. The initial intention of the European Commission was to make all public sector information in the Member States available for re-use. However, this caused some Member States and public institutions great concern, as many of these institutions are expected to provide for at least part of their own funding. Therefore, in the negotiation process between the European Parliament and the Council, the general principle was toned down to a mere encouragement for the Member States to make their information available for re-use. Nevertheless, the PSI directive has gained lot of impacts in the Member States as demonstrated in the next sub paragraph.

A key objective of INSPIRE initiative was to make more and better spatial information available for Community policymaking and implementation in a wide range of sectors. Initially, it would focus on information needed to monitor and improve the state of the environment - including air, water, soil, and natural landscape - and it can be extended later to other sectors such as agriculture and transport. The INSPIRE Directive was adopted by the European Council and Parliament in spring 2007 and entered into force May 2007 [10]. The INSPIRE Directive is a framework, where the details are defined through a set of so-called implementing rules, where the Member States provide experts for drafting the rules, which are finally adopted by the INSPIRE Committee. Thus, a high degree of Member States involvement is ensured. The INSPIRE Directive Implementing Rules deals with metadata specifications, data specifications, network services, data and service sharing, and spatial data services.

2.4   Existing Data Portals for Coastal Zone Management and Planning

Geoportals are web-based access points, often public access points, containing networks of geographic data with the purpose of allowing portal users to find existing geographic data. Within marine spatial planning, marine geoportals are important tools for easing access to existing marine data, creating collaboration projects between different shareholders owning marine data, and improving interoperability between technical platforms of different data users and data owners by using internationally recognised standards [11].

The European Geoportal (http://geoportal.jrc.it/) is considered one of the main building blocks of the European SDI. The vision of the European Geoportal is to facilitate discovering, viewing, accessing, and querying geographic information from the local level to the global level, for a variety of uses, such as environmental policy development and impact assessment, land use planning, natural disasters preparedness, monitoring, and response. Besides the European EU Geoportal serves as an information site regarding INSPIRE by providing links to newsletters, reports, and events.

2.5   The National Danish Data Infrastructure

Open public data is a key element in digital governance and for making broad use of the data made available through various geoportals [12]. Without this, the societies cannot utilise the huge amount of data being collected by the public sector every day. One approach to this is the Danish Basic Data concept [13].

By using a common geographic basis for administration, it is possible for example to link relevant data about the environment, traffic, health, property, companies and people. Basic data constitutes the core information needed be public authorities in their daily work, and contains information about *Persons, Businesses, Real properties, Addresses, Roads* and *Areas*. All these data have a spatial reference, and accordingly geography and maps are important elements in the Basic data concept (Fig. 2).

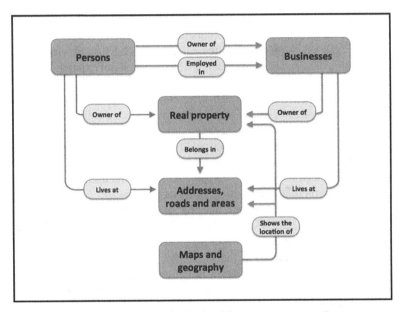

Fig. 2. The basic data concept in the Danish open government data strategy.

This figure illustrates clearly the interconnection between the different components of the Basic Data set. Each person, business unit, property, house and road have for decades been provided with unique identifiers, and a cross-reference register has ensured the interconnection between the different objects in the infrastructure. Besides, all persons and business units are assigned an address. Finally, the addresses, properties (parcels) and buildings are assigned a geographic reference, ensuring its connection with geography (maps). Thus, the basic Data set constitutes an integrated system facilitating the core functions in public administrations.

At a later stage in the process it is expected to expand the Basic Data set to include personal data, income data, business financial statements, and road infrastructures. Recently, meteorological data from the Danish Meteorological Institute have been added to the list of open government data. In order to maintain the authoritative status required for public administration, management and decision-making, the Basic Data needs to comply with the following principles: 1) Basic Data needs to be as correct, complete, and up-to-data as possible; 2) All public authorities must use the Basic Data in their daily work; 3) As far as possible Basic Data must be made freely available to businesses as well as the public (sensitive personal data excluded); 4) Basic Data must be distributed efficiently and accommodate the needs of the users.

The efficiency of this model was analysed by Hansen and Schrøder [14] and it was concluded that the total socio-economic benefits during the first three years with open geospatial data is estimated to about 470 million € of which 340 million € comes from the production effect production effect and 130 million € from the improved efficiency.

2.6 Marine Data

On the seaside there are a lot of stakeholders and players with interest and activities. When you have 'shares' in an area it often calls for a need for knowledge about the place – i.e. mapping. The maps needed can be knowledge about existing infrastructure, technical installations, restricted areas, future plans etc.

It means that different stakeholders with different interest call for different maps/data, and it means that data collected on the seaside, in most cases are collected with a specific purpose, and not a coordinated effort between organisations and private stakeholders. In principle, it means that similar dataset could be collected within a few days, with different data owners or with a very small difference in technical setup.

The stakeholders need to be able to compare, combine and exchange datasets, to get an overview of where there are conflicts or interests to consider.

To get overview over the available data for the marine areas, an MSDI (Marine Spatial Data Infrastructure) can be established. According to Cooper et al. [15] the MSDI includes all marine geographic and business information. Cooper et al. [15] defines a catalogue of data to implement in the MSDI, but there can be national differences to consider. In addition, it can be difficult to define an appropriate model for marine and maritime data, but Holzhüter et al. [16] have provided a conceptual approach to harmonise data for maritime spatial planning.

In 2015 the Danish Geodata Agency together with 10 other agencies started the implementation of a national MSDI (Marine Spatial Data Infrastructure) for the Danish sea territory. The purpose is to make relevant marine data including metadata available on a common platform. The work with the MSDI is still ongoing and not finalised yet.

The MSDI is available through the Danish Geodata Agencies homepage[1] and there are two versions available: a 'free' version, and a version which require logon.

3 Modern Data Acquisition Methods

The data described above are updated according to a more or less regular time schedule at least for the terrestrial domain, whereas some data for the marine areas are imposed by

---

[1] https://msdi.dk/kort/.

licensing regulation. However, this is not the only challenge concerning data availability in the coastal zone. As mentioned in the introduction the coastal zone is very dynamic due to currents and waves constantly changing for example the coastline due to erosion and deposition. Also, the sea bottom as well land topography are changed, and in a climate changes perspective these processes are enhanced by sea level rise and expected increased storminess. This calls for new surveying and mapping technologies which are cheaper and more automatic than traditional methods based on photogrammetry or total stations. Below, a set of modern data acquisition methods are described.

3.1 Satellite Based Platforms

The performance of optical imaging satellites has increased dramatical over the last decades and is currently capable of providing images with high spatial and temporal resolution. Currently, the constellation of Pléiades-HR 1A and 1B together with SPOT 6 and SPOT 7 can provide daily images from an area with a raw ground pixel size down to 0.7 m for Pléiades [17] and 1.5 m for SPOT and from mid 2020 Airbus is expected to begin launch of the four satellite constellation Pléiades Neo with possibility of two daily revisits and ground pixel resolution of 0.3 m [18].

The optical satellite images enable global mapping of coastal features at high temporal and spatial resolution, and with the possibility of getting stereo and tri-stereo acquisition it is possible to derive elevation models of the coastal zone. Furthermore, the shallow water bathymetry can be estimated from the multispectral optical satellite images [19] to complete the mapping of the coastal zone. However, deriving elevation models from stereo images over sandy beaches often proves to be a challenge due to decorrelation caused by lack of visible features in the sand and bathymetry estimated from optical satellite images is degraded by the sea floor vegetation.

The launch of ICESat [20] in 2003 marked a major step forward by the introduction of the spaceborne LiDAR instruments GLAS, and ICESat-2 [21] launched in 2018 introduced the multibeam LiDAR instrument ATLAS with photon detector. The LiDAR instruments are based on travel time and are thereby not dependent on trackable features in order to derive an elevation. Furthermore, the introduction of the photon detector in combination with the green laser used by ATLAS enables direct estimation of bathymetry [22].

While ICESat-2 is a promising new satellite it should be noted that the observations are significantly different from the imaging satellites e.g. Pléiades. The imaging satellites provide a swath of pixels - usually with equal pixel spacing in along and across track direction, whereas the ATLAS instrument provides three high power profiles with 0.7 m along-track sampling and 3.3 km across-track spacing combined with three low power profiles with same configuration shifted 2.5 km along-track.

3.2 Airborne Based Platforms

For many years airborne solutions have been used for providing data for mapping of different kinds. Airborne solutions can be images of LiDAR solutions, and can be carried out primarily with airplanes, but can also be done with helicopters. Airborne images solutions can provide orthophotos and photogrammetric solutions. Based on LiDAR, point clouds can be extracted, and Digital Terrain and/or surface models can be developed.

Airborne solutions are frequently used for large scale projects. In Denmark airborne solutions have been used by COWI to create orthophotos with full land coverage since 1995[2] and the first full land coverage orthophoto based on LiDAR in Denmark was carried out in 2007 and is now part of the terrestrial SDI mentioned in paragraph 2.5. This is a very important data layer in coastal zone management and planning in Danish municipalities, and 75 out of Denmark's 98 municipalities is connected to the sea.

Over the last two decades airborne LiDAR has matured into a mapping technology and routinely used for 3D modelling of urban areas, capturing boreal forests, bathymetry mapping and many other applications all over the world [23].

During the last years the use of two new types of LiDAR instruments Geiger-mode LiDAR (GML) and Single Photon LiDAR (SPL) has been commercialized [24]. These new sensor types are effective and can be operated from a higher altitude than traditional LiDAR systems. In 2001 the first successful photon-counting airborne laser altimeter was demonstrated under NASA and flown in 6700 m above ground over the Atlantic Ocean and Assawoman bay off the Virginia coast [24].

Airborne solutions are not suitable for smaller project, which means that they are not relevant for filling in gabs, but useable when data for bigger areas are needed.

3.3 UAV

The Airborne data acquisition is expensive and require planning and preparation to get started. Flight planning and flight permission are required before you can enter the airspace. Therefore, it might make sense to look at other methods to collect data for smaller areas, when data are needed within short time or after an event like a major storm. Until recently, the acquisition of high resolutions digital surface models has been dominated by the use of airborne LiDAR, but with the development of digital cameras and UAVs this method is worth considering for collecting data to fill in gabs in marine and coastal data [25]. According to the results from Gonçalves et al. [26] UAV's can replace the many of the conventional flights, without any loss in quality of topographic and aerial data and gain in the coast of data acquisition. The test from Gonçalves et al. [26] is carried out on very sensitive areas on the Portuguese northwest coast, both photogrammetric DSM and orthoimage mosaic are generated and evaluated. The Portuguese test concluded that UAVs can be a major breakthrough in the study and monitoring of morphological changes induces by coastal dynamics.

During the last years projects with LiDAR have been carried out and tested in coastal areas. The benefits of UAV LiDAR are to deliver more accurate digital terrain models when vegetation is present, it can be processed much faster and the reliability is expected to be better over weakly textures surfaces [27]. UAV data acquisition as a method is efficient but national rules and regulations can influence the efficiency of the method, like the requirement of flying the UAV in line of sight [27]. It means that you have to

---

[2] http://www.kortal.dk.

have visual control over the UAV when flying it, and it can impact your flight planning, so you need to break your work into smaller parts.

3.4 Mobile Mapping - Combined Solutions

Mobile mapping is a surveying method of integrating the process of collecting data from a vehicle - car, train, boat, moped or similar. Mobile mapping systems can include different type of sensors, but most common the 'basic' systems consist of GPS, INS (Inertial Navigation System), cameras and laser scanners, the number of cameras and laser scanners depends of the manufactures [28].

The benefit of considering mobile mapping systems to fill in gabs in marine data along the coast, is that it is a solution that are flexible and can access the area immediately after an event has happened if required. Next to this, airborne systems have troubles with detecting vertical objects like steep cliffs and dunes [29], but by using mobile systems from a boat or a vehicle on the beach such cliffs dunes can be monitored.

Most of the manufactures of mobile mapping systems offer a multi sensor platform, which makes it possible to combine the basic system with more sensors related to data in the coastal and marine zone thus being relevant to combine with bathymetry. In 2019 a project was carried out in Idaho combining a mobile mapping system with bathymetry [30]. The project was to scan the Clearwater Memorial Bridge in Idaho using Leica Pegasus. A part of the project was to scan the river bottom with multibeam combined with laser scanning of the sea banks and the underside of the bridge. The outcome of the project was successful and demonstrated that the mobile mapping system acquire much more data than the multibeam method and can cover all tasks in one step while they had to go back and forth several times when using multibeam.

3.5 A Data Infrastructure for Coastal Zone Management and Planning

Combining all elements into a holistic data infrastructure can provide a sound digital platform for decision-making in coastal zone management and planning. Figure 3 illustrates the components and their interconnections.

Figure 3 illustrates how the different data sources can be integrated and used by the coastal zone planners in various authorities from the local over regional to national levels. The data from the marine SDI and the terrestrial SDI are normally available through geoportals and often freely available regarding public sector data [29], although the Marine SDI most often requires payment for the part of the data set, which represents the Digital Nautical Chart used for ship navigation. The other data sources – satellites, UAV and mobile mapping are not available directly but requires special software for handling. Satellite data from the European Copernicus programme can be accessed free of charge and directly through an online portal[3] and this is also the case for some ESA (European Space Agency) data. Other satellite data from for example SPOT requires payment but are also accessible through online portals.

Data from UAV's and mobile mapping systems are 'local' by nature and managed by a connected computer, which also contains the necessary software for processing

---

[3] https://www.copernicus.eu/en/how/how-access-data.

raw data into appropriate data formats for subsequent upload to a local server (other data). Below the advantages and disadvantages related to the various data sources are discussed.

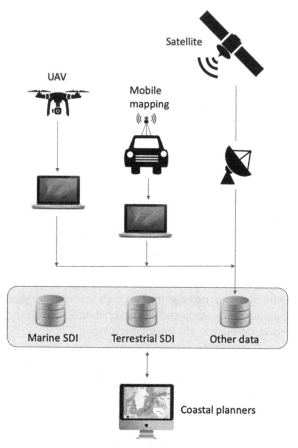

Fig. 3. Data sources for coastal zone management and planning.

4 Discussion

The national terrestrial and maritime SDI's are the most important data sources in integrated coastal zone management and planning, but it requires that the data has a high accuracy and is up to date and being generally accessible. Following the INSPIRE Directive and the PSI (Public Sector Information Directive) many EU Member States have established spatial data infrastructures for mainly terrestrial data and in many cases adopted the principle of open government data. This is a very important step towards digital governance and accordingly an important contribution to efficient coastal zone management and planning. Regarding the marine domain the accessibility to data is more diverse. One of the main problems found with the Danish MSDI is the 'conflict' between different shareholders and organisation - raising several challenges.

- The shareholders are not liable to handover their data to the MSDI, which means that more actual data could exist without being available
- Some data are free while other are pay per use

When working with management and planning in a dynamic area as the coastal zone, it requires that data are up to date, and it is important to find a way to keep the data updated by monitoring coastal changes and fill in gabs when needed. Traditional mapping carried out by national mapping agencies is centralised and updated according to a more or less well-defined time schedule – for example every 5 or 10 years. This is of course not satisfactory for coastal zone management keeping in mind the rapid changes in this zone. With the development in data acquisition, methods and development it is expected that it will become easier to keep data updated and monitor coastal changes in the future.

The satellite technology has developed in a way where it can provide data that can be used in management and planning of the coastal zone, but it is still a technology that need to be used by specialists who can process and evaluate the data to the extend needed. The development and easy access to satellite data has provided an additional source of data. The Copernicus programme providing freely available satellite data has become a major data source for as well the public as the private sector, and due to the stability of this data platform, an increasing amount of software has been developed to support the use of Copernicus data. Other satellites like SPOT and Pléiades-HR are operated from commercial companies and requires licenses for accessibility.

Airborne data provision has proven to be effective in the coastal zone especially the LiDAR platform, and it is expected that the Photon and Giger-mode will make it even more effective. The disadvantages with the airborne solutions are the high price for data acquisitions and they are therefore more suitable for bigger areas.

UAV and Mobile-mapping solutions are solutions that can be operated within a short notice – it doesn't require much planning to get them started, these solutions are therefore appropriate if we look into filling in gabs. If an event for example a storm is expected, it would be possible to survey the area before and after providing useful information for establishing and updating management plans. The mobile-mapping system is not as sensitive for the wind as the UAV, but the mobile mapping will not get the data from above.

If we compare the different technologies that can be used to fill in gaps, we can see that data from satellites and airborne solutions are effective for large scale mapping, where UAV and mobile mapping solutions are most effective in smaller areas.

It is expected that more stakeholders get case to case mapping done with UAV's and maybe mobile-mapping in the future, because it is easier to mobilize and get data produced. In some cases, some stakeholders might have their own UAV solutions.

On the other hand, larger scale project is expected to be carried out based on satellite data, it is not a day to day delivery, and require specialist knowledge to get the needed output. Both mapping based on satellite data and UAV's are mainly expected to take place in bigger project maybe lead by a national organisation.

The data obtained by UAV's and mobile mapping solutions will typically be produced from case to case in order to provide additional information for specific task like new coastal protection actions to reduce the risks from erosion and flooding. Although, these data do not have the stamp as authoritative the quality and accuracy may be higher than the data available through the official national SDI's, and therefore better targeted towards such specific tasks. A rather recent source of information can be collected by citizens, using their mobile devices to collect specific information about vulnerable nature like birds and flowers. This data source called citizens science is currently growing in popularity often due to lack of resources in the local authorities.

Authoritative versus non-authoritative data is a relevant discussion. While the large public sector data sets available from the national terrestrial and marine SDI's have a stamp as being authoritative meaning that decisions made using these data can be considered of high quality regarding the information level behind the decisions. This also means that all levels of governance – from local over regional to national – are using the same data for their decision-making. The additional data sources presented in the current paper based on satellites, UAV, and mobile mapping platforms do not have this stamp of being authoritative except the satellite data from the Copernicus programme, which has this authoritative stamp from the European Commission. However, satellite data are not as a cadastral map or a topographic map but requires classification and interpretation, which in some degree will vary between different users and their skills in image processing.

Digital governance is a complex matter involving a lot of interests and stakeholders with their own agendas and expectations, and often the responsible coastal planners and managers can be confronted with different locally produced data set showing opposite trends in the development in the coastal zone. This can be a very delicate task to balance such interests.

Finally, it should be emphasised that coastal zone management and planning in border regions generally only have access to data for their own country while flooding and erosion do not accept national borders. Therefore, a need for access to data from the neighbouring countries are obvious, and the Directive on Maritime Spatial Planning [31] encourage to transnational planning. A conceptual model for a transnational data infrastructure can be found in [32] which is based on the experiences from the Baltic Sea and the common HELCOM data portal.

5 Conclusion

Coastal zone planning and management is a complex task taken place along the coasts, which are very dynamic in nature. Digital governance with easy access to huge amount of authoritative data available for the coastal planners through terrestrial and marine SDI's. This is a major step forward. However, recognising the dynamics in the coastal zone – not at least under the current changing climate, which will have major effects by sea level rise and increased storminess.

To handle these challenges the required data goes beyond traditional available cadastral and topographic maps available through terrestrial national SDI's. Similarly, some data are available for the marine space through marine SDI's but much less and focused on data on the environment, fishery, shipping, and recently other offshore activities like energy production and fish farms.

The current paper has described a set of modern data acquisition platforms like satellites, UAV's, and mobile mapping systems, and how they can contribute to create up-to-date information about the dynamic coast in easy and cost-effective ways. It is realised that these new platforms do not have the authoritative stamp but nevertheless the only data source in specific planning and management decisions, where you cannot wait for the next release of official data. The next steps in our research will focus on how to integrate the new data sources into the official marine and terrestrial SDI's

Acknowledgement. This research is carried as part of a Ph.D. project with financial support from the National Danish Geodata Agency.

References

1. European Environment Agency: Balancing the future of Europe's coasts – knowledge base for integrated management. EEA Report, No. 12/2013 (2013)
2. Feser, F., Barcikowska, M., Krueger, O., Schenk, F., Weisse, R., Xia, L.: Storminess over the North Atlantic and North-western Europe – a review. Q. J. Roy. Meteorol. Soc. **14**, 350–382 (2014). https://doi.org/10.1002/qj.2364
3. Ministry of Environment and Food of Denmark: Coastal Analysis, p. 2016. Ministry of Environment and Food of Denmark, Copenhagen (2016)
4. United Nations: Agenda 21. United Nations Conference on Environment & Development, Rio de Janeiro, Brazil, 3–14 June 1992. United Nations Sustainable Development (1992)
5. European Commission: Recommendation from the European Parliament, The Council, of 30 May 2002 concerning the Implementation of Integrated Coastal Zone Management in Europe. Official Journal of the European Communities, L 158/24 (2002)
6. Rajabifard, A., Feeney, M.-E., Williamson, I.: Spatial data infrastructures: concept, nature and SDI hierarchy. In: Williamson, I.P., Rajabifard, A., Feeney, M.-E. (eds.) Developing Spatial Data Infrastructures: From Concept to Reality, pp. 17–40. Taylor and Francis, London (2003)
7. European Commission: Directive 2003/4/EC of the European parliament and of the Council of 28 January 2003 on public access to environmental information and repealing Council Directive 90/313/EEC. Official Journal of the European Union, L 41/26 (2003)
8. European Commission: The reuse of public sector information, Directive 2003/98/EC of the European Parliament and of the Council. Official Journal of the European Union, L345, pp. 90–96 (2003)
9. European Commission: Directive 2019/1024 of the European Parliament and of the Council of 20 June 2019 on open data and the re-use of public sector information. Official Journal of The European Union, L 172/56 (2019)
10. Commission of the European Communities: Directive 2007/2/EC of the European Parliament and of the Council of 14 March 2007 establishing an Infrastructure for Spatial Information in the European Community (INSPIRE). Official Journal of the European Union (2007)
11. Strain, L., Rajabifard, A., Williamson, I.: Marine administration and spatial data infrastructure. Mar. Policy **30**(4), 431–441 (2006)
12. Hansen, H.S., Hvingel, L., Schrøder, L.: Open government data – a key element in the digital society. In: Kő, A., Leitner, C., Leitold, H., Prosser, A. (eds.) EGOVIS/EDEM 2013. LNCS, vol. 8061, pp. 167–180. Springer, Heidelberg (2013). https://doi.org/10.1007/978-3-642-40160-2_14

13. The Danish Government & Local Government Denmark: Good Basic Data for Everyone – A Driver for Growth and Efficiency. The eGovernment Strategy 2011–2015 (2012)
14. Hansen, H.S., Schröder, L.: The societal benefits of open government data with particular emphasis on geospatial information. In: Kő, A., Francesconi, E., Anderst-Kotsis, G., Tjoa, A.M., Khalil, I. (eds.) EGOVIS 2019. LNCS, vol. 11709, pp. 31–44. Springer, Cham (2019). https://doi.org/10.1007/978-3-030-27523-5_3
15. Cooper, P., Pepper, J., Osborne, M.: The Hydrographic and Oceanographic Dimension to Marine Spatial Data Infrastructure Development: Developing the capability. White paper, IHO MSDI Working Group, May 2010 (2010)
16. Holzhüter, W., Luhtala, H., Hansen, H.S., Schiele, K.: Lost in space and time? A conceptual approach to harmonise data for maritime spatial planning. Int. J. Spat. Data Infrastruct. Res. **14**, 108–132 (2019)
17. Lebègue, L., et al.: Pléiades-HR image quality commissioning. Int. Arch. Photogram. Remote Sens. Spat. Inf. Sci. **XXXIX-B1**, 561–566 (2012)
18. Airbus: Pléiades Neo. Trusted Intelligence (2019). https://www.intelligence-airbusds.com/automne/api/docs/v1.0/document/download/ZG9jdXRoZXF1ZS1kb2N1bWVudC02MMD IwOA==/ZG9jdXRoZXF1ZS1maWxlLTYwMjA3/PleiadesNeo_TrustedIntelligence_web_201910.pdf
19. Lyzenga, D.R., Malinas, N.P., Tanis, F.J.: Multispectral bathymetry using a simple physically based algorithm. IEEE Trans. Geosci. Remote Sens. **44**(8), 2251–2259 (2006). https://doi.org/10.1109/TGRS.2006.872909
20. Schutz, B.E., Zwally, H.J., Shuman, C.A., Hancock, D., DiMarzio, J.P.: Overview of the ICESat mission. Geophys. Res. Lett. **32**, L21S01 (2005). https://doi.org/10.1029/2005GL024009
21. Markus, T., et al.: The Ice, Cloud, and land Elevation Satellite-2 (ICESat-2): Science requirements, concept, and implementation. Remote Sens. Environ. **190**, 260–273 (2017). https://doi.org/10.1016/j.rse.2016.12.029
22. Parrish, C.E., Magruder, L.A., Neuenschwander, A.L., Forfinski-Sarkozi, N., Alonzo, M., Jasinski, M.: Validation of ICESat-2 ATLAS bathymetry and analysis of ATLAS's bathymetric mapping performance. Remote Sens. **11**(14) (2019). https://doi.org/10.3390/rs11141634
23. Lemmens, M.J.P.M.: Photon Lidar. GIM Int. **29**, 17 (2015)
24. Stoker, J., Abdullah, Q., Nayegandhi, A., Winehouse, J.: Evaluation of single photon and Geiger mode Lidar for the 3D Elevation Program. Remote Sens. **8**(9), 1–16 (2016)
25. Rothermel, M., Haala, N.: Potential of dense matching for the generation of high quality digital elevation models. Int. Arch. Photogram. Remote Sens. Spat. Inf. Sci. ISPRS Arch. **38**, 271–276 (2012). International Society for Photogrammetry and Remote Sensing
26. Gonçalves, J.A., Henriques, R.: UAV photogrammetry for topographic monitoring of coastal areas. ISPRS J. Photogram. Remote Sens. **104**, 101–111 (2015)
27. Assenbaum, M.: Monitoring coastal erosion with UAV Lidar. GIM Int. **32**(2), 18–21 (2018)
28. Petrie, G.: Mobile Mapping Systems: An Introduction to the Technology. Geoinformatics. **13**, 32–43 (2010)
29. Bitenc, M., et al.: Evaluation of a LIDAR land - based mobile mapping system for monitoring sandy coasts. Remote Sens. **3**(7), 2072–4292 (2011)
30. Pfeifle S.: Clear Scanning of Clearwater (2019). https://www.xyht.com/hydromarine/clear-scanning-on-the-clearwater/

31. European Commission: Directive 2014/89/EU of the European Parliament and of the Council of 23 July 2014 establishing a framework for maritime spatial planning. The Official Journal of the European Union, L 257/135 (2014)
32. Hansen, H.S., Reiter, I.M., Schrøder, L.: A system architecture for a transnational data infrastructure supporting maritime spatial planning. In: Kő, A., Francesconi, E. (eds.) EGOVIS 2017. LNCS, vol. 10441, pp. 158–172. Springer, Cham (2017). https://doi.org/10.1007/978-3-319-64248-2_12

Enabling Collaboration Among Cultural Heritage Experts and Maritime Spatial Planners

Lise Schrøder(✉), Marina Georgati, and Henning Sten Hansen

Aalborg University Copenhagen, A.C. Meyers Vænge 15, 2450 Copenhagen, Denmark
lisesch@plan.aau.dk

Abstract. Across Europe, countries are joining forces in order to implement European Commission initiatives as the Blue Growth Strategy and the Directive on Maritime Spatial Planning. Collaboration on how to perform stakeholder involvement as well as create cross-border solutions has become a key issue around the European sea basins and holistic spatial planning approaches similar to terrestrial planning practices are now being implemented in the marine environment. Among the sectors in marine governance is the maritime cultural heritage under water as well as in the coastal zone, where the example of the Baltic Sea Region illustrates how this sector has become an inherent part of the new Blue Growth discourse and the MSP-policy development across the region. In order to utilise this potential, support for collaboration and shared understandings within the maritime cultural heritage community of practise is needed. This research has focused on how to develop a spatially enabled digital and collaborative working environment to support the co-creation of new shared spatial planning concepts for maritime cultural heritage. The development of the platform itself has been carried out in a close cooperation with the actual users including cultural heritage experts, public authorities and research institutes in the Baltic Sea Region.

Keywords: Maritime spatial planning · Marine governance · Maritime cultural heritage · Organisational learning · Distributed systems · Open source solutions

1 Introduction

Directive 2014/89/EU of the European parliament and of the council of 23 July 2014 established the framework for maritime spatial planning (MSP) in order to minimise conflicts among different sea uses and the member states has to establish the national maritime spatial plans by 2021 [1]. Being broader and more economic in scope than the preserving strategies, this new Blue Growth discourse also created the momentum for integrating the maritime heritage to the ongoing macro-regional MSP-policy development [2–4]. In order to achieve the aims of the European Commission, spatial data infrastructures, various decision support tools as well as vehicles enabling collaboration and capacity building are needed, and since the beginning of this century, a large number of projects on how to deal with those matters have been carried out [5, 6].

The Baltic Sea Region provides an interesting example of how a community of practice within the field of maritime spatial planning gradually has been established

© Springer Nature Switzerland AG 2020
A. Kő et al. (Eds.): EGOVIS 2020, LNCS 12394, pp. 106–120, 2020.
https://doi.org/10.1007/978-3-030-58957-8_8

during the past decades by adapting to the vision of a sustainable further development of the Baltic marine environment and the shared experiences created by mutual engagement in a number of projects, where marine and maritime spatial planning issues have been on the agenda. The institutional conditions and traditions differ a lot among across the countries of the region, though, shared visions of a healthy and prosperous Baltic Sea have facilitated a long tradition for working together, and the region has been a pioneer in developing Maritime Spatial Planning in Europe [7]. Supported by the two pan-Baltic intergovernmental institutions VASAB[1] and HELCOM[2], and a number of EU-financed projects have contributed to building up a knowledge base for the region and digital tools for spatial decision support for MSP.

Likewise, former underwater and coastal heritage projects have contributed to the common understanding of the unique and diverse richness of the underwater and maritime heritage in the Baltic Sea Region [4, 5]. As emphasised by Hansen et al., to create the best possible data and knowledge foundation for MSP, a well-functional Geographic Information System (GIS) with comprehensive, detailed and regularly updated data is needed [8]. Concerning maritime cultural heritage, profound national differences in the data management and accessibility has to be taken into consideration, and also the implementation of the concept of Maritime Spatial Planning differs a lot in the different Baltic Sea states [4]. As further pointed out by Lehtimaki et al. [4], the history of the heritage registers in use today started decades ago and under varying conditions.

Addressing this challenge, the aim of this research is to develop a spatially enabling collaborative working environment to support the co-creation of new shared spatial planning concepts for maritime cultural heritage. In order to pursue this question, an analytical framework, referring to the understanding of digital habitats and digital tools enabling communication and learning in communities of practice as defined by Wenger [9] and Wenger et al. [10] will provide a conceptual backbone for the analysis. Methodologically, these concepts will be transferred into a more operational experience-oriented analytical framework suitable for the analysis of spatial planning understood as a creative collaboration process based on the management of tangible phenomena and communication enabled by sharable artefacts as for instance maps [11]. This framework will be introduced in part two, where also the understanding of spatial planning will be introduced. This will provide the context for the introduction of the maritime cultural heritage community of practise and the contours of its digital habitat. In part three the demands for a spatially enabled collaborative working environment will be specified, providing the basis for presenting the suggested solution, the BalticRIM Data Portal. In part four, the concept of the digital habitat will provide a framework for the discussion, which will be followed by a conclusion and some further perspectives.

2 Background and Theory

The creation of a platform supporting the development of concepts for integrating maritime cultural heritage in the national maritime spatial plans will be based on an understanding of the specific conditions in the Baltic Sea region, which draws on the long

---

[1] https://vasab.org/.

[2] https://helcom.fi/.

tradition for working together based on shared visions. Pan-Baltic governance structures as The Baltic Marine Environment Protection Commission (HELCOM) and national governments collaborating in the regional forum, Visions and Strategies for the Baltic Sea Region (VASAB), provides an organisational backbone for the Baltic Sea maritime spatial planning community of practise, which is further enforced by the joint efforts in a huge number of EU-financed projects aiming at developing for instance spatial data infrastructures and shared toolboxes [6, 7].

The first paragraph of this chapter introduces the understandings of communities of practise and digital habitats as conceptualised by Wenger [9] and Wenger et al. [10]. The second paragraph introduces how this kind of learning processes can be recognised in theories of spatial planning dealing with learning processes based on engaging in the planning matters.

2.1   A Community of Practice and Its Digital Habitat

The understanding of *communities of practice* as conceptualized by Wenger [8] provides a useful framework for characterizing the scenery of collaboration processes related to maritime spatial planning. Referring to this concept three dimensions of practice provides the sources of coherence of a community: mutual engagement, a joint enterprise, and a shared repertoire. Referring to Wenger [8], membership in a community of practice is a matter of *mutual engagement*, providing the basis for doing whatever they do, and thus defining the community. Therefore, enabling mutual engagement is essential in any practice. Though, as pointed out by Wenger mutual engagement creates relationships among people reflecting the complexity of doing things together. Also, a *joint enterprise* contributes to keeping the community of practice together as it is characterized by the collective process of negotiation, that reflects the complexity of mutual engagement. This joint enterprise is defined by the participants, not just as a stated goal but based on relations of mutual accountability, that becomes an integral part of the practice. Finally, a *shared repertoire* is the third characteristic of practice as a source of community coherence. The repertoire of a community of practice includes routines, words, tools, ways of doing things, stories, gestures symbols, genres, actions or concepts [9] and becomes a resource due to reflecting a history of mutual engagement and are remaining inherently ambiguous. On that background, Wenger states, that, '…communities of practice, as a locus of engagement in action, interpersonal relations, shared knowledge and negotiation of enterprises, hold the key to real transformation', and he argue, that communities of practice can be understood as 'shared histories of learning' [9].

As presented by Wenger et al. in "Digital Habitats – stewarding technology for communities", technology has changed our understanding of communities, and the other way around communities have changed our uses of technology [10]. Wenger et al. introduce the notion of the *digital habitat* referring to the portion of a community's habitat, that is enabled by a configuration of technology. On this background they propose four perspectives to be considered: 1) The *tools* supporting specific community activities, 2) the *platforms* providing access to tools, 3) the *features* making tools and platforms 'liveable' 4) the *full configuration* of technologies sustaining the habitat. Furthermore, due to this perception, the communities of practice perspective contribute to understand digital habitats – '… on how communities use technology, how they are influenced by it, how technology presents new learning opportunities for communities, and how communities continue to assess the value of different tools and technologies over time, and even how communities influence the use of technologies' [10].

Recent research by Morf et al. presented in 'Towards a Ladder of Marine/Maritime Spatial Planning Participation' [12] emphasize, that there are numerous methods and techniques to stimulate interactions between planners, authorities and stakeholders. In the current research, the focus will be on the constructs of the digital habitat, and how it can function as a platform for communication as such, as well as how its potential for enabling co-creation and collaborate production of sharable artefacts can be understood as a vehicle for facilitation of mutual engagement and learning contributing to the ongoing configuration of the Maritime Spatial Planning community of practice.

2.2 The Spatial Planning Perspective

An approach to distinguish how the different material as well as digital resources feeds into this kind of creative planning processes, is the conceptualization of how space is created as presented by Healey [13], who adapted Lefebvre's spatial triad [14], and further conceptualised by Schrøder [11]. Referring to this understanding, space is produced in terms of being 'perceived', 'conceived' or 'lived' interacting in a continuous process, which will be exemplified in the context of maritime spatial planning below.

Space can be understood at the *perceptual level* as a 'spatial practice' or as 'routine material engagement and experience of being in and moving around (urban) areas' [13]. An example, which can be recognised both in the urban as the maritime spatial planning context, could be a maritime cultural heritage site as a harbour functioning as the scenery for daily-life functions.

At the *conceptual level*, space can be understood as a 'representation of space', which can also be expressed as 'intellectual conceptions of (urban) areas, produced for analytical and administrative purposes' [13]. This makes sense not only in the urban context but also in the broader perspectives of spatial planning, where an example of intellectual conceptions produced for analytical and administrative purposes for instance could be the concept of Ecosystem Services, which is a central concept in maritime spatial planning [15]. And within the context of maritime cultural heritage referred to above, for instance the topics on a workshop arranged by The International Council for the Exploration of the Sea (ICES) [16], 'methods for identifying marine places of socio-cultural importance' and 'mappings of spatially relevant information' as well as the MSP data study [17], illustrate this point.

Dealing with space at the *pragmatic level* and the ideas of 'lived space' understood in terms of 'representational spaces', Healey [13] rephrases the formulation as 'cultural expressions of place qualities and spatial meanings'. ICES [16] emphasises the close relationship between cultural values and place attachment and 'sense of place', which also can be related to the understanding of cultural values as social constructs arisen from the specific cultural context of time and place [13, 15]. This exemplifies, how Healey's [13] concept of 'representational spaces' links to Liggett [18] and the understanding of 'meanings within a cultural memory'.

Healey [13] stresses the importance of distinguishing the intellectual conceptions of the planning professionals from the local knowledge, which is based on the material experience as well as the cultural imageries. In this process resources related to the perceived space as well as the lived space might contribute to experiential engagement involving passive as well as active participation of the stakeholders. In that respect, both aspects will function as a planning resource, which can contribute to the intellectual constructs of the planning process [13]. This could also be understood in terms of the 'the ladder of participation', where Arnstein [19] distinguish between citizen participation being passive or active. On the other hand, intellectual conceptions such as study trips or workshops can function as experiential resources setting the stage for further experiential engagement in the planning process, which also reflect the understanding of stakeholder involvement being of a more iterative nature as also pointed out by Morf et al. [12].

3 Design of the BalticRIM Data Portal

In the following paragraphs demands for a spatially enabled collaborative working environment bridging the domains of maritime cultural heritage and maritime spatial planning will be specified, providing the basis for presenting the suggested solution, the BalticRIM Data Portal. The first part will introduce some of the main functionalities in this kind of portals, the second part will specify specific demands for the particular solution. And finally, the chosen solutions for the BalticRIM Data Portal will be presented.

3.1 Existing Data Portals for Maritime and Underwater Cultural Heritage

Geoportals are web sites that display an entry point to geodata on the web with the purpose of providing existing geodata to portal users [20]. Specifically, marine geoportals have gained a great popularity lately allowing the access to marine data and improving interoperability by using internationally recognised standards [8]. As documented in the research by Hansen et al., most European portals include metadata in the INSPIRE standard, but still it is often difficult to gain an overview over all the data provided and the date of origin of the data. Furthermore, not all data are downloadable, and the degree to which the portals include data from private companies appear to be limited [8].

The significance of Geoportals as part of the spatial data infrastructure has been repeatedly investigated in existing literature, but as this research aims at developing a web portal for geospatial data, that promotes Maritime and Underwater Cultural Heritage and its integration in Maritime Spatial Planning, this section focuses on presenting existing data portals for Maritime Cultural Heritage. It differs from country to country how Maritime Cultural Heritage and Underwater Cultural Heritage is included in Maritime Spatial Planning, and there are only a few examples of portals that combine these two fields, and often concentrating the interest on other aspects of MSP rather than UCH or MCH. Even though geoportals have sparked a great interest the last few years and as the previous section notices a great effort has been put on geoportals for Maritime Spatial Planning, there are only a few instances of map portals devoted to cultural heritage and even less promoting maritime, underwater or coastal cultural heritage. Based on review of relevance for MSP initiatives first and then as independent actions, this section presents some of the most significant examples.

- The PORTODIMARE project[3] aims at creating a geoportal for data and information related to coastal and marine areas of the Adriatic-Ionian Region and provides access to modules for Integrated Coastal Zone Management and Maritime Spatial Planning analysis and risk evaluation. It integrates existing databases, portals and tools developed by previous EU-funded projects, local and national administrations and other initiatives. UCH is one of the 26 broad categories. The web service is based on GeoNode, a web-based platform for the development of GIS and the deployment of SDI using Openlayers. It has a big map viewer, but the data structure seems complicated with great restrictions in visualising more than one layer on the same map.

- Developed by using commercial tools and including information about underwater cultural heritage among others, the SNIMar geoportal[4] is a tool for the environmental management of the Portuguese marine waters. It contributes to the implementation of the European initiatives on marine governance, since it simplifies the sharing, searching and accessing to metadata and marine data, particularly useful for public administration, universities and research institutes. It has flexible options regarding the size of the map viewer, support in two languages (Portuguese and English) and efficient search options allowing both the visualization of data and its download.

- The Archaeological Atlas of the 2 Seas[5], maps UCH and disseminates information about underwater archaeological sites in the shared seas of France, England and Belgium focusing on World War I shipwrecks and gathering data through research and fieldwork [21]. The A2S geoportal[6] lists 1600 archaeological sites in the English Channel and the Southern North Sea, and more than 3000 underwater sites, while historical photographs enhance the dataset. The archaeological sites are contextualized online by high-resolution background bathymetry, ancient charts and aerial photograph, and pop-up windows add valuable details.

- A WebGIS service for the preservation of the underwater cultural heritage for the Belgian part of the North Sea and was developed by Vandenbulcke et al. [22]. Its setup is based on the latest advanced technologies and open standards in order to provide interoperability among the involved organisations.

- Following a similar approach Jaelani and Bachtiar describe a geoportal for the cultural heritage preservation of Penanggungan and Trowulan, which provides a data infrastructure, which collects, stores, and visualizes the spatial distribution of cultural heritages in these two areas. PostgreSQL is used for data storing, QGIS and GeoServer for data processing, uDig for improved maps view and Openlayers for data visualization on the web [23].

The examination of these marine geoportals reveals the limited number of geoportals linked to UCH or MCH, and the inadequate interest, that the MSP-related portals show to these fields, including only a small number of archaeological sites. These examples confirm, as stated in the previous section, the great fluctuations among web portals when considering their interfaces and the offered possibilities in the client side.

---

[3] https://portodimare.adrioninterreg.eu/.

[4] http://geoportal.snimar.pt/index.html?language=en.

[5] http://www.a2s-geoportal.eu/#/welcome.

[6] https://www.geodata.soton.ac.uk/geodata/web/project208.

3.2   The Needs of the User Community

During two decades pilot projects based on collaboration among national stakeholders in the Baltic Sea Region have been carried out [6–8]. A number of EU-financed projects have facilitated a learning-by-doing approach, which gradually has built up the common knowledge base and digital tools for spatial decision support for MSP. The empirical input for this research is based on active participation in some of those projects – the Baltic LINes[7] and BalticRIM[8] Interreg projects and the BONUS BASMATI[9] project as well as documented results from some of the other projects focussing on the digital infrastructures and digital government perspectives of the Baltic Sea Region. And the current research has been carried out in a close cooperation between cultural heritage experts, public authorities, and research institutes in the Baltic Sea Region.

The Data and Map Service BASEMAPS. In order to provide direct access to the national databases via WMS services instead of storing the data at HELCOM [8], the data and map service BASEMAPS[10] was developed in the Baltic LINes project. The BASEMAPS portal was further developed as part of the Pan Baltic Scope[11] project in order to serve as a collaboration platform testing designs of shared concepts for the display of the actual maritime spatial plans and to harmonise planning outputs in a digital setting. The programming code for BASEMAPS is open source, so it seemed to be a feasible solution to utilise this resource as a similar working environment for the BalticRIM project. Though, it turned out to be very difficult to reuse the BASEMAPS software as such, so the technical solution had to be redesigned. Thus, even if the basic elements from BASEMAPS formed a conceptual basis, it had to be transformed into a new solution based on more flexible standard software components.

In the following, this solution will be presented as the BalticRIM Data Portal: www.balticrimdataportal.eu.

MCH as well as MSP Data Not Being Available. The Baltic LINes project revealed a general challenge, as it turned out to be very difficult to provide harmonised and up to date datasets for cross-border maritime spatial planning tasks. In many of the Baltic Sea countries a lot of data for maritime spatial planning are restricted or not available at all. Most data for maritime spatial planning relate to Annex III of the INSPIRE Directive, and even if some open data services exist, many of the data categories differs across borders, and the data are presented in national languages and not available in English translation [7]. Likewise, concerning maritime cultural heritage, the profound national differences in the data management and accessibility had to be taken into serious consideration as well as the different ways of implementing MSP in each country [4]. As emphasised by Hansen et al. [7] the importance of applying widely approved and used technical standards to SDIs, is continuously recognised, while the importance of ensuring semantic interoperability is often overlooked. The point made by Brink

---

[7] https://vasab.org/project/balticlines/.

[8] https://www.submariner-network.eu/balticrim.

[9] https://bonusbasmati.eu/.

[10] https://basemaps.helcom.fi/.

[11] http://www.panbalticscope.eu/.

et al. [24], that increasing semantic interoperability has to be seen as a complex and ongoing process, which contributes to gradually discovering overlaps between concepts and models, is in itself an important aim for the output of the collaboration in the BalticRIM project. As pointed out by Hansen et al., all users require easy, transparent, and open access to up-to-date information [8]. Heritage registers in use today were created and gathered during recent decades and with varying competence and capacity, and as documented in the BalticRIM project [4], none of the Baltic Sea states have carried out systematic inventories on underwater heritage. Thus, these registers are far from complete and inclusion of maritime heritage aspects requires drawing on various additional data sources and comprehensive knowledge and experience regarding national policies and practices [4].

The Aim of THIS BalticRIM Solution. In order to analyse and test spatial data and maritime spatial planning concepts in the complex cross-disciplinary and cross-border setting and to share and disseminate project outcomes, a web-GIS seemed to be the most feasible solution. The pitfalls experienced in the Baltic LINes, where the extensive use of special-made programming code for the BASEMAPS platform made it very difficult to reuse, should be avoided. The BalticRIM prototype should be easy to modify along with identifying further needs among the project partners. A specific aim of the BalticRIM solution was to provide a spatially enabling working environment making it possible to display and discuss also sensitive and not publicly available data to support the co-creation of new shared spatial planning concepts for maritime cultural heritage, so a closed setting with restricted access to some parts of the portal was essential.

3.3   The Conceptual Design of the Web-GIS Platform

Based on the user demands and the strategic vector of developing a web service by using open source tools in a simple and intuitive structure, this section describes the main components of the proposed Web-GIS in both the backend and the frontend. The spatial Database Management System is the basis of the system, which stores most of the spatial data, facilitates its management and provides access to authorized clients to read limited-access data. More particularly, the DBMS is connected to a database that contains tables about the users and the metadata of the imported datasets and the vector layers. Information stored in the database is called from the backend component by using queries in Structured Query Language (SQL). The present application makes use of PostgreSQL with its spatial extension PostGIS because of the plenty advantages that it offers. For instance, it is free of restrictions and costs with high speed, supports a wide range of file formats, and is independent to other platforms.

To make the data accessible to the user, a web-map server is needed, and function as an intermediate tool that publishes spatial data from any spatial data source using open standards. GeoServer as a full-featured OGC server was selected to be used in this application offering great interoperability benefits.

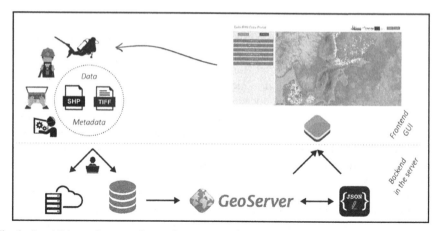

Fig. 1. In addition to the vector layers that are stored in the project's database, the BalticRIM portal visualises through the GeoServer supplementary WMS layers stored in external sources, like the INSPIRE or HELCOM portals. These layers refer to generic datasets displaying the administrative borders of the involved countries or the background of the areas including bathymetric maps

Regarding the frontend element of the service, which can take place in most standard web browsers, some of the main considerations designing the interface has been the simplicity in use, the clear distinction between open (Pan-Baltic) and restricted (case studies) datasets, the intuitive navigation and the aesthetic attractiveness. For this reason, the interface is divided into only three sections, giving a minimalistic impression and offering two simple navigation paths either under the 'Case Studies' or the 'Panbaltic' tab. These two tabs include datasets for the specific case studies of each country and datasets of Pan-Baltic interest respectively. The latter datasets are publicly accessible, while only registered members with advanced right permission are able to view the former ones.

The web page is developed by using HTML, CSS and JavaScript, while Openlayers is the selected JavaScript library for the visualisation of spatial data on the web. Every time the users make a request in the layers' menu, the geospatial data is retrieved from the GeoServer and visualised using a predefined style and layout as formed in the GeoServer in WMS format. Maps rendered as raster images through WMS are purely graphical and the client does not have access to the data, while the rendering time of even large maps is low and the service can be updated fast. However, WFS can also be an alternative functional option for visualising selected layers on the map.

3.4   Implementation of the BalticRIM Data Portal

The presented Web-GIS service is only one of the main outputs of the BalticRIM project. The service attempts to collect all relevant geospatial data concerning maritime and underwater cultural heritage in the Baltic Sea with the support of the involved organisations and institutions revealing the similarities and the main differences among the countries around the Baltic Sea. The proposed Web-GIS not only presents the national underwater and coastal cultural heritage but also attempts to bridge the legislative gaps among the neighbouring countries, promotes sites of cultural and touristic significance and introduces an innovative, Pan-Baltic spatial analysis of the most important national features of maritime cultural heritage. This section focuses on the description of the front-end interfacing and the structure of the web portal from the side of the client.

The Basic Design. Central in the design has been the online service providing various possibilities for the users. The interface is divided in three parts: the navigation bar in the upper part of the window, the selection menu in the left side and the interactive map in the right side, as shown in Fig. 2 and Fig. 3.

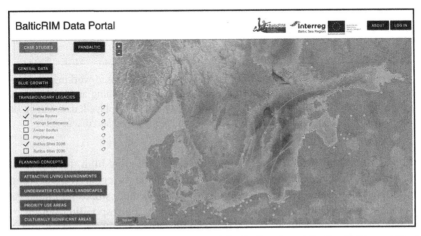

Fig. 2. The interface of the BalticRIM Data Portal displaying the public Pan-Baltic part illustrates some of the shared understandings of 'transboundary legacies' as the Hansa, or the Rutilus sites based on a list of the 100 most valuable maritime cultural heritage sites developed by the national heritage agencies across the Baltic Sea Region. The orange bars below refer to some of the planning concepts, which has been part of an exercise transforming the spatial representations of the heritage registers based on single coordinates into area-based concepts, which are essential in the context of maritime spatial planning.

The selection menu on the left side of the portal includes two tabs/sections; the first one refers on specific case studies at the national level (Fig. 3), while the second one is related to the cross-border perspectives and Pan-Baltic datasets. The menu presents various depth levels dependent on the division of the study case areas. The users are able to check the checkbox of the desired layer to view the data on the map. Once the checkbox is selected the layer is activated and presented on the right side of the window through a JSON request and response to and from the server correspondingly. Openlayers which is the web viewer of the datasets contains various user interface elements facilitating navigation in the map data, like zoom in and out, panning and scale bar.

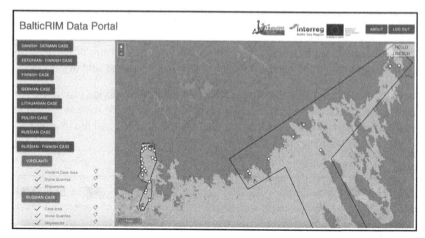

Fig. 3. The interface of the BalticRIM Data Portal displaying the closed working environment providing a platform for displaying case study data as well as developing and testing planning concepts for maritime cultural heritage. Here sensitive data can be displayed, data can be shared in a cross-border setting, and new planning concepts can be visualised and discussed.

Additional Functionalities. Of great importance for providing high-quality information and a holistic overview of the displayed datasets. Metadata registrations accompany the datasets from each involved organisation and are collected, stored and managed in the database in one metadata table, while by clicking the corresponding button in the layers' menu a metadata window shows up including this valuable information enriching the displayed data and enhancing its quality, reuse and discoverability. The metadata registrations in the database includes an additional Boolean attribute about the status of the dataset controlling its visibility depending on the permission rights of the user.

Download Functions. In addition to the metadata window, that opens by clicking on a button next to the selected layer, download function are included. A further button for each layer provides the possibility to the user to download the desired layers. This functionality only works for selected layers, which can be publicly accessible by other portals or for layers without restrictions. Pop-up windows for specific elements of the datasets will be added. At the national as well as the Pan-Baltic scale, there has been an interest for showing aggregated layers at national or Pan-Baltic levels as the total amount of Danish shipwrecks or all lighthouses in the Baltic Sea. However, also visualisation and the promotion of singular elements will be added in order to display information concerning the most attractive elements among the cultural heritage phenomena. This can include information on distinctive diving attractiveness of shipwrecks or the exceptional cultural heritage value of shipwrecks or lighthouses or external links to webpages with further information about the selected feature.

Display of Data. The Data display of the BalticRIM Data Portal allows users to view data published by national data providers through OGC open geospatial standards – WMS and WFS, which are related not only to underwater cultural heritage but also to coastal and nearby areas with high cultural significance. Apart from the publicly accessible datasets, which are being shown in a Pan-Baltic scale (see Fig. 1), a separate forum for the case study areas from the different countries or cross-border settings functions provides a closed working environment (see Fig. 2). Only members with advanced right permission may access this part of the portal, which allows for working also with more sensitive datasets. Concerning styling of the datasets and harmonisation of metadata, some challenges still remains.

4 Discussion

The BalticRIM Data Portal[12] was designed to provide a data and map service and thereby facilitate collaboration and exchange of data and insights across borders in order to create new maritime spatial planning concepts taking maritime cultural heritage into consideration. Referring to Healey [13] and Schroeder [11] planning processes can be related to the creation of spaces and places based on human contributions in the form of routine material engagement, intellectual conception and cultural expression. It has been argued, that this conceptual understanding can be related to Wengers et al's concepts of communities of practice and the construct and functions of its digital habitat [9, 10]. In the following, the understanding will provide a framework for discussing the usability of the BalticRIM data portal in terms on how it enables the collaboration and further development of planning concepts, shared understandings and capacity building within the community of maritime cultural heritage and maritime spatial planning.

An Arena for Collaboration. The platform as such can be understood in terms of a digital habitat providing an arena for dealing with the actual matters in the maritime cultural heritage community, which facilitates material engagement. Underwater remains of settlements, wrecks, lighthouses are all physical phenomena. Likewise, is it obvious, that the engagement in how to deal with those physical objects or sites in a maritime spatial planning context has a very material dimension as entities, that needs protection or can be utilised for various purposes [4, 25]. In this context, the digital habitat enables the basic interaction in maritime spatial planning discussions on how to manage those values as well as how the digital features facilitate the development of shared concepts for maritime spatial planning and processes relating to it.

The Systemic Perspective. In a broader context, the BalticRIM project can be understood in terms of a system, where the systemic approach facilitates the analysis of interconnected entities, their relations and representations. In this optic the digital platform for collaboration serves as the object of interest in the MSP project referring to a shared vision of establishing or further developing this kind of supportive structures. Thus, the creation of the digital habitat including tools, platforms, features, or a full configuration, can be understood as an immaterial vehicle mediating different understandings and thereby facilitating collaboration among the maritime spatial planners and professionals from the involved sectors. Issues on how to organise and display the case studies, which data to include, how to schematise cultural heritage data in formats,

---

[12] www.balticrimdataportal.eu.

that fits the purpose of MSP and the needs of the spatial planners, how to navigate on the portal, how to style the data, how to format the metadata, or whom to grant access, becomes enablers for establishing mutual understandings of the often tacit national and professional differences. Dealing with those matters is a good example of, how the need for and the co-creation of the features of the Web-GIS solution turns the BalticRIM Data Portal into this kind of tangible and sharable artefact, which can contribute to constitute the community of practise.

Enabling Learning Processes. The mutual learning process and the co-development of outcomes of the BalticRIM project, can be understood as an apparatus for capacity building in a broader perspective. The interaction among cultural heritage experts and maritime spatial planners, many of them taking part in the BalticRIM project as well as dealing with the ongoing tasks of the national MSP processes, creates new cultural expressions in the form of theoretical concepts, practical schemes as well as technical solutions. The need for a digital infrastructure facilitating the collaboration regarding the development and testing of new shared spatial concepts, evolved during the project and turned out to be a central feature of the project. Probably, the national setups will continue to differ, data might never be fully harmonised, still the organisational cultures are gradually changing, and new integrated concepts are starting to bridge across borders as well as among the cultural heritage maritime spatial planning communities.

5   Conclusions and Further Development

The prototype of the BalticRIM Data Portal has been developed in a close cooperation with professionals from cultural heritage institutions, maritime spatial planners and other stakeholders by means of open source components based on state-of-the-art principles and systems architecture standards. The basic concept of the portal has already proved to spatially enable the communication across the professional domains of maritime cultural heritage experts and maritime spatial planners by providing an internal digital habitat, where initial data, ideas, and concepts could be shared, developed and tested in the Balti-cRIM projects. Some of the results are already being implemented in national maritime spatial plans, others provide a basis for further development and dissemination. Technically, challenges relating to accessibility to data, their formats, and the multi-language environment this kind of tasks relate to still remain. The current research builds on those former experiences and ambitions regarding an overall systems architecture in a long-term perspective. Still, in terms of maritime spatial planning and capacity building across national borders and among practitioners in a complex, interdisciplinary professional community, the BalticRIM Data Portal already serves this purpose by providing an arena for knowledge sharing, engagement and mutual learning processes. In order to further develop the portal as a means of disseminating the BalticRIM outcomes, the Data portal is now going to be tested among a broader audience of maritime cultural heritage authorities and planners in the Baltic Sea Region.

Acknowledgement. This research is carried out as part of the BalticRIM project co-funded by the European Union (European Regional Development Fund) through the INTERREG Baltic Sea Region 2014–2020 programme. Also, many thanks to the BalticRIM partners providing valuable input for the current research.

References

1. European Commission: Directive 2014/89/EU of the European Parliament and of the Council of 23 July 2014 establishing a framework for maritime spatial planning. The Official Journal of the European Union, L 257/135 (2014)
2. European Commission: A European Strategy for more Growth and Jobs in Coastal and Maritime Tourism. Communication from the Commission to the European Parliament, The Council, the European Economic and Social Committee and the Committee of the Regions. European Commission (2014)
3. European Commission: Blue Growth Strategy on the opportunities for marine and maritime sustainable growth. Communication from the Commission to the European Parliament, The Council, the European Economic and Social Committee and the Committee of the Regions. European Commission (2012)
4. Lehtimäki, M., Tevali, R., Tikkanen, S.: To transmit Maritime Cultural Heritage (MCH) knowledge for MSP processes STEP 1 - BalticRIM status report WP2 GoA 2.1 (2019). https://www.submariner-network.eu/images/BalticRIM/BalticRIM_O2.1_gaps_on_MCH_for_MSP_processes_2020.pdf
5. Roio, M. (ed.): The Changing Coastal and Maritime Culture V BSR Cultural Heritage Forum in Tallinn 2013, Estonian National Heritage Board (2013)
6. Zaucha, J.: The Key to Governing the Fragile Baltic Sea. Maritime Spatial Planning in the Baltic Sea Region and Way Forward. Riga: VASAB Secretariat (2014)
7. Moodie, J.R., Kull, M., Morf, A., Schröder, L., Giacometti, A.: Challenges and enablers for transboundary integration in MSP: practical experiences from the Baltic Scope project. Ocean Coast. Manag. **177**(2019–07), 1–21 (2014)
8. Hansen, H.S., Reiter, I.M., Schröder, L.: A system architecture for a transnational data infrastructure supporting maritime spatial planning. In: Kő, A., Francesconi, E. (eds.) EGOVIS 2017. LNCS, vol. 10441, pp. 158–172. Springer, Cham (2017). https://doi.org/10.1007/978-3-319-64248-2_12
9. Wenger, E.: Communities of Practise – Learning, Meaning, Identity. Cambridge University Press, Cambridge (1999)
10. Wenger, E., White, N., Smidt, J.D.: Digital Habitats – Stewarding Technology for Communities. Cambridge University Press, Cambridge (2009)
11. Schroeder, L.: Cultural heritage as an experiential resource in planning. In: Lorentzen, A., Larsen, K.T., Schrøder, L. (eds.) Spatial Dynamics in the Experience Economy. Routledge, Abingdon (2015)
12. Morf, A., Kull, M., Piwowarczyk, J., Gee, K.: Towards a ladder of marine/maritime spatial planning participation. In: Zaucha, J., Gee, K. (eds.) Maritime Spatial Planning. LNCS, pp. 219–243. Springer, Cham (2019). https://doi.org/10.1007/978-3-319-98696-8_10
13. Healey, P.: Urban complexity and Spatial Strategies: Towards a Relational Planning of Our Times, The RTPI Library Series. Routledge, Abingdon (2007)
14. Lefebvre, H.: Critique of Everyday Life: Foundations for a Sociology of the Everyday. Verso, London (2002)
15. Magnussen, K., Heiskanen, A.-S., Navrud, S., Viitasalo, M.: Ecosystem services in MSP: ecosystem services approach as a common Nordic understanding for MSP, TemaNord, Nordic Council of Ministers, Copenhagen (2017). https://doi.org/10.6027/TN2017-536
16. ICES: Report of the Joint HZG/LOICZ/ICES Workshop: Mapping Cultural Dimensions of Marine Ecosystem Services (WKCES), 17–21 June 2013, Geesthacht, Germany. ICES CM 2013/SSGHIE:12, 70p. (2013)
17. European Commision: MSP Data Study: Evaluation of data and knowledge gaps to implement MSP, European Commission, Directorate-General for Maritime Affairs and Fisheries. Assistance Mechanism for the Implementation of Maritime Spatial Planning (2016)

18. Liggett, H.: City sights/sites of memories and dreams. In: Liggett, H., Perry, D. (eds.) Spatial Practices. Sage, London (1995)

19. Arnstein, S.R.: A ladder of citizen participation. J. Am. Inst. Plann. **35**(4), 216–224 (1969)

20. Van Oort, P.A.J., Kuyper, M.C., Bregt, A.K., Crompvoets, J.: Geoportals: an internet marketing perspective. Data Sci. J. **8**, 162–181 (2009). https://doi.org/10.2481/dsj.008-013

21. Momber, G., Bowens, A.: The Atlas of the 2 Seas and the first world war forgotten wrecks projects: innovative methods of underwater cultural heritage research, presentation and dissemination. In: Da Silva, A.R., Simonds, L., Guérin, U. (eds.) Underwater Cultural Heritage from World War I, pp. 183–192. United Nations Educational, Scientific and Cultural Organizations, Paris (2015)

22. Vandenbulcke, A., van Ackere S., Decock, M., Stal, C., De Wulf, A.: Preservation of the archaeological heritage of the north sea using webGIS. In: 16th International Multidisciplinary Scientific GeoConference SGEM (2016)

23. Jaelani, L.M., Bachtiar, J.A.: Implementation of geoportal for cultural heritage preservation of Penanggungan and Trowulan. IPTEK J. Proc. Ser. **3**(6), 3–7 (2017). https://doi.org/10.12962/j23546026.y2017i6.3306

24. van den Brink, L., Janssen, P., Quak, W., Stoter, J.: Towards a high level of semantic harmonisation in the geospatial domain. Comput. Environ. Urban Syst. **62**(2017), 233–242 (2017)

25. Seesmeri, L.: Toolkit for mapping underwater landscape and anticipating risks for underwater landscape. University of Turku, Landscape Studies (2019)

Exploring Usability and Acceptance Factors of m-Government Systems for Elderly

Tamás Molnár[1]([⊠]) and Andrea Kő[2]

[1] Humboldt-Universität zu Berlin, Berlin, Germany
tamas.molnar@cms.hu-berlin.de
[2] Corvinus University Budapest, Budapest, Hungary
andrea.ko@uni-corvinus.hu

Abstract. The last decade has shown that e-government systems have an enormous advantage for both the government and also the citizens. It is however not easy to develop services which can be used by users with low computer literacy. We have investigated in this research, how elderly users can profit from mobile government systems and how such system could be designed in accordance with the requirement that every citizen has to be able to use them. Elderly users are an important target group for governments as Europe will be the oldest continent by 2060. There are several m-government initiatives and projects offering various government services, like information sharing, alerting and mHealth services, which provide mobile remote patient monitoring in order to measure vital signs, bio-signals of patients outside hospital environments. Such systems can strongly benefit from improved acceptance by elderly users; therefore, investigation of social and psychological aspects of mobile adoption is an emerging field of research. The goal of our research is finding a way to map the needs of the elderly and set guidelines for the design of m-government systems. We apply IGUAN framework (Molnar 2014) for usability investigation, which we developed, in our earlier research as a guideline for improving the usability of e-government systems. We constructed a scenario in usability investigation, a search for medical treatment. Our research follows a user-driven method and uses the data acquired on usability of m-government by the elderly from Germany and Hungary. The main contribution of this paper is the assessment of the requirements for m-government systems' development for elderly, by investigating the factors, which lead to a low acceptance of m-government by this group.

Keywords: m-government for elderly · Usability · IGUAN usability framework

1 Introduction

The last decade has shown that E-government services are essential for an efficient service-oriented government. This enables citizens to use public services independent from time and location constrains. This however also carries the problem of how to offer these to the whole of the population, including people with lower computer literacy, as these services has to be offered to and accessible by every citizen.

© Springer Nature Switzerland AG 2020
A. Kő et al. (Eds.): EGOVIS 2020, LNCS 12394, pp. 121–134, 2020.
https://doi.org/10.1007/978-3-030-58957-8_9

Several solutions for this problem have been shown by research projects, and it seems that stationary e-government services can be created according to this requirement. The progress of technology has however lead to the extension of the traditional e-government systems to mobile devices. It offers the possibility of reaching a larger part of the citizens, which can enable the real breakthrough for electronic governance, but on the other hand, these devices create new challenges on how to implement services, which can be used by every member of the population. Mobile systems, which are targeted by our research are defined as "the government that provides information and services to citizens and firms using wireless user infrastructure, service software application and mobile devices" [1]. It includes government services and applications (Apps) through mobile technology such as tablets, smartphones, etc. [1]. Ibrahim Kushchu from Japan was one of the first researcher, who discussed the aspects of m-government [2].

The interface of a system determines the overall complexity by either masking or increasing the complexity of the task behind the system. E-government system are for this aspect unlike any other interactive services, as these systems should be offered so that the "digital divide" [3] is narrowed to a minimum. The challenge in this is the incorporation of the complex task into a simple interface, which is usable by the whole population. We can measure this by taking a user group with the least experience, the elderly, who will also become increasingly important users for these systems in the future.

European population is aging fast; it is now and will be in 2060 the oldest continent in the world. Old-age dependency ratio (the ratio of over 65 years old to the working age population), is estimated to be about 49% [4], one inactive elderly will eventually be supported by two active people from 2060 [5]. As for internet penetration, most elderly users seem to prefer touchscreen devices as smartphones and tablet computers as their primary internet device. This is not only the case in Europe but seems to be worldwide trend, as the GSMA estimates that currently in 2020 most adults (5.7 billion people) have access to mobile services [6] and a high percentage include access to the internet.

These numbers draw attention for the m-government services as well, especially in remote areas where internet services are limited. Using mobile devices in government services has several advantages like the mobility of telecommunications and the supporting of many communication services content. There are several m-government initiatives and projects offering various government services, like information sharing, alerting and mHealth services provide mobile remote patient monitoring in order to measure vital signs, bio-signals of patients outside hospital environments [7]. Khan collected typical m-government applications, like transportation systems, education systems, health and urban policy information [8]. He analyzed the m-government challenges and determined that the security concern and the weak ICT infrastructure are decisive. Such systems can strongly benefit from improved acceptance by elderly users; therefore, investigation of social and psychological aspects of mobile adoption is an emerging field of research. Younger people have clear social and psychological motivations towards the use of the mobile services, while in the group of the elderly there is no such a commitment, [9]. We have found in our previous research project [10] when investigating the acceptance of stationary e-government systems by the elderly that users started to favor mobile devices (tablet computers) from 2013 onwards. This was only the case for the younger control group of our research, but also for the elderly users, who preferred the intuitive user interface of touchscreens, which require no abstraction of the mouse movement to the cursor on the screen. E-government research primarily focused on non-m-government services, but the importance of these services is increasing, according to the previously mentioned factors. According to the above-mentioned issues and our own results, we concluded that it would be reasonable to perform a dedicated follow up project with m-government systems.

These premises made it apparent that the utility of mobile e-government for the ageing population warrants a deeper research project, which should focus on this essential population group. As shown by other research projects the use of e-government can be promoted to elderly if the interface of the system is in accordance with the needs of them [10, 11]. Al-Hubaishi et al. [12] developed a comprehensive framework of mobile government service quality. They identified twenty mobile government service quality sub-dimensions classified within six dimensions (source was the literature on m-government). Additionally, papers also describe the strong correlation between usability and acceptance for elderly [13]. Hung, Chang and Kuo [14] analyzed the factors that determine user acceptance of the m-government services using the theory of planned behavior. They had a sample of 331 users from Taiwan (all users had m-government experiences). Their research model included nine external variables and they investigated twelve hypotheses. Their conclusion was that perceived usefulness, perceived ease of use, trust, interactivity, external influence, interpersonal influence, self-efficacy, and facilitating conditions are critical factors in improving user acceptance of m-government services. However their study did not deal with those users who are older than 40.

Our research is investigating the following questions:

- How do elderly users profit from m-government?
- Which are the decisive factors in usability and acceptance of m-government services for elderly?
- Is it possible to create m-government systems in accordance with the needs of the elderly?

We mapped these questions into a research project with the goal to discover the acceptance of m-government systems by the elderly. The project is built upon a user-driven approach and uses in the first phase of the research the data acquired in our earlier studies on usability of e-government by the elderly [10].

This method enables us to compare our findings with the data from stationary e-government systems, and prove the notion that elderly users favor touch screen devices when using e-government systems.

This paper is structured as follows:

First, in the introduction section, some decisive problems and challenges in m-government are detailed; then we discuss the research methodology. The following part presents the methodology, the research phases and the IGUAN framework, which we apply for usability investigation. Next, we detail our approach understanding the target group. Discussion part presents results. Finally, conclusion part summarizes strengths and weaknesses of IGUAN with further improvement directions.

2 The Methodology

The examined case grounds on the previously developed IGUAN framework (Fig. 1) [10], which serves for improving usability of e-government systems. The selected guideline helps to design applications and services in agreement with the target group needs and provides elderly users easy access too. According to previous research results, the framework proved to increase the acceptance of the system measurably [10]. Multiple studies [15–17] show that elderly can benefit from certain improvements of the user interface.

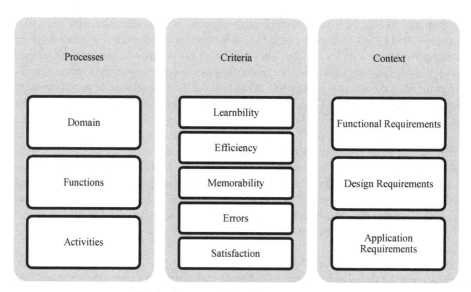

Fig. 1. Structure of the IGUAN framework

With proper optimization, the elderly may have better user experience, easily accept the system as a valid alternative compared to uncomfortable, and time consuming offline services. We applied the methodology previously in one of our projects, which opens the possibility to compare acquired data, ensuring a good evidence that mobile government systems are favored over traditional systems by the target group.

The guideline is built along three main aspects, which are constructed upon the general usability improvement methods of Richter and Flückinger [18]. The framework defines three interlinked aspects, each forming a dimension of the usability of the system. By integrating the core requirements of the application design with user requests, internal and external aspects of the improvement process are incorporated into the base structure of the guide. Later this is broken down into easily executable functions.

The functional requirements incorporate general guidance aspects and configuration requirements, which are specified by the objective of the application. These are immutable, as the requirements describe the internal functions and processes of the e-government service. Derived from the Technology Acceptance Modell [19], the design requirements include as focus the perceptions and attitudes towards the system.

These have to be declared in relation to the targeted user group. The needs characterizing for the connection of the target group and the system are included in the application requirements. Trustworthiness, representing citizens' impression of the credibility of the application is an aspect of e-government systems. The second aspect describes criteria controlling the usability of an application. The mentioned criteria have been chosen in accordance with the experience from comparable studies in general software usability assessment [20–22], and represent a link to the ISO/IEC 25010:2011 [23, 24] (previously ISO/IEC 9126). In the early phases of our research five core factors by Fisk et al. (2009) determining acceptability of a system were also used to construct the interviews, which enabled an overview of the user requirements.

The actual best practices for the IGUAN framework are provided by the process aspect, which can be split up into the domains, functions and activities. The domains describe the improvement process by describing the redesign cycle with four domains:

- Interview and Understand
- Analyze and Specify
- Design
- Evaluate and Effect

These domains are aligned with the contextual design and the usability improvement sequence cited earlier for the better understanding of system requirements of the elderly. The hybrid flow-model based on the ISO 9241-110/ISO 9241-210 was refined to create the domain model of the IGUAN. Activities resulting in usability improvements are called functions. These specify what is to be done to achieve a better acceptance of the application. The steps guiding the improvement process are modelled with 23 distinct steps. The direct actions required to achieve a measurable usability improvement can be seen as the execution of the more general functions and allow for a wide customization of the guidelines for the particular application. These activities contain the actual methodology of the functions enabling to use the sophisticated toolset required by the actual usability improvement. The functions are grouped by the domains, each domain representing a key component in the usability improvement process.

This method enables creating a procedure, which is proved to provide profound data, but also offers the possibility to directly compare findings of previous research on e-government systems. During the procedure development, the findings of several analogous research projects [17, 25] were taken into account. The integration of inspection methods and interface tests are the most comprehensive methodology for usability assessment, which is supported by multiple authors [13, 26] as the only method, which results in a comprehensive overview of the system. Heuristics, cognitive walkthroughs and action analysis are used as inspection methods, which are for pre-implementation general usability assessment by developers.

We applied these theories and concepts in our integrated usability improvement research method. This framework serves as a basis for an iterative usability improvement process created along the hypothesis that heuristics in combination with dedicated user input will not only result an improved system as postulated by multiple authors, but also lead to a solution, which can be used to create a generalized guideline. The process can be seen in Fig. 2.

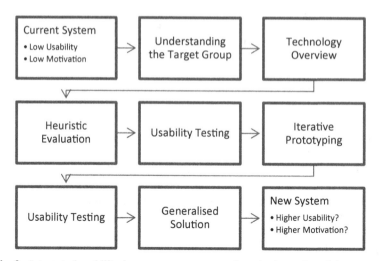

Fig. 2. Integrated usability improvement process – broad schematics of the research

As described above, and seen on the schematics of the research, the initial premise was that currently offered m-government systems offer low usability and have measurable problems motivating elderly users. This idea was further developed into the theory that systems should work for the user, and be aligned with the tasks, which are considered significant by the target group. The general framework of the project was therefore built upon three phases, which include multiple proven principles of human factors approaches:

- Understanding the target group (interview) and technology overview
- Heuristic evaluation and usability testing
- Development of a solution.

3   Understanding the Target Group

The first phase forms the basis of our investigation, and is used to understand whether elderly users favor and profit from mobile government systems. It was designed to give an overview about the requirements and the fundamental issues of the target group. The data gathering for this phase was based on deep interviews and standardized questionnaires. This step also includes a technology overview, which was fundamentally a generalized expert analysis of the currently offered electronic government systems in Germany and Hungary. We have tested the scenario with 30 test participants between the age of 60 and 90; they were recruited in Germany (15 participants) and Hungary (15 participants). The summative median age was 74 years.

In this phase of our research we reuse the qualitative data acquired for our previous study on the impact of e-government system on the elderly as a basis for a comparison between stationary e-government systems and mobile government and create through this an opportunity to directly compare the theoretical acceptance of stationary and mobile systems.

The approach for the interviews in this step have been created on a purely theoretical basis. This decision was essential, as any application or functional system might influence the test group with actual and real problems, which consequently would create falsified data based on a single system. Through this processes we have an analogous approach in both countries (Germany and Hungary), which made possible and centered the scenario on a theoretical system. It gives the elderly several advantages through improved service quality and efficiency. This procedure has been successfully demonstrated in earlier research [10] and has produces reliable data about the theoretical acceptance of the user group.

As for the scenario, we selected a theoretical system, which would have a strong usefulness for the target group: "searching for medical treatment". The selections were based on information acquired from local government officials in both countries.

We identified maturity levels for this service as well, which helps to create a model for the assessment of m-government application. Data was acquired by the means of a standardized questionnaire, which included multiple questions about the acceptability of the targeted system. Next part summarizes the scenario and the maturity levels.

3.1 The Scenario: Searching Medical Treatment

The scenario used for the analysis was based on real-world services, offered for the citizens in Hungary. We translated it into German thereby creating an identical approach and enabling the comparability of the data from the two countries.

The local government of Belváros-Lipótváros in Budapest operates a health center (BLESZ) for ambulatory patients living in the 5th district. The facility provides health care services through twenty-one different medical areas. Having some kind of health issue, several questions may be raised by the patient: Which physician should I choose? How may I contact my physician and make an appointment? When is my medical expert available or have consulting hours? We aimed investigating the services maturity levels in this scenario. The categorization of the e-government maturity levels was based on the classification of the European Commission. This model describes systems from pure information providers (Level 1) through simple interactivity (Level 2) to highly interactive systems (Level 3). Legacy methods without any electronic component can classified as Level 0 and very highly integrated system with fully electronic data transfer and processing can categorized as Level 4. An additional level, Level 5 was introduced by the European Commission for pro-active e-government systems [27]. In our scenario, the Levels are the following:

Level 0: To answer above questions potential patient may turn for help to BLESZ costumer service in person or by phone. Beyond these communication forms, there exists no other option to gain information (e.g.: website, mobile application).

Level 1: Some static information is available online on the official website, however, it is not updated regularly. The system contains details about physicians at a specific medical area. Online forms or other interactive interfaces are not available.

Level 2: In addition to the previous levels, patients may be informed by the website/mobile application providing opportunity to schedule an appointment with the selected medical expert. Reading other patients' previous experiences one can make a better decision of choosing professional help.

Level 3: Additionally to the previous levels, patients may ask their questions on forums and online (video) chat to their medical expert. Organizing online consultations with medical record transfer is also possible.

A Level 4 scenario was not used, as this would not offer additional electronic components, which would result different results from level 3.

The choice of Hungary as a comparable test environment to Germany was made on multiple premises: e-government distribution, the Internet penetration rate and the demographic structure. The centralized approach to e-government in contrast to the federal system of Germany enabled an evaluation of multiple governmental procedures in a similar environment. A further question when dealing with e-government services is the complexity of the integrated electronic components. The maturity model for e-government systems created by the European Commission can illustrate this increasing complexity and development of e-government solutions. We used this maturity level based model for the different systems, enabling the easy and proven assessment of electronic services, thereby creating a framework for the research and an option to compare systems with different components and goals.

This approach guarantees that users are confronted step-by-step with more and more electronic components and were not overwhelmed by new concepts, which might create refusal or other sudden and uncontrolled changes in the attitude of the test candidates. The results from the previous research [10] support the theory, that there is a threshold in the acceptance of electronic government by the elderly. We have seen that younger elderly approves electronic government systems which offer electronic components up to level 3. The categorization of younger elderly, as being under 75, was based on the classification of Maeda [28]. Citizens might not accept present systems beyond level 2; interactive systems seem to encourage a fear of new technology and fuel disapproval in about 50% of the tested participants.

The acceptance of the levels is measured with a standardized questionnaire, consisting of standard questions of the ASQ method, based on the research by J.R. Lewis [29] at IBM. We have modified the method for the use with the scenario, as the basic framework places its emphasis on multiple choice grading. This was modified to grading scheme with four possible levels, from very satisfied to very unsatisfied.

In addition, the standard ASQ questions, described in the next chapter, were accompanied with supplementary queries, needed for a deeper understanding of attributes unique to e-government.

The three main aspects of the ISO 9241-210 – efficiency, utility and effectiveness – link the standard with the ASQ. Before the questionnaire, the participants are familiarized with the scenario by a short verbal introduction consisting of the narrative overview. This is followed by the relevant questionnaire. This is repeated for each maturity level with the relevant narrative part and then the questionnaire. The standard questions are asked for each maturity level. The supplementary questions are asked at the relevant maturity levels, thereby creating a deeper understanding of the user experience of highly advanced systems. This is followed by the socio-demographic questions, consisting of age, gender, housing, schooling and previous experience with e-services.

The filled in questionnaires are analyzed and evaluated in order to understand and visualize the theoretical acceptance of e-services by elderly users. As for the earlier, comparable research, the theoretical acceptance is calculated from the three ASQ questions by assigning one or zero for positive or negative answers. The theoretical system is considered as accepted if the three scores were positive for the user. The earlier research with standard e-government systems concluded that there is a threshold in the acceptance of e-government and probably other types of e-services for different cohorts.

The earlier results support the theory that younger elderly approve e-government systems, which offer electronic components up to level 2. Level 3/4 systems were somewhat more controversial, but even such systems were acceptable for about 50% of the younger test participants in both countries. Older elderly might however not accept present systems beyond level 1. Interactive systems seem to encourage a fear of new technology and disapproval in about 50% of the tested participants. Further research was therefore concentrated on this issue, as these cohorts could profit the most from new offerings. Level 3 and 4 electronic applications could offer the most for this age group, as it would enable easy and comfortable G2C communication and could support the efficiency of ambient assisted living through a communication platform with the government.

4   Discussion

The acceptance of the levels was measured with a standardized questionnaire, consisting of standard questions based on the ASQ method, shown in the previous section, based on the research by J.R. Lewis [29] at IBM. In addition, the standard ASQ questions were accompanied with supplementary queries, needed for a deeper understanding of attributes unique to e-government. The three main aspects of the ISO 9241-110 mentioned and described earlier – efficiency, utility and effectiveness – link the standard with the ASQ, leading to comprehensive and reproducible results. Utility in the ASQ is consistent with utility in the ISO 9241-210. Ease of use is consistent with effectiveness and time gain is consistent with efficiency.

The results from the different levels analyzed in accordance with the maturity model of the European Commission seems to support the hypothesis that there is a threshold in the acceptance of mobile government and probably other types of e-services for different cohorts. This threshold can be observed in Fig. 3. The results demonstrate a distinct drop in acceptance for the elderly at level 2. Simulated approaches rejected by at least one-third of the participants should be considered as not accepted and such applications will probably suffer from general acceptance problems if offered to the population in their current design.

The results support the theory that younger elderly approve e-government systems, which offer electronic components up to level 2. Level 3/4 systems were somewhat more controversial, but even such systems were acceptable by approximately one-third of the test participants in both countries. This validates our hypothesis that mobile government systems can be useful for the elderly and will be accepted if created with the users in mind. This warrant therefore further research in order to analyze the requirements of such systems and find a generalized solution, which will help to alleviate the acceptance threshold. As a next step in our research, we moved to the second function of the IGUAN: Analyze and Specify.

M-government services are the next evolutionary step of e-government systems and are built on the premise of combining the advantages of traditional e-government systems

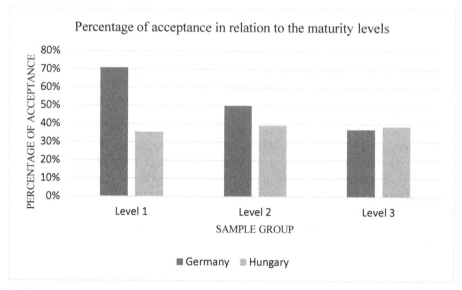

Fig. 3. Comparison of the acceptance of the scenario levels by the elderly users in Hungary and Germany, 2019

with the possibilities of the app-based ecosystem on mobile devices. M-Government systems might be a solution to improve the effectiveness of governmental services for the population, as traditional e-government has reached its limit in user acceptance, in particularly for the peripheral user groups, as the elderly [10]. The popularity and ubiquity of mobile devices and applications can strongly contribute to an inherently better acceptance by building on the previous experience of the users with such systems. This can be seen on the example of interactive applications which can be compared or even surpass the complexity of level 4 e-government systems and are readily accepted by elderly users on mobile devices [30]. Multiple factors contribute to this higher acceptance:

- The perceived usability of touchscreen devices is measurably higher for elderly users. This is caused by the direct control of the interaction without the representation of interaction through a mouse controlled pointer. As shown by other researchers, this can directly influence the acceptance of applications when compared to identical tasks with mouse and keyboard based input [31].
- The development of mobile services has caused a high penetration of mobile devices in all cohorts of the population. Elderly users, who have not necessarily access to a standard computer, have a smartphone and/or a tablet, which they use for multiple tasks on daily basis.
- The ubiquity of mobile devices has led to a higher general acceptance of mobile applications by elderly users. Users have also gained experience with mobile applications through practice, and these factors cause a higher perceived usefulness for such devices.

The higher perceived usefulness and the perceived ease of use are critical features in acceptance of systems. This combined with more experience with the underlying mechanics of touchscreen applications offers a better basis for acceptance of e-government systems on this platform, than traditional systems. This stems from the factors, which influence the perceived usability of applications:

- "The perceived complexity of the interface, which is created by the complexity of the task to be done and the design of the user interface..." [32]. The task itself should be considered a constant; therefore, the only way to decrease this factor is the improvement of the interface.
- "The previously acquired general experience of Internet applications..." [28]. This is in our case the previously acquired general experience with interactive mobile e-services. This experience gives the user the edge when trying to solve a problem presented by the unfamiliar task and/or interface, thereby helping to overcome the perceived difficulties of the system.
- Additionally, in case of e-government systems the perceived security and privacy is a decisive factor for the users when assessing the usability of the system. In particularly for elderly users, who are influenced by security problems heralded by the media, the trust in the application could be critical.

Other authors have also described these factors. Alharbi and his colleagues (2014) investigated which factors are decisive in m-government services in Saudi Arabia. Their research applied TAM model (technology acceptance model), which is widely used to measure the acceptance of new technology [33]. Authors identified five main potential factors in Saudi context and ten sub factors that may influence the adoption of m-government. These main factors are the following: perceived trustworthiness, usage experience, enjoyment, awareness and security. This conclusion can be projected onto our user group, the elderly. As described earlier the experience of the users with mobile applications is inheritably higher as for standard e-government applications, as users are familiar with touchscreen interfaces. This means that the perceived usability of the system will governed mainly through the perceived complexity and the perceived security of the application.

As shown earlier, the first step of our research was the analysis of the theoretical service acceptance, which will give us insight into the accepted maturity level of the m-government services. Next step was a general assessment of m-government systems for the elderly by testing an existing system along the premises of the IGUAN guideline. The main objective of the tests in the second phase will be to gather data about the usability of systems in an everyday environment with the users of the selected cohort. The tests will therefore be not only based on the proven scenarios, but also backed-up by methodology designed for the assessment of the user experience and verified by analogous studies. To completely understand the users' previous familiarity with comparable systems, an analysis of the experience on an individual level is needed [28]. This is based on the CLS (Computer Literacy Scale) developed at the Chair of Engineering-Psychology at the Humboldt-University Berlin [34]. This model can assess the computer literacy of the user precisely through a series of questions, creating a matrix from typical tasks on a computer.

We conduct the actual tests using the data gathered in the 1st phase, and make up the main part of the user tests. They was performed with a "thinking-aloud" method to document the accomplishment of the tasks. The touch movements on the screen was captured by screen-capture technology. In addition, the required mental effort was measured by the application of the RSME (Rating Scale Mental Effort) developed by Zijstra [35]. During the scenarios, the quantity of assistance required by the test participants was recorded and categorized according to their impact. The significance of the problem was characterized by the frequency (F), the impact (I) on the successful competition of the task and the persistence (P) between individuals. The score (S) of a problem is calculated by a function (1) based on Nielsen and Loranger [20].

$$S = (F * I * \sqrt{P})/\sqrt{10} \qquad (1)$$

The impact of the problems is classified on a scale of three, with minor issues as one and problems with critical outcome for the success of the task with three. Additional data is acquired by the after scenario questionnaire (ASQ) which was adapted for the user tests in our previous research. The three questions, which the ASQ is based on, were modified according to the results from the 1st phase, thereby contributing to the comparability of the results. The ASQ itself was based on the work of Lewis J.R. [29].

- "I am satisfied with the ease of completing the tasks in this scenario".
- "I am satisfied with the information and consider this system useful".
- "I am satisfied with the amount of time it took to complete this scenario".

The answers are provided through five intervals from strongly disagree (1) to strongly agree (5).

5 Conclusion

M-government services are combining the advantages of traditional e-government systems with the possibilities of the app-based ecosystem on mobile devices. They might be a solution to improve the effectiveness of governmental services for the population, in particularly for the elderly.

The results from the first phase and our previous research have shown that elderly are interested in e-government applications and the theoretical acceptance of such systems can be improved with a structured approach. Data from similar research projects also show that mobile systems have a higher acceptance by the elderly compared to traditional electronic service. The next phase of our research will be the development of the m-government service related to the scenario detailed above, which will offer insight into the acceptance of actual systems by the target, and enable us to gather information about the particular requirements of elderly users. This system will then be modified in accordance with the acquired data from the second step. Next we perform a test again with the same methodology as before to create a system with a higher acceptance and usability.

References

1. Wang, C., Feng, Y., Fang, R., Lu, Z.: Model for value creation in mobile government: an integrated theory perspective. Int. J. Adv. Comput. Technol. **4**(2), 16–23 (2012)
2. Kushchu, I., Kuscu, H.: From E-government to M-government: facing the inevitable. In: Proceeding of European conference on E-Government (ECEG 2003) (2003)
3. Mehra, B.: Virtual Communities on the Internet: Social Interactions Across the Digital Divide. University of Kansas (2004)
4. European Commission: The 2015 Ageing Report. European Commission (2015)
5. Abadie, F., et al.: Strategic Intelligence Monitor on Personal Health Systems (SIMPHS) Market Structure and Innovation Dynamics, European Commission Joint Research Centre, Institute for Prospective Technological Studies (2011)
6. GSMA Association: The Mobile Economy. GSMA (2017)
7. Kő, A., Gábor, A., Szabó, Z.: Innovative eHealth services – PISCES solution. In: Kő, A., Francesconi, E. (eds.) EGOVIS 2015. LNCS, vol. 9265, pp. 206–219. Springer, Cham (2015). https://doi.org/10.1007/978-3-319-22389-6_15
8. Khan, M.A.: Exploring the push and pull drivers in M-government framework that influence acceptance of services on mobile devices. Int. J. Comput. Sci. Netw. Secur. **16**(2), 23–26 (2016)
9. Conci, M., Pianesi, F., Zancanaro, M.: Useful, social and enjoyable: mobile phone adoption by older people. In: Gross, T., et al. (eds.) INTERACT 2009. LNCS, vol. 5726, pp. 63–76. Springer, Heidelberg (2009). https://doi.org/10.1007/978-3-642-03655-2_7
10. Molnar, T.: Improved Usability of Electronic Government Services for the Ageing Population. HU Berlin, Berlin (2014)
11. Righi, V., Sayago, S., Blat, J.: Towards understanding e-Government with older people and designing an inclusive platform with them. Int. J. Public Inf. Syst. **3**, 131–142 (2011)
12. Al-Hubaishi, H.S., Ahmad, S.Z., Hussain, M.: Exploring mobile government from the service quality perspective. J. Enterp. Inf. Manag. **30**(1), 4–16 (2014)
13. Fisk, A.D., Rogers, W.A., Charness, N., Czaja, S.J., Sharit, J.: Designing for Older Adults. CRC Press, Boca Raton (2009)
14. Hung, S.-Y., Chang, C.-M., Kuo, S.-R.: User acceptance of mobile e-government services: an empirical study. Gov. Inf. Q. **30**, 33–44 (2013)
15. Hipp, C.: Elderly Friendly HMI: Graphical User Interface for Ambient Assisted Living. Fraunhofer IAO, Stuttgart (2009)
16. Robinet, A., Picking, R., Grout, V.: A Framework for Improving User Experience in Ambient Assisted Living. University of Plymouth, Plymouth (2008)
17. Bruder, C.: Gestaltungsprinzipien für das Training älterer Benutzer elektronischer Geräte. Technische Universität Berlin, Berlin (2008)
18. Richter, M., Flückiger, M.: Die 7 ± 2 wichtigsten usability-methoden. In: Richter, M., Flückiger, M.D. (eds.) Usability Engineering kompakt, pp. 21–76. Spektrum Akademischer Verlag, Heidelberg (2010). https://doi.org/10.1007/978-3-8274-2329-0_3
19. Davis, F.D.: Perceived usefulness, perceived ease of use, and user acceptance of information technology. MIS Q. **13**(3), 319–339 (1989)
20. Nielsen, Loranger: Prioritizing Web Usability, the University of Michigan. New Riders (2006)
21. Park, K.S., Lim, C.H.: A structured methodology for comparative evaluation of user interface designs using usability criteria and measures. Int. J. Ind. Ergon. **23**, 379–389 (1999)
22. Nokelainen, P.: www.uta.fi (2004). http://www.uta.fi/laitokset/aktk/papers/tech_ped_usabil ity/edmedia2004_pn.pdf. 5 Dec 2011
23. ISO: ISO/IEC 9126-1:2001 Software engineering - Product quality - Part 1: Quality model. ISO (2001)

24. ISO: ISO/IEC 25010:2011 Systems and software engineering - Systems and software Quality Requirements and Evaluation. ISO (2011)
25. Sayago, S., Sloan, D., Blat, J.: Everyday use of computer-mediated communication tools and its evaluation over time: an ethnogrpahical study with older people. Interact. Comput. **23**, 543–554 (2011)
26. Nielsen, J.: Usability Engineering. Academic Press, San Diego (1993)
27. European Commission: Electronic Government Maturity Levels (2011)
28. Maeda, J.: Simplicity - Die zehn Gesetze der Einfachheit. Spektrum, München (2007)
29. Lewis, C.H.: Using the "thinking aloud" method in cognitive interface design. IBM (1982)
30. Choudrie, J., Pheeraphuttharangkoon, S., Zamani, E., Giaglis, G.: Investigating the adoption and use of smartphones in the UK: a silver-surfers perspective. University of Herfordshire (2014)
31. Kobayashi, M., Hiyama, A., Miura, T., Asakawa, C., Hirose, M., Ifukube, T.: Elderly user evaluation of mobile touchscreen interactions. In: Campos, P., Graham, N., Jorge, J., Nunes, N., Palanque, P., Winckler, M. (eds.) INTERACT 2011. LNCS, vol. 6946, pp. 83–99. Springer, Heidelberg (2011). https://doi.org/10.1007/978-3-642-23774-4_9
32. Jung, R.: Formale Bewertung der Benutzerkomplexität bildschirmgeschützter Informations- und Unterhaltungssysteme im Kraftfahrzeug. ZMMS Spektrum, vol. 15, no. VDI (2002)
33. Alharbi, S., Drew, S.: Using the technology acceptance model in understanding academics' behavioural intention to use learning management systems. IJACSA Int. J. Adv. Comput. Sci. Appl. **1**, 143–155 (2014)
34. Sengpiel, M., Dittberner, D.: The computer literacy scale (CLS) for older adults - development and validation. Mensch Comput., 7–16 (2008)
35. Zijstra, F.R.H.: Efficiency in Work Behaviour. A Design Approach for Modern Tools. Delft University of Technology, Delft (1993)

Towards Evidence-Based, Data-Driven Thinking in Higher Education

Ágnes Meleg[(⊠)] and Réka Vas

Corvinus University of Budapest, Fővám Square 8, Budapest 1093, Hungary
agnes.meleg@stud.uni-corvinus.hu, reka.vas@uni-corvinus.hu

Abstract. Decisions in higher education institutions may have an impact on several stakeholders at the same time (students, academic personnel, teaching and non-teaching staff), for this reason, it is crucial to try to make the best-informed decision possible. The evidence-based practice is a method for decision-making processes, using evidence from multiple sources in a conscientious, explicit and judicious manner. This practice can be leveraged in higher education; however, its implementation and adoption may take a long time and demand a lot of effort. The aim of this paper is to motivate higher education institutions to follow evidence-based, data-driven thinking. We present the evidence-based practice – in general and from the point of view of higher education –, give guidance on how an institution can start applying the method in decision-making or going further if it is on the journey, and encourage data-driven thinking pointing out the different areas where data analytics can be beneficial.

Keywords: Evidence-based practice · Data-driven decision-making · Learning analytics · Academic analytics

1 Introduction

The soundness and efficiency of decisions made in higher education are primarily dependent on the expertise and experience of their managers, even today. Critical decisions ranging from everyday university operations to strategy development are based on the unchallenged assumptions and unquestioned judgments of decision makers. University managers are often constrained by unstructured data that are stored in silos and the lack of time and adequate expertise to collect, structure, analyze and use data in an appropriate way. Technology evolution has substantially increased the ability of organizations to collect, store, analyze and apply data in a consistent manner.

The evidence-based practice (EBP) offers a structured way of decision-making, through the conscientious, explicit and judicious use of the best available evidence from multiple sources (Barends et al. 2017). One of the sources is information coming from data.

In this article the aim is to present what data-driven thinking means in the organism of an institution, going through the different terms and levels, and giving practical examples with the purpose of supporting its implementation in higher education.

© Springer Nature Switzerland AG 2020
A. Kő et al. (Eds.): EGOVIS 2020, LNCS 12394, pp. 135–144, 2020.
https://doi.org/10.1007/978-3-030-58957-8_10

The first level towards data-driven thinking is to introduce evidence-based practice at the institution. Once that basis is accepted, the organization can build its own best practices using the methodology of evidence-based practice, and – as part of the process – create its own way how to use data to make better-informed decisions.

2   Evidence-Based Practice

2.1   Evidence-Based Practice as Decision-Making Method

Primarily, the term "evidence-based" was introduced in medicine, by now its principles extend across disciplines (for example management, criminology, social work, and public policy) (Barends et al. 2017).

Its objective is to help make better decisions. Using evidences in general, allows people to make better decisions. However, simply using evidences is not sufficient: the evidence should be trustworthy and relevant. The evidence-based practice gives guidance on how to achieve that, pointing to three important factors (Briner 2019).

To get the best available evidence, first, we need to be conscientious, explicit and judicious. We should look hard for the evidence, not accepting the first that gets in our way. Once we have the evidence, we need to specify and describe it in detail, to ensure its relevancy and trustworthiness. Lastly, we have to be critical towards the evidence we have, to make sure its quality is adequate and it is reliable to use.

The second key factor of evidence-based practice is the usage of multiple sources. Different types of sources can bring in different perspectives. Evidence from one source may reinforce or question another one. Thus, we can have a better and clearer picture, if we use several sources. The four main resources of evidence are the following: (a) scientific literature, (b) organizational data, (c) stakeholders' concerns, and (d) professional expertise.

The third factor is the structured approach. In practice, we can gather evidence from each of these sources after having the questions related to a particular issue listed. It is important to mention that the process of identifying the problem and the process of finding its solution need to be separated. First, we need to understand the problem in a clear and deep way, and then it can be addressed, looking for a possible solution.

To apply the structured approach of the evidence-based practice, six steps are recommended to follow. (1) First, the problem should be translated into questions. (2) Second, evidences from each type of source need to be gathered trying to answer the questions. (3) As a next step, the evidences should be examined and analyzed. (4) After that, the best evidences should be chosen from each type. (5) As a result, the answers obtained from the evidences are ready to be used during the decision-making process. (6) Finally, the effects of any decision taken need to be evaluated.

It is important to highlight that the first and last steps are independent from the evidences, however, the steps in between are strongly dependent – and all the source types are recommended to be involved.

2.2 Evidence-Based Practice and Data Analytics in Higher Education

The evidence-based practice can be leveraged in higher education as well. "Evidence-based decision-making combines professional experience with data, research, and literature to draw conclusions, make judgments, and determine courses of action" (Leimer 2012, pp. 46).

Applying the six-step method, the figure below (Fig. 1) presents an example of how decision-makers can use the evidence-based practice in higher education. For many universities one of the burning problems is student retention, hence the questions: "To what extent is it the university's responsibility that the students do not complete the program? How the university may prevent this?", in other words: "How can the university keep the students engaged and make them improve their grades?".

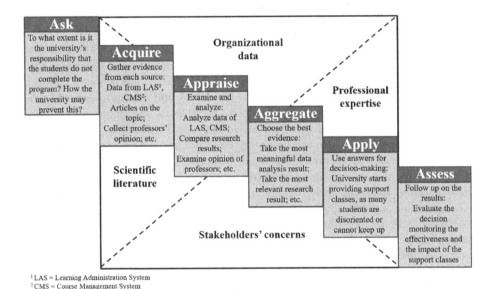

¹ LAS = Learning Administration System
² CMS = Course Management System

Fig. 1. Evidence-based practice: sources and steps

Following the EBP structure, the recommended four sources for this study are the following: (a) scientific literature: research articles of other educational institutions and any other scientific findings on this matter, (b) organizational data: students' grades and performance, engagement in learning, online activities (c) stakeholders' concerns: concerns of students, teachers, and any other academic personnel, and (d) professional expertise: pedagogical and methodological opinions.

At the first stage of the square ("Acquire"), we collect all the available information from all four sources and as a second step, we examine them ("Appraise"). Asking questions in these two phases may help. a) What do the results of scientific studies tell about student retention? What theories have been used to address it? b) What do organizational data tell about the nature of this problem? Are there any patterns in students' grades that might be useful to have some insights? c) What do teachers believe are the key points of student retention? What do students think about it? d) From the experience of the academic personnel, what do we think is the nature of student retention? Based on the expertise, how can we address it?

After each question-answer, the relevancy and trustworthy should be examined; in case of data, we should pay special attention to data quality (accuracy, consistency, completeness, timeliness). At the next two stages, we choose the best evidence in each source category ("Aggregate") and decide on how to apply the findings ("Apply"). Finally, we evaluate the effects ("Assess").

Data analytics in this study has multifold role. We use organizational data as source to find insights related to the problem. We gather data from the Learning Administration System and the Course Management System (information systems applied in higher education and the proposed Analytics Framework including these systems are detailed on Fig. 2 and 3) to examine student performance and try to find the root causes for non-success. Additionally, with student surveys we have a better understanding analyzing their answers and searching for patterns.

The university can also apply data analytics to provide as effective solution as possible. Looking into previous years' results patterns could be identified describing that in a particular subject which students are likely to have success and who are the ones with possible difficulties. Furthermore, we can take a look into student forums and analyze which students ask the most, which topics are the most frequent to get a deeper insight. Thanks to the descriptive and predictive analytical methods, the university can provide the students with customized support. Finally, data analytics may have a huge contribution in analyzing the effectiveness and the impact of the support classes as well.

It is notable that information gained from data can bring very powerful insights; considering this, an organization might be engaged in data analytics at various levels. In higher education academic analytics (AA) and learning analytics (LA) are distinguished. "According to the 1st International Conference on Learning Analytics and Knowledge," learning analytics is the measurement, collection, analysis and reporting of data about learners and their contexts, for purposes of understanding and optimizing learning and the environments in which it occurs. "Academic analytics, in contrast, is the application of business intelligence in education and emphasizes analytics at institutional, regional, and international levels" (Long and Siemens 2011, pp. 34).

Thus, information from data can be leveraged for various purposes, at various levels, however, the implementation and the adoption of the EBP might be challenging for the institutions.

3   Towards Data-Driven Thinking

3.1   Implementation of Evidence-Based Practice

Implementing the evidence-based practice means a cultural change. Developing such a culture takes a lot of effort and time, at multiple level of the organization. To apply this method in decision-making processes, we need to acquire data as one of the evidence types. Different operational units or a dedicated office can provide data. As a next step, the data must be turned into information, through analysis and interpretation. Finally, the information can be used for decision-making processes (Leimer 2012).

To have evidence-based, data-driven thinking at the organization, it is suggested to establish an office that is responsible for helping decision-making processes. Office personnel with evaluation and research background can help frame questions by participating in initial and ongoing discussions of programs and initiatives. As a result, the questions can be answered empirically, complementing professional experience of the decision-makers.

Such an office – which can be called in different ways, e.g. institutional research (IR) or institutional effectiveness (IE) – is able to cover various tasks, supporting the organization. Their tasks can be grouped into three main areas: (1) analyzing, (2) advising, and (3) advocating ("3A"). The first "A" stands for analyzing: turning data into information to answer questions, enhance processes, and help new visions. The second "A" represents advising: consulting with executives, managers and other decision-makers of the organization, giving advice and supporting them with empirical evidences. The third "A" means advocating: encouraging the use of empirical results and the evidence-based practice as method.

Establishing the office requires the executives' engagement in evidence-based practice, and a multi-year plan. As a starting point, all the existing functions need to be reviewed: their current locations, roles and responsibilities (research, assessment, accreditation, planning, program reviewing, institutional budgeting, business intelligence, market research, etc.). Once the stock-taking is completed, the real establishing can take place, either creating a completely new office, or expanding an existing one, or merging several existing offices together (Leimer 2012).

3.2 Data Usage

If the evidence-based, data-driven mindset is accepted by the organization, and the dedicated office is established, the next question is how to use the data, and what kind of data can be turned into information.

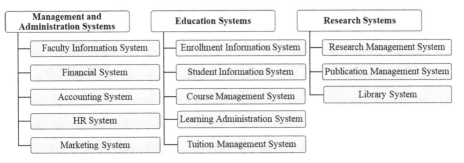

Fig. 2. Information systems in higher education

Colleges and universities take a wide range of approaches. The easiest solution is start using the built-in reporting capabilities of the different IT solutions. Universities usually apply a wide variety of information systems to support their everyday operations. These systems focus on three major areas: (1) Management and Administration, (2) Education and (3) Research (see Fig. 2).

Although a wide range of data is available in these systems, institutions must realize that the use of simple queries or built in reporting solutions will not provide the desired results and benefits on the long run.

To cover further needs a traditional way is to buy or build an enterprise BI system, which allows the institution to get easier and rapid access to the data that is primarily recorded and stored in the operational systems (detailed on Fig. 2) of the university. Having the structured data, the dedicated analytics team can carry out further analysis. In addition to centralized data warehouse, at least one business intelligence tool can also be beneficial, so that reports, dashboards can be built providing a better capability for the institution support (Drake and Walz 2018).

Apart from structured data, unstructured or semi-structured data might be used as well (e.g. student forum texts, survey results), bringing additional insights. Especially, in the domain of "student success", semi- and unstructured data may provide beneficial information; however, new technologies and techniques are required to their analysis (Drake and Walz 2018).

Analyzing students' success is just one example of how universities may benefit from analytics. There are numerous other cases – like the analysis of student retention, learning profiles, student habits, organizational performance etc. – that demonstrate how universities can take advantage on specific fields by applying analytics solutions in different depths (ranging from descriptive analytics through predictive analytics to

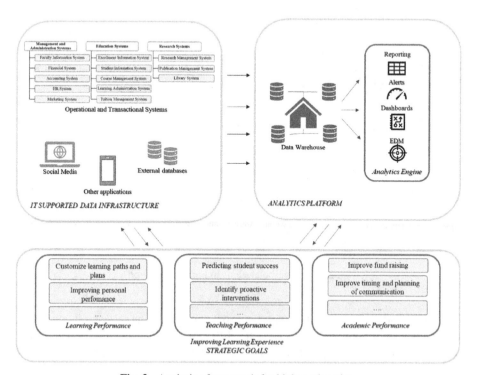

Fig. 3. Analytics framework for higher education

prescriptive analytics). Current practice in higher education shows that most of these analytics solutions are performed in an ad-hoc and isolated manner. Analytics projects are typically self-initiated and managed by a small team that has access only to a limited set of data stored in the operational systems of the institutions. This also means that most of the institutions in higher education still lack a comprehensive framework (see Fig. 3) that enables them to build on each possible aspect of analytics in an efficient way.

All higher education institutions are generating and collecting vast amount of data each day, but data cannot be the starting point of developing the analytics framework for the institution. The first step of creating this framework is to define the strategic goals of the organization and specify the expectations concerning teaching, learning and overall academic performance. Based on these expectations it can be specified what kind of analytics projects (like improve fund raising, or predict student success, etc.) should be started to sufficiently inform day-to-day decision-making. In order to be able to run all necessary data projects an adequate analytics platform should be implemented as well. This platform should support all data cleaning, transition and structured storage of data based on which different analytics and machine learning solutions can efficiently run.

3.3 Self-Assessment

In order to see where the organization stands on the large spectrum of the adoption, carrying out a self-assessment can help. As the following figure shows (Fig. 4), there are many possibilities and variations of how learning analytics and academic analytics may influence each other.

Based on the study of Buerck and Mudigonda (2014) it might happen that an academic analytics initiative turns into a learning analytics success (see graph at the bottom). In other scenarios learning analytics and academic analytics can evolve together, in a different way and pace (see graphs on the top).

During the assessment, the organization can think over and evaluate where they stand regarding the adoption of evidence-based, data-driven decision-making, furthermore, the assessment may also give a view on the relation of the learning analytics and academic analytics initiatives.

In the 'y' axis the maturity level is represented, which involves several aspects. One point of view is the data usage: does the organization use only structured data or unstructured data as well? Another aspect is the expansion: does the organization use the data occasionally, or frequently with the evidence-based mindset in all departments?

Depending on the organization the number and type of questions may vary, in setting up the different points maturity models can give guidance. The EDUCAUSE model takes into consideration six dimensions: data efficacy, decision-making culture, investments/resources, policies, technical infrastructure, and IR involvement. The HEDW model looks at nine dimensions: business intelligence team, scope, role of source business units, data products, user coverage, users' engagement, data management, business value, and strategic support (Drake and Walz 2018).

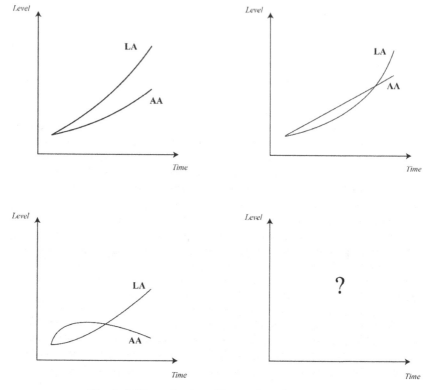

Fig. 4. Different levels and interaction of LA and AA

In the 'x' axis the time is shown. The organization can consider different levels of scaling, according to how detailed picture the evaluators would like to get. Future dates are also recommended to use, so that the progress can be visioned.

The self-assessment process may help the institution in making suggestions for further steps and to create a vision where they would like to see themselves in the next years. It may also motivate to create goals, laying down some milestones that the institution would like to achieve.

3.4 Success Factors

To have a success in the domain of LA and AA, there are three main factors: "executives committed to an evidence-based decision-making, staff members with adequate data analysis skills, and the flexible and effective technology platform" (Géryk 2017, pp. 1).

In addition to these key points, there are also some smaller, but still important aspects which are worth keeping in mind.

(1) Uniqueness – It is very useful to be informed about general recommendations, and other institutions' initiatives and successful projects, however, every organization is different, which needs to be taken into consideration. For example, when setting up

the necessary apparatus, it is beneficial to think through which set-up would be the best for the organization, whether creating a new office, or expanding, or merging existing ones would be the most suitable solution. One solution can fit very well one institution, while it might be a complete failure for another.

(2) Focus – Another significant factor is to always keep focus. For example, when going through the implementation process, it is important to focus on the original objective, keeping the real purpose of the office, and avoiding giving additional responsibilities that might distract the effective functioning (Leimer 2012).

(3) Flexibility – When carrying out a project, unexpected events might happen. If an outcome does not perform in practice as it was planned in theory, flexibility must be essential. For example, some constraints may preclude a successful completion of an analytics initiative, but with re-envisoned approach the primary goals can still be achieved (Buerck and Mudigonda 2014).

(4) Interpretation – Data analytics can support the institution only in case of good interpretation of data analysis results. For example, if institutional decision makers misuse or misinterpret the data, the analytical efforts do not bring any value (Cox et al. 2017).

If all the above are given or taken care of, the institution can have a great success in analytics, bringing value to all the stakeholders. At the end, students, professors, and the institution as a whole can benefit from better-informed decisions.

4 Conclusion

Making good decisions is always hard, especially if there are several questions and issues that should be addressed at the same time. In higher education institutions, decisions are primarily dependent on the personal experience and expertise of the managers; however, it is a good practice to have it completed with some empirical evidence. The evidence-based practice suggests a structured way for better-informed decision-making, using multiple sources: scientific literature, organizational data, stakeholders' concerns, and professional expertise. To leverage organizational data, the institutions have to make several steps, and the implementation and adoption might be a long journey. Self-assessment can help the managers in evaluating the institution and setting up goals to achieve related to evidence-based practice and data analytics, with the objective to enhance decision-making processes, giving benefit to all the stakeholders of the institution.

References

Barends, E., et al.: Managerial attitudes and perceived barriers regarding evidence-based practice: an international survey. PLoS ONE **12**, 1–15 (2017)

Briner, R.: The basics of evidence-based practice. People Strategy **42**, 1–7 (2019)

Buerck, J.P., Mudigonda, S.P.: A resource-constrained approach to implementing analytics in an institution of higher education: an experience report. J. Learn. Analytics **1**, 129–139 (2014)

Cox, B.E., et al.: Lip service or actionable insights? linking student experiences to institutional assessment and data-driven decision making in higher education. J. High. Educ. **88**, 835–862 (2017)

Drake, B.M., Walz, A.: Evolving business intelligence and data analytics in higher education. New Dir. Inst. Res. **2018**, 39 (2018)

Géryk, J.: Visual analytics of educational time-dependent data using interactive dynamic visualization. Expert Syst. **34**, e12175 (2017)

Leimer, C.: Organizing for evidence-based decision making and improvement. Change **44**, 45–51 (2012)

Long, P., Siemens, G.: Penetrating the fog, analytics in learning and education. Educause Rev. **2011**, 31–40 (2011)

Identity Management and Legal Issues

Authentication of Electronic Legal Statements by a Trust Service Provider Using Two-Factor Dynamic Handwritten Signature Verification

Péter József Kiss[(✉)] and Gábor Klimkó[ⓘ]

MTA Information Technology Foundation, Budapest, Hungary
mtaita@t-online.hu

Abstract. It is a necessary premise of electronic administration that legal statements of natural persons could be authenticated. The use of electronic signatures is an appropriate and sound approach for guaranteeing authenticity, but its use is not prevalent among natural persons. It is proposed that a trust service provider could create an electronic signature on behalf of a natural person, where the client is authenticated by two-factor dynamic handwritten signature verification. This procedure, supplemented with further controls, would provide a secure and reliable basis for authenticating of electronic legal statements.

Keywords: Authentication of electronic legal statements · Trust service provider · Electronic signature

1 Introduction

A key element of official administration is the capability of the ex-post authentication of clients' legal statements. This authentication capability should be available to both the client and the service provider of the administrative procedure.

During traditional (paper-based) administrative procedure a natural person is linked to his legal statement by his handwritten signature. The emergence of the electronic version of legal statements created a new situation regarding authentication which led to certain requirements that at first glance were satisfied both technically and legally by authenticating the electronic documents with electronic signatures [1, 2]. This authentication method is regulated by legislation and it is currently generally accepted by the European Union. The eIDAS regulation on electronic identification and trust services for electronic transactions in the internal market ensures the enforced acceptance of electronic legal statements at cross border level [3].

Growth in the use of the electronic signature for document authentication, however, is neither fast nor widespread. The technical condition for the creation of an electronic signature is an exclusively (securely) owned private encryption key by the signatory and this is provided usually using a smartcard (or chip) with suitable security features. Some EU member states provide such personal identification (ID) cards for administrative procedures within the public administration (for example the Bürgerkarte in Austria

© Springer Nature Switzerland AG 2020
A. Kő et al. (Eds.): EGOVIS 2020, LNCS 12394, pp. 147–158, 2020.
https://doi.org/10.1007/978-3-030-58957-8_11

[4], and the electronic ID card in Hungary [5]). The private key can also be stored in a modified chip in a smartphone and the client can create his electronic signature with his smartphone (see e.g. [6]). However, at least two doubts have risen about the widespread use of the electronic signature:

1. only few people are willing to use voluntarily the electronic signature technology; and
2. the question still remains as to how secure the use of electronic signature really is.

Hungary is a good example of the low acceptance of the electronic signature technology. The Hungarian state provides electronic personal ID cards ("eSzemélyi", smartID card) for the purpose of conducting official administration procedures. The owner of this smartcard can use it for creating qualified electronic signatures. Every Hungarian citizen is entitled today to have the smartID card. Earlier issued paper-based ID cards are valid for 5–10 years, thus, smart IDs are spreading, and by now more than 4.4 million smartID cards have been issued (about 3.4 million by the end of 2018 to the approximately 8.8 million citizens entitled to it). The private key (the corresponding certificate) that is necessary for the creation of the electronic signature is provided free of charge on the smartID card, but the holder has to ask for it. In 2019, only 20.900 Hungarians from the 1,123,260 who applied for smartID cards asked for the signature certificate [7].

The National Media and Infocommunications Authority (NMHH) is the responsible authority for the supervision of electronic services in Hungary. The official statistics published by NMHH shows the real extent of the demand, which in 2018 was the following:

- there were 162,499 qualified signature certificates issued for natural persons
- there were 16,809 qualified signature certificates issued for organizations,
- there were 14,175 qualified signature certificates issued for government entities and
- the number of other qualified signature certificates was 6,118 [8]

The above figures indicate that the electronic signature is used principally by those who are obliged to do so by the law (for instance, Hungarian lawyers are required by law to use electronic signatures for certain legal transactions).

The second concern refers to the question of how secure the use of the electronic signature is. A device, that is able to create a qualified electronic signature, must ensure the protection of the private key at an appropriate technical level. This capability is usually certified by independent and accredited testing parties. However, this type of protection focuses on the security risks linked to the theft of the device, though the scope of possible misuses (and their risks) is far wider. Kiss pointed out that in the case of face-to-face customer services there are other serious risks to be dealt with beyond the security risks originated from acts committed by unknown persons, such as theft or the accidental loss of the device. Abuses committed by acquaintances (family members or colleagues) are potential risks, as well as the risk of collusion with the clerk during the official administrative procedure. Thus, the real question is the reliable authentication of electronic legal statements [9].

2 The Challenge of Authenticating Electronic Legal Statements

During the course of an administrative procedure usually there is a legal statement of the client which must be authenticated. At the beginning of the procedure the client has to be authenticated, and when that has been done, he could make his statement. If an electronic document produced during the administrative procedure were simply stored in the system of the authority (or the service provider) without any further measure, it would be rather cumbersome to give a legal proof of what the client has in fact approved. There is no guarantee that in the case of a legal dispute the court would accept an electronic document to be authentic which is stored in the computer system of a party that might have conflicting interests.

The electronic signature of the client on the electronic document could provide a solution in principle to the above problem. Unfortunately, there is a very limited interest in the use of electronic signature technology as it was shown in the introduction section.

Even if the technology is used, provided the person concerned uses electronic signatures regularly, the second issue shown in the introduction section may still make its reliability questionable. To create an electronic signature with a solution currently in use, it is necessary to own a device and to know a password (or PIN code). Even this two-factor authentication could be risky when the signatory uses his password frequently in such an environment where others can observe it and write the code down. To demonstrate this risk, let us suppose X has a qualified electronic signing device that he regularly uses at his workplace to authenticate his documents. Let Y be his colleague who is in a position to observe the PIN code entered for these transactions. When X leaves this signing device without supervision – even for a very short time, then Y could sign electronically with the device a legal electronic statement prepared in advance and (for instance, one that claims Y gave a loan to X that should be reimbursed in five years). Y then sells his claim to a claim adjuster, who five years later demands the sum from X. X has not known for five years that a loan contract exists with his qualified signature but now he is required to pay. In the absence of proof to the contrary, the document signed with a qualified electronic signature must be considered authentic according to the law and X has absolutely no means to prove that it was not him who signed the document at that time [9].

For the purpose of authenticating electronic documents, an electronic signature created by a third-party trust service provider could also be used. This is similar to the situation when a person dictates his statement to a notary who authenticates it on behalf of the entrusting client and, as a result, the statement is linked to the client. A similar solution is used in the Hungarian electronic public administration called "Document Certification Traced Back to Authentication" (DCTBA)[1]. A state-operated (trusted) electronic service, having identified the client, acts as „quasi notary". This service authenticates the electronic document uploaded by the client with a computer made electronic signature. In this solution, the client does not need to have a device able to produce an electronic signature, but at the same time the method of the authentication of the client by the service could raise security questions [10].

---

[1] This service is available at URL https://niszavdh.gov.hu/index.

We have already noted that the use of a certified signing device does not protect against the abuse of an acquaintance and this represents a real risk. Even if one applies a smartphone for creating electronic signatures, this risk is only reduced as there are many life situations when an acquaintance could have access to the phone (for instance the owner takes a shower, or leaves the phone on the table for a moment).

In order to reduce the risk of the unauthorised use of smartphones, manufacturers started to incorporate biometric authentication into their devices. Among the available numerous biometric options [11], the following techniques are widely used for authentication currently

- fingerprint recognition,
- face recognition and
- iris recognition [12].

Currently, fingerprint recognition-based authentication is the most accessible service in smartphones. However, the protection level afforded by the applied solution is low as simpler versions can be deceived by gummy fingers [13].

Face recognition can also be misled with spoofing (masquerading as a valid client) [14]. The possibility of deceiving the face recognition procedure means a serious problem. Certain banks authenticate their remote clients when they want to open an account based on an ID card photograph sent in followed by the use of a video, where the client shows himself through the camera of a computer or smartphone.

The use of the iris recognition technology [15] – apart from being more of an experiment than a generally used feature in smartphones [16] - is based on the preparation of high-resolution pictures and the only obstacle is how to get hold of it. There is a well-known case when a person in a picture taken earlier of an Afghan girl was identified many years later based on her iris picture, after her iris pattern was taken from the earlier high-resolution photo [17].

At the same time, a neglected or improperly used technique among biometric characteristics is the electronic form of handwriting [18]. From now on we will use the term "electronic handwritten signature" to describe digitally captured handwritten signatures including not only the picture of the signature but also other characteristics of signing like speed or pressure.

3   The Current Use of Electronic Handwritten Signatures

Today it is possible to draw with an electronic pen (thus also sign) an increasing number of devices (smartphones, tablets, notebooks). Even the capability of pressure sensing is becoming widespread. These advances make the use of the electronic handwritten signature possible from a remote environment (e.g. home).

Digital capture of handwritten signatures is a general, common form of authenticating electronic documents in certain applications. This technology is widely used by package delivery companies and lately, it has been gaining acceptance in banks as well.

There are several approaches – with very different levels of security – for the use of the digital picture of handwritten signatures in the electronic world. A typical approach is the authentication of the signatory [19, 20], however, the technical problems of authentication cannot be taken as solved [21, 22].

Instead of looking for a possibly partially technical solution, we should examine the basic idea of using handwritten signatures to find a more widely acceptable solution. Considering all its characteristics (not only the picture in itself, but also its dynamics [23], and its changes in pressure force, which the expert in the case of a signature on paper estimates from the line and ink thickness), handwritten signatures are more or less unique.

We start with considering what is accepted by the law for paper documents with handwritten signatures. In Hungarian legislation, a handwritten signature on a paper document does not provide fully probative force of linking the signatory to the document. Two witnesses are needed, who certify that it was the person concerned who signed the document [24]. One of the reasons for this limitation is that handwritten signatures are very different, some are intricate, difficult to copy while others are very simple and easy to imitate.

The basic condition for authenticating a handwritten signature is to identify the biometric characteristics of the signature (picture, speed and acceleration, pressure force) and this needs an appropriate electronic signing pen and screen (tablet or smartphone). It is also important to create a perception that is similar to that of signing on paper (when identification is slow and the display of the traces is delayed, the signature will not be the same as the usual one). Solutions using special devices were described in the literature [25], but these have disadvantages similar to card/smartphone electronic handwritten signature without any substantive benefits. Authentication of the creator of a handwritten signature to an electronic document can happen basically in two ways.

1. Either the biometric data are linked to the document, and a registration sample serves only as post verification (note that without a sample it is not possible to express an opinion on the authentication of the signature as individual signatures change with time); or
2. the verification occurs at the time of signing via using an electronic sample repository of the signatory

A common feature of these solutions is that the documents – usually in encrypted form – include the characteristics of the electronic handwritten signature. However, encryption methods currently in use may become breakable in the future. This weakness forecasts the necessity of re-authenticating these documents (similarly to electronic signatures). The biometric data linked to the document will necessarily become known, thus it will be possible to create fake documents based on this solution. Furthermore, the change with time in the handwritten signatures of the same signatory, or simply the change of the signing device that affects the "signing experience" *ab ovo* requires using a reference sample repository.

From the client's aspect, the electronic handwritten signature is a very comfortable and common solution thus its wider use could help the propagation of electronic solutions. Authentication of an electronic handwritten signature alone, however, has security risks and does not offer the same level of protection to each signatory due to the ease of counterfeiting simpler forms of signatures. We would need such a procedure which retains the comfort offered by the electronic capture of handwritten signatures but provides a higher level of security, as well as it allows remote use.

4   A Procedure for the Authentication of Electronic Legal Statements

We have summarized our findings on the authentication of electronic legal statements in the previous sections.

1. The use of electronic signatures is an appropriate and sound approach as it has a well-founded and established legal as well as technical background. As the use of electronic signatures is not prevalent among natural persons, it is practical and convenient to have a trust service provider to create electronic signatures.
2. Verification of electronic handwritten signatures (HSV) is often and easily accepted by a client, who is going to issue an electronic legal statement, for the purpose of his authentication by the trust service provider. It is necessary, however, to consider the security risks involved in the use of HSV technology for personal authentication.

In the literature, in general, any reduction of the risk of mis-authentication due to the use of the HSV technology is usually achieved by some technical improvement of the procedure. We propose to use a personal authentication procedure by the trust service provider in which HSV technology is used in a two-factor process. Having authenticated the client, the trust service provider should create an electronic signature on the submitted legal statement on behalf of the client. This is done by appending a clause containing the client's personal data (e.g. personal identification data of the client) to the legal statement that receives an electronic time stamp, too; then an electronic signature is to be created for the extended document. Finally, in order to increase the reliability of the entire legal statement authentication procedure, we recommend using a follow-up control, too, namely a regular notification mechanism. This follow-up control should be requested by the client. A further optional service would deposit the electronically signed document in a document repository, managed by the trust service provider.

Before the first use of the trust service, the client must register himself at the trust service provider. To do so, the client is expected to provide a handwritten sample signature and an – also handwritten – permanent password. The trust service provider will store the biometric characteristics of the signature and the permanent password in a sample register. (For the protection of the authentication procedure, these biometric data should never be appended to the legal statements to be authenticated!).

As a handwritten signature (something the client *has*) is often easy to imitate, a second authentication factor (something the client *knows*) should also be used. For this purpose, Kiss proposed the use of one-time passwords, which can be also stored in the sample register of the service provider. These one-time passwords must also be provided in handwritten form. The client can give his one-time passwords more than once, but only in either a secured environment at the premises of the service provider, or alone (e.g. at home) on an electronic device (e.g. his smartphone) capable of capturing the biometric characteristics of the signature. In the latter case, transmission of the data to the trust service provider should happen through a secure channel.

The main steps of the registration part of this proposed procedure are shown in Fig. 1.

When the registration was done, the trust service provider will be able to authenticate the client. After successful authentication the trust service provider prepares the necessary clause referring to the client and attaches it to the legal statement given by the client. In principle, an even higher degree of security could be achieved if not some personal data but rather an Anonymous Linking Code (ALC) is stored in the clause compiled by the trust service provider. The paper by Kiss et al. describes such a solution [26]. The use of ALCs however, is rather complicated and computationally demanding.

As we already mentioned, it is advisable to have an additional follow-up security control in the procedure, which enables the client to check whether there was an earlier abuse of which he was the suffering subject. This service is the regular notification service requested by the client. The client will get a detailed (itemised) account off all his transactions with the service provider having occurred within a given period [27]. (An analogue of this service is the monthly bank statement). If a client chooses to have this service, then he will be regularly informed about his authentication transactions, sample registers queries and his legal statement authentication requests. If he finds a transaction in his name but without his consent, he will be able to act.

Finally, the electronically signed document could be either given back to the client or it could be deposited in a document repository managed by the trust service provider.

Note here that in this paper we wanted to describe a procedure for authentication of electronic legal statements from a technical point of view. For those readers who are also interested in the necessary legal background, please refer to our previous work on possible ways of implementing an electronic document certification service [31]. In this paper there is a short description of the previously mentioned "Document Certification Traced Back to Authentication" (DCTBA) service, which is now in operations[2] in Hungary. In order to implement the authentication service described in this paper, it is possible to extend the current functionality of DCTBA both in technical and legal terms.

The DCTBA is one of the so-called Regulated Electronic e-government Services (REeGS) that are defined both in legal and technical terms in Hungary. The legal background for each REeGS is laid down in the Act CCXXII of 2015 on Electronic Administration and the General Rules of Trust Services [32]. Having developed the extended DCTBA, an official permission would be needed from the Electronic Administration Supervision Authority[3] which would provide the required legal background.

The main steps of the authentication procedure of electronic legal statements is shown in Fig. 2 (note that Fig. 2 does not include the regular notification service).

---

[2] This service is available for Hungarian citizens possessing a so-called Client Gate at https://nis zavdh.gov.hu/index/ (in Hungarian only).

[3] The homepage of the authority is at https://euf.gov.hu/ (in Hungarian only).

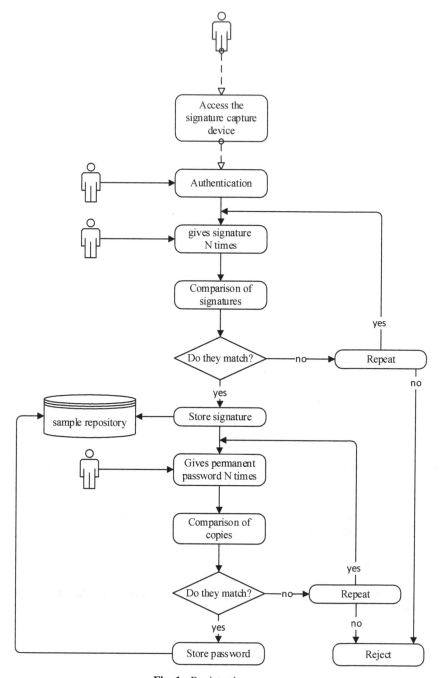

Fig. 1. Registration process

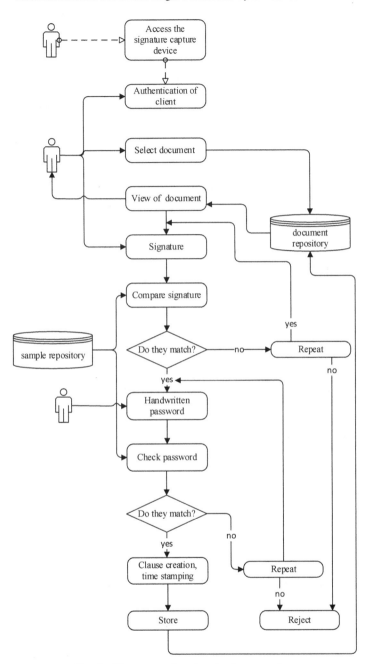

Fig. 2. The proposed authentication procedure

5   Conclusions

It is a necessary premise of electronic administration that legal statements of natural persons should be authentic, that is, these statements cannot be either manipulated or refused.

The handwritten signature is a common and generally accepted form of authentication, and it is possible to capture it digitally on an increasing number of mass-produced consumer devices [28–30]. Clients, who own such devices, and organisations with a clientele who prefer the traditional signature, should consider the use of electronic handwritten signatures for authentication. However, the exclusive use of HSV technology for the authentication of natural persons and the authentication of legal statements involves numerous security risks and its legal validity is also questionable. In this paper a possible solution to reduce the associated risks and to ensure legality was proposed, in which

- a trust service provider authenticates the client's legal statement with electronic signature technology; and
- the client is authenticated with a two-factor procedure based on HSV technology.

The client's document together with a proper clause that links the client's identity to the documents, will be electronically signed by the service provider. This way there is no need for the client to have the necessary infrastructure for creating an electronic signature. The use of a follow-up security controls as a regular notification service and document repository of electronically signed documents would further enhance reliability of the proposed authentication service of electronic legal statements.

References

1. Dumortier, J.: Legal status of qualified electronic signatures in Europe. In: ISSE 2004—Securing Electronic Business Processes, pp. 281–289. Vieweg+Teubner Verlag (2004). https://doi.org/10.1007/978-3-322-84984-7_28
2. Reed, C.: Legally binding electronic documents: digital signatures and authentication. Int. Lawyer **35**, 89 (2001)
3. Regulation (EU) No 910/2014 of the European Parliament and of the Council of 23 July 2014 on electronic identification and trust services for electronic transactions in the internal market and repealing Directive 1999/93/EC. https://eur-lex.europa.eu/legal-content/HU/TXT/?uri=uriserv%3AOJ.L_.2014.257.01.0073.01.HUN. Accessed 04 Apr 2020
4. Handy-Signatur & Bürgerkarte Der digitale Ausweis. (in German), https://www.buergerkarte.at/. Accessed 16 Mar 2020
5. https://eszemelyi.hu/in_english. Accessed 16 Mar 2020
6. https://www.is2.de/en/softwaresolutions/elektronische-signatur/. Accessed 16 Mar 2020
7. Summary of electronic public services and customer service activities, 2019 III. quarter (2020). (in Hungarian). Accessed 16 Mar 2020
8. NMHH. Statistics of trust services in Hungary (2018). (in Hungarian). http://nmhh.hu/cikk/186670/Bizalmi_szolgaltatasi_statisztikak. Accessed 16 Mar 2020
9. Kiss, P.J.: On the selection of an appropriate identification technology for electronic contact with a personal customer service. Vezetéstudomány/Bp. Manage. Rev. **49**(7/8), 61–69 (2018). (in Hungarian), https://doi.org/10.14267/veztud.2018.07-08.07

10. 451/2016. (XII. 19.) Government Decree on the modalities of electronic administration, 12.§(1) d) point (2016). (in Hungarian). http://njt.hu/cgi_bin/njt_doc.cgi?docid=199341. 378035. Accessed 16 Mar 2020

11. Jain, A.K., Flynn, P., Ross, A.A. (eds.): Handbook of Biometrics. Springer, Heidelberg (2007). https://doi.org/10.1007/978-0-387-71041-9

12. Rui, Z., Yan, Z.: A survey on biometric authentication: toward secure and privacy-preserving identification. IEEE Access **7**, 5994–6009 (2018)

13. Galbally-Herrero, J., et al.: On the vulnerability of fingerprint verification systems to fake fingerprints attacks. In: Proceedings 40th Annual 2006 International Carnahan Conference on Security Technology, pp. 130–136. IEEE (2006)

14. Erdogmus, N., Marcel, S.: Spoofing face recognition with 3D masks. IEEE Trans. Inf. Forensics Secur. **9**(7), 1084–1097 (2014)

15. Bowyer, K.W., Burge, M.J. (eds.): Handbook of Iris Recognition. ACVPR. Springer, London (2016). https://doi.org/10.1007/978-1-4471-6784-6

16. Thavalengal, S., Corcoran, P.: Iris recognition on consumer devices—challenges and progress. In: 2015 IEEE International Symposium on Technology and Society, pp. 1–4. IEEE (2015)

17. Mehrotra, H., Vatsa, M., Singh, R., Majhi, B.: Does iris change over time? PloS One **8**(11) (2013). https://doi.org/10.1371/journal.pone.0078333, https://journals.plos.org/plosone/art icle?id=10.1371/journal.pone.0078333. Accessed 16 Mar 2020

18. Impedovo, D., Pirlo, G.: Automatic signature verification: the state of the art. IEEE Trans. Syst. Man Cybern. Part C (Appl. Rev.) **38**(5), 609–635 (2008)

19. Fierrez, J., Ortega-Garcia, J.: On-line signature verification. In: Handbook of Biometrics, pp. 189–209. Springer, Boston (2008)

20. Trevathan, J., McCabe, A.: Remote handwritten signature authentication. In: ICETE 2005 - Proceedings of the Second International Conference on e-Business and Telecommunication Networks, Reading, UK, 3–7 October, pp. 335–339 (2005)

21. El-Henawy, I., Rashad, M., Nomir, O., Ahmed, K.: Online signature verification: state of the art. Int. J. Comput. Technol. **4**(2c2), 664–678 (2013)

22. Querini, L.G., Sabourin, R., Oliveira, L.S.: Offline handwritten signature verification—literature review. In: 2017 Seventh International Conference on Image Processing Theory, Tools and Applications (IPTA), pp. 1–8 (2017)

23. Karnan, M., Akila, M., Krishnaraj, N.: Biometric personal authentication using keystroke dynamics: a review. Appl. Soft Comput. **11**(2), 1565–1573 (2011)

24. Act CXXX of 2016 on the Code of Civil Law, Section §324. http://njt.hu/cgi_bin/njt_doc. cgi?docid=198992.375437. Accessed 17 Mar 2020

25. Querini, M., et al.: A new system for secure handwritten signing of documents. Int. J. Comput. Sci. Appl. **12**(2), 37–56 (2015)

26. Kiss, J.K., Kiss, P.J., Klimkó, G.: A model of secure interconnection of registers containing personal data. In: ECEG 2015 Proceedings of the 15th European Conference on eGovernment, University of Portsmouth, UK, 18–19 June, pp. 149–157 (2015)

27. Kiss, J.K., Kiss, P.J., Klimkó, G.: Towards a model of client-driven access to public e-services. In: Kő, A., Francesconi, E. (eds.) EGOVIS 2015. LNCS, vol. 9265, pp. 117–131. Springer, Cham (2015). https://doi.org/10.1007/978-3-319-22389-6_9

28. Heckeroth, J., Boywitt, C.D.: Examining authenticity: an initial exploration of the suitability of handwritten electronic signatures. Forensic Sci. Int. **275**, 144–154 (2017)

29. Krish, Ram P., Fierrez, J., Galbally, J., Martinez-Diaz, M.: Dynamic signature verification on smart phones. In: Corchado, Juan M., et al. (eds.) PAAMS 2013. CCIS, vol. 365, pp. 213–222. Springer, Heidelberg (2013). https://doi.org/10.1007/978-3-642-38061-7_21

30. Sae-Bae, N., Memon, N.: Online signature verification on mobile devices. IEEE Trans. Inf. Forensics Secur. **9**(6), 933–947 (2014)

31. Kiss, P.J., Kiss, J.K., Klimkó, G.: Electronic document certification service: an enabler of e-government uptake in Hungary. In: Kő, A., Francesconi, E. (eds.) EGOVIS 2016. LNCS, vol. 9831, pp. 276–286. Springer, Cham (2016). https://doi.org/10.1007/978-3-319-44159-7_20

32. Act CCXXII of 2015 on Electronic Administration and the General Rules of Trust Services (in Hungarian). http://njt.hu/cgi_bin/njt_doc.cgi?docid=193173.377340. Accessed 16 June 2020

Analyzing eID Public Acceptance and User Preferences for Current Authentication Options in Estonia

Valentyna Tsap$^{(\boxtimes)}$ ⓘ, Silvia Lips, and Dirk Draheim ⓘ

Tallinn University of Technology, 12619 Tallinn, Estonia
{valentyna.tsap,silvia.lips, dirk.draheim}@taltech.ee

Abstract. Estonia is an advanced digital society where eID is considered as part of the critical infrastructure. With the current number of e-services that the state offers to citizens and businesses, more than 2/3 of citizens regularly use eID today. We investigate the reasons that stand behind its public acceptance. We have conducted a survey among Estonian eID users with 268 respondents to find out which of the existing eID authentication methods are preferred the most (smart cards, Mobile ID, cloud-based solutions, bank links, usernames and passwords, etc.) and what are the decisive factors for these preferences. We have presented and discussed the results by interpreting the data with a set of pre-defined eID public acceptance factors. The outcomes suggest that users prioritize convenience, speed, and security as well as availability of co-existing multiple authentication methods that suit them depending on the setting and circumstances. Moreover, we explain the importance of other contributing factors specific to the case of Estonia.

Keywords: eID · Authentication · Estonia · Public acceptance

1 Introduction

Identity management has been one of the crucial building blocks of e-government and electronic service provision. The current heterogeneity among the EU states' e-governance initiatives has become a hindering factor in the movement towards cross-border interoperability and digital single market. In recent years, fundamental changes have been introduced into policies, regulations and legislation on the international level to assure a common path for everyone (e.g. eIDAS Regulation).

Though the regulations and normative documents have accumulated an exhaustive realm of knowledge and experience to improve electronic identity management, not all aspects have been sufficiently covered [8]. With respect to the subject of eID being present in the literature, so far it can be stated that there is a definite array of work that concentrates on the technological aspects (e.g. architecture, cryptography [19], privacy [3,26], security [4], etc.), policy

© Springer Nature Switzerland AG 2020
A. Kő et al. (Eds.): EGOVIS 2020, LNCS 12394, pp. 159–173, 2020.
https://doi.org/10.1007/978-3-030-58957-8_12

(e.g. implementation and adoption) [12], aspects on different scales [1,4]. While each of them were studied either in isolation or in conjunction with others, it has been noticed that the input to the citizen-oriented research is rather minor [2,9]. It is more common to come across literature that covers a broader angle on the acceptance of technology while we are interested in evidence on a specific aspect.

In Estonia, eID is a vital part of the e-government ecosystem [24]. It is a component of the X-Road data exchange layer. This way, eID enables access to e-services and e-voting. It also serves as the main infrastructure for e-residency [17,27,31].

Estonians have at their disposal several methods of authentication for accessing e-services such as ID-card, digital identity card (suitable only for authentication and digital signing), Mobile ID, Smart ID (cloud-based solution), Bank ID, user name and password, PIN-calculator, social media accounts. It is worth to note that due to the focus of this study, we do not cover the technical specifications of the abovementioned eID solutions.

Nowadays, two thirds of the Estonian population are using eID on a regular basis [16]. Thus, the country presents itself as a unique case worth investigating from the angle of end-users. We would like to change the perspective and look at the situation from the citizen's end. More specifically, we will approach the gap by focusing on what is actually driving them to use and accept eID. Although we are aware of the strategy and measures carried out by the Estonian government during its path of eID establishment, we want to find out what the citizens' perceptions and preferences are for the available eID means and what factors contribute to the existing level of eID public acceptance.

Identifying users' specific preferences, perceptions and attitudes is a potential source of feedback to service providers, policy makers and other stakeholders of the identity management domain [14].

Therefore, we investigate the following research questions:

1. Which eID authentication methods are preferred by the citizens?
2. What are the factors of eID public acceptance in Estonia?

We launch a survey targeting owners of Estonian eID and examine reasons, motivations, and features of eID usage and the potential appeal to end-users. As the Estonian eID consists of several solutions offered to citizens, we differentiate eID in the survey, so to obtain a more in-depth insight of attitudes and opinions. To interpret and frame the survey results, we use categories of eID public acceptance derived within previously conducted research. Additionally, we use statistical data on different eID means provided by the state eID issuer and trust service provider in order to analyze their usage more accurately. Within this research, we focus exclusively on the citizen as the end-user.

We begin our paper with defining our research methodology in Sect. 2. Next, we report on the findings in Sect. 3. We interpret and discuss the obtained results in the context of related work in Sect. 4. We finish with conclusion in Sect. 5.

2   Research Methodology

We used case study research [34] with a semi-structured qualitative survey as the data collection method [10,30]. We analyze the open-ended questions with thematic analysis. We argue that the chosen methodology serves best in achieving the research objectives, as we investigate the unique setting and state of affairs in the Estonia's identity management and enquire citizens' opinions.

We use pre-defined factors of eID acceptance derived from [32] to design the survey and interpret its result. Each factor is described in the context of our findings in the discussion section, i.e., Sect. 4. The list of factors is as follows (full definitions of the factors can be found in the original study [32]):

1. Complexity
2. Ease of use
3. Functionality
4. Awareness
5. Trust
6. Privacy
7. Security
8. Control and empowerment
9. Transparency.

We have ruled out the factors of "path dependency" and "cultural and historical factors" from the interpretation, as they are not relevant in the context of this research. We did not formulate the questions using or inquiring details from end-users related to the path chosen by the Estonian state when introducing eID defined as "path dependency", i.e. previous technical, organizational and regulatory settings [7]. Neither did we analyze the cultural and historical perspectives of the subject under research.

As there are several alternatives to access e-services available, we want to find out which functionalities and features appeal to users and what are the priorities when they choose a certain authentication method. Therefore, we designed a survey for the owners of Estonian eID, i.e. citizens, residents, individuals holding a digital citizenship (e-Residency), holders of digital identity cards. In total, we have collected n = 268 responses (Estonia has approx. 1,328,000 citizen, and approx. 97% of Estonian citizens have an eID [21], i.e., approx. N = 1.288.000, 95% confidence level with 6% margin). The survey was created in the online platform surveymonkey.com. We have used social media platforms and email channels to distribute the survey. As Estonia is a multi-lingual country the survey was distributed in three languages: Estonian, Russian, and English. The survey consisted of 12 questions.

The questions have covered eID relation to e-services, frequency of use, purpose, preferences for authentication options. When asking about e-services and their use we have distinguished between those provided by public and private sectors. We have also enquired what functionalities and features appeal to citizens the most. To get a general current picture of citizens' trust and attitudes, we have included the respective questions inquiring their opinions. We also included demographics-related questions on gender and age.

We also submitted requests for statistics from the Estonian eID issuer, Police and Border Guard Board (PBGB), and the trust services provider, SK ID Solutions AS (SK). They have provided data on the total number of online certificate status protocol (OCSP) requests, number of national eID part of the OCSP requests (all national documents including mobile-ID), mobile ID and Smart ID usage in numbers within the period of 01.01.2017–01.05.2019.

2.1   Limitations

One of the limitations of this research is the chosen method of sampling. Convenience sampling is not considered desirable and does not guarantee the representativeness of results for the entire population, i.e. the rest of Estonian citizens may have similar perceptions of eID [25].

Another aspect is that the provided statistical data is general and very limited in its range. We do not have access to specific numbers that reflect for example the usage of certain e-services depending on the authentication means. This would have been beneficial and helpful for a more precise analysis of user trends. However, acquiring such data would require contacting all e-services owners, both public and private.

To conclude, the identified features and factors are partly grouped according to categories derived from the previous research on eID public acceptance factors [32], which may not include all the variables that play a role in acceptance. In other words, this limitation emanates from the limitations of the previous research. Thus, we have also assumed the possibility to identify other novel and significant aspects worth outlining after analysis.

3   Results

We present the results of the survey by going through each of the questions and describing the breakdown of responses.

The first two questions aimed to obtain demographical data about respondents. 50.7% of respondents are male, 49.2% - female. The age groups are represented as follows: 32.4% (87 respondents) - 18–24 y. o., 32.8% (88 respondents) - 25–34 y. o., 22.7% (61 respondents) - 35–44 y. o., 7.4% (20 respondents) - 45–54 y. o., 1.8% (5 respondents) - 55–64 y. o., 2.2% (6 respondents) – older than 65 y. o.

Following the demographics, the respondents were asked what authentication methods they use in order to access e-services. Multiple choice was available. Figure 1 displays the answers. As it can be seen, ID card is used the most to access e-services. Smart ID holds the second position. Username/Password is the third choice with a rate of 47%. Mobile ID reached a similar percentage – 45.9%.

Further, the respondents were asked to specify how often they use e-services. 50% of respondents stated they are using e-services on a daily basis. Around 29%

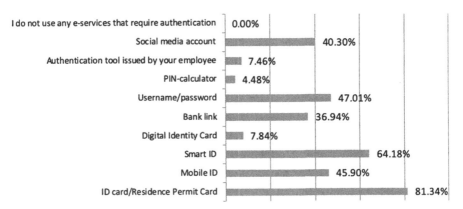

Fig. 1. eID authentication means

reported to use them at least several times a week, 8.9% - once a week, 9.7% - a few times a month, 1.8% - once a month, 0.7% - less than once a month. None of the respondents reported not using e-services at all.

Considering the wide range of available e-services, we decided to see also which are accessed using the available authentication means and which of those are the most prevailed depending on the service providers (public and private).

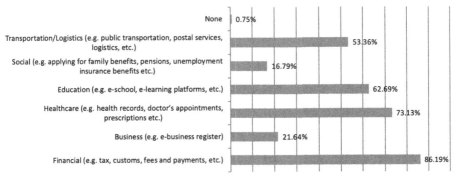

Fig. 2. Use of public e-services

As seen on Fig. 2, four types of services such as financial, healthcare, education, and transportation related e-services are clearly distinguished based on the responses. We have also listed e-services provided by private sector that require authentication and grouped them in categories such as transportation (e.g. taxi), entertainment, lifestyle, food delivery, telecommunication (e.g. mobile phone, internet), financial (e.g. banking). The results have reflected high numbers of private sector e-services used by respondents: transportation – 70,1%, entertainment – 60,4%, lifestyle – 78,7%, food delivery – 47,7%, telecommunications – 87,3%, financial – 90,6%.

When asked were there cases when users could not access an e-service by means of their preferred authentication method, 56,41% of respondents confirmed such cases occurred while the rest 43,5% replied negatively. Those who could not authenticated themselves were asked to clarify what was the service they had tried to access. 63% indicated it was a public service (e.g. many educational institutions do not support Smart ID; technical issues when using eID card or Digi-ID). The rest 36% of respondents reported private services not supporting their preferred options (e.g. certain banks not providing login with Smart ID).

The respondents were asked to explain their choice and/or preferences when using a particular authentication method among others. As the question was open-ended, we have analyzed the textual responses and created themes to sort them after skewing. We marked each response according to its theme and then summarized how many times each theme has occurred. Because many responses repeatedly included more than one theme, we present them separately as combined themes.

Table 1. Response summary to Q11.

Theme	# of times mentioned	% from total # of respondents
Convenience	41	18
Convenience + Security	17	6
Convenience + Speed	27	10
Convenience + Speed + Security	7	3
Ease of use	10	4
Security	8	6
Speed + Security	5	2
Speed	16	6
Usability	2	1
No additional device needed	5	2
Availability	5	2
Convenience in total	101	38
Security in total	38	14
Speed in total	65	25
Smart ID	45	17
ID card	20	8
Mobile ID	24	9
Username/Password	5	2
Social Media	2	1
PIN-Calculator	1	0

Among the responses, six types of authentication methods have been distinguished. Similarly, as in question about which methods are being used, respondents, again, featured Smart ID, Mobile ID, and ID card. The responses that contained themes on authentication methods were also occurring in combination with themes listed in the first part of the Table 1. For example, Smart ID + Convenience was mentioned three times; Smart + Mobile ID – four times.

Three themes such as Convenience, Speed, Security have been mentioned relatively frequently in combination with each other as well as standalone. Hence, we also summarized the number of times these themes were mentioned by the respondents in total. Convenience appeared as the most frequently named aspect and priority for respondents.

When asked what additional features users would prefer to utilize during authentication, we received the following results. The majority – 78.36% – of users indicated willingness to use fingerprints for authentication purposes. With respect to other biometrical data, 28.73% of users chose iris scan, 27.61% – facial image recognition as possible authentication options. Voice recognition appealed to 11.94% of respondents. A considerable number of users – 40.30% – would like to use NFC technology. It is worth noting that as of 2018 [30], a new generation of Estonian eID smart-cards are issued. The new ID document format supports NFC.

Users have also written: *"I would only use fingerprint if it were an "additional" layer of security, not the only authentication needed to log in", "I have concerns about some of the abovementioned options. In particular concerns about security and reliability of those, especially given the modern technological advancements in AI (e.g. image rendering; voice reproduction). Hence, perhaps the only reasonable option is iris scan."*

Three respondents indicated their refusal to use the suggested options. Respondents have been also asked their opinion whether there are enough authentication methods available. The majority of almost 74% agreed there are enough, around 20% said there should be more, 3% there should be less, and around 3% replied *"I don't know."*

The next question on the possibility of having a universal solution has gained similar results where 64% of respondents would like to have several authentication options available, almost 28% found the idea to be appealing, and around 8% indicated they do not know. Some of the respondents have shared their comments with respect to the matter, pointing out the necessity of having more than one method available. One of the users found the idea of a universal solution to be utopian and the other expressed an opinion that considering the existing problems with eID, it is helpful that there are alternatives. Another point was made that having a single solution would have involved more risks and security concerns.

About 20% of respondents have indicated that they fully trust the service providers who handle their personal data. The same number of users noted they do have trust although not without some concerns. 36% feel skeptical about this matter but continue to use eID and e-services. About 3% express do not have trust and feel concerned about their data, and the same number of people do not understand how their data is handled and processed. Among the written responses, users note: *"Don't trust to e-elections"* and *"I trust public sector, and I'm skeptical of private sector."*

From the data provided by eID service providers, we have included for analysis the number of OCSP requests submitted via Mobile ID and Smart ID (See Fig. 3). OCSP is an Internet Protocol used for revocation of a digital certificate in the Public Key Infrastructure domain.

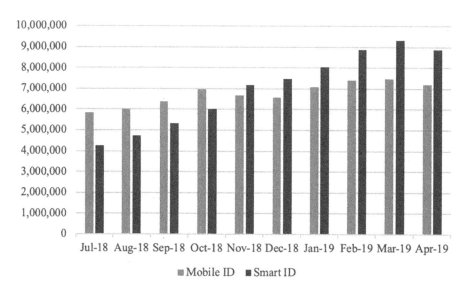

Fig. 3. Number of OCSP requests.

Mobile ID and Smart ID channels were the only differentiated arrays and thus significant for our study. The rest of data service providers decided to share with us were not included into analysis. The figures represented aggregated numbers that could not be applied within analysis which is why we could not relate to the rest of the results.

4 Discussion

4.1 eID Public Acceptance Factors

We will discuss our findings from the perspective of the eID public acceptance factors from Sect. 2 in combination with and against the background of related work. We interpret the Estonian eID according to the outcomes of empirical data analysis. We compare our insights with the ones discussed by other researchers.

Complexity. This factor explains to what extent users perceive the solution at use as a difficult-to-use system [27,32]. During the analysis of survey and written responses, no results were related to this factor.

Functionality. This factor refers to the perceived usefulness and benefit [11]. The results that reflect the types of e-services the respondents are accessing the most by various authentication methods, allow to conclude that the latter ones are seen useful and practical. 25% of respondents have mentioned speed as one of their priorities in choosing the right authentication method.

Awareness. Content analysis of written responses revealed that in general users are knowledgeable and tech-savvy. They demonstrate knowledge of potential risks when it comes to security and privacy, capabilities and limitations of the existing system, principles of its functioning, etc. For example, one user has mentioned the following when asked would a universal authentication method be better to use: *"The issue of technical capability. One central convenient working system would certainly be more convenient. However, given ID-card authentication issues, this problem would be greater if alternative authentication tools did not exist."* [5] argues that awareness is one of the bridges to understanding, trust and hence user acceptance. Additionally, [9] point to lack of awareness that leads to a perception of the technology being too complex. They further note building awareness as a way to enhance ease of use. The activities on the increasing awareness of Estonian population on the use of e-services have been evidently effective as the number of users has been growing [22].

Control and Empowerment. This factor refers to the citizen's ability to control his or her personal data and access to it. Moreover, it includes issues related to disclosure by consent, data integrity [15], access to services [1]. The analysis of collected data within this research did not extract results relevant to be interpreted with this factor.

Transparency. This factor refers to citizen's ability to understand the principles of his or her data is being processed by the service providers. It is also characterized as the visibility and accountability of brought to citizens through service delivery [1]. The question on the trust to service providers who handle personal data showed that only about 4% of respondents replied that they do not know or do not understand how their data is being handled. Though it seems to be the only aspect discovered that is relevant to this factor, it positively reflects on the given case.

Trust. It is assumed that public acceptance heavily relies on whether users trust the technology. Research results of a study aimed to identify public acceptance determinants of ten selected technologies detected trust to be a second most frequently occurring factor. In public sector, the concept of trust applies not only to the technology but to the service provider who must ensure and guarantee proper personal data processing. As within this research part of the respondents indicated to trust fully the service providers in handling their data (20%), demonstrated some concerns (19%), or felt skeptical about the matter

(36%), only around 4% of them showed themselves to be highly concerned, and the same number of people said they are not aware or do not understand how their data is handled. It can be said, that generally in case of Estonia the trust level is relatively high.

Privacy Concerns. This factor is tightly linked with trust. As privacy concerns comprise risks, the latter go hand-in-hand with trust. There is no consensus on how are they related. A study [29] revealed that trust is underpinned by the perceptions of risk. In the context of our research, as seen above, people do have a certain level of distrust towards service providers. A response was submitted where users have mentioned: *"Don't trust to e-elections"* and *"I trust public sector, and I'm skeptical of private sector."* Other types of technologies, for example, biometrics, used in identity management field, are associated with risks [18]. The respondents expressed they willingness to use biometrics but some shared the following opinions:

> *"I have concerns about some of the abovementioned options. In partic-ular concerns about security and reliability of those, especially given the modern technological advancements in AI (image rendering; voice repro-duction). Hence, perhaps the only reasonable option is iris scan.";* *"Prefer non-biometric options for privacy reasons but don't feel current tech allows for needed security. Smart ID is the best currently available in my opinion";* *"I would only use fingerprint if it were an "additional" layer of security, not the only authentication needed to log in."*

The raised concerns do have a valid point. As [14] note, the concept of trust has been in focus of research in eCommerce primarily, where the trust of con-sumers is directed toward vendors not known previously, a situation of "initial trust". In this kind of a relationship, a predisposition to trust already exists. However, [29] argue, in public sector, the citizens, or "consumers" are too famil-iar with the service provider, i.e. state. In this sense, the technology itself is not an object of trust anymore but rather becomes an issue related to the service provider.

Security. This factor accounts for the ability of state, or service provider in general, to grant security of data, software, hardware, their reliability, trustwor-thiness, and safety. The importance of security is difficult to overestimate which is why it is not surprising that this issue has been raised by respondents when we asked about their priorities when choosing an authentication method. Security was mentioned in total 38 times.

Ease of Use. This factor has been defined as one of the major factors of public acceptance of technologies by many theories [11,33]. [11] defines ease of use as the "the degree to which a person believes that using a particular system would be free from effort". In this research, convenience (or ease of use) was the most frequently brought out theme by the respondents. As Table 1 demonstrates, it was mentioned as the priority more than 100 times. [9] mark convenience as one of the motivation factors of the acceptance of eID.

[6] indicates that "the ultimate convenience product or service would then be available continuously (time), everywhere (place), and would require almost no effort to acquire or use".

4.2 Authentication Methods

The results of the survey indicated several authentication methods users go for when it comes to e-services access. Almost each option has been featured by the respondents. A few points can be made in this regard. Firstly, the received numbers can be explained by range of available methods and a possibility to use them in parallel. Secondly, and this can be connected to the previous point, the responses showed that at least half of them are using e-services on a daily basis, while around one third uses them several times a week. Thirdly, given, that e-services are provided both by public and private sector and the authentication methods facilitated by these service providers can vary, we can say that one person uses at least two authentication methods. A governmental portal may offer to access its services by ID card and Mobile ID while, at the same time, the same user may visit, for instance, an insurance company's website authenticating himself with the same methods if available or with a username and password. The high percentage that reflects the use of ID card by respondents corresponds with the fact that 67% of Estonian population use ID card regularly as 99% of public services are available online [13,23]. A study on citizens' satisfaction of e-services conducted by the Ministry of Economic Affairs and Communication of Estonia indicated that "has increased on one hand due to an increased use of existing e-services as well as on the account of new e-services." [22] It was examined that within two years, the number of users of such e-services as healthcare, social affairs, transportation, financial affairs, increased significantly (20% growth in use on average).

It is difficult to distinguish a single leading authentication method. The respondents favor ID card, Mobile ID, Smart ID, and social media accounts. They also mostly agree that there is enough methods available and, moreover, a universal solution is not a good idea because users prefer to have alternatives. In 2017, Estonian e-identity management discovered a major security vulnerability known as ROCA (Return of Copper-Smith Attack) that affected more than 70% of e-ID cards [21]. Having at disposal alternative eID tokens was one of the key reasons why the stakeholders managed to go through the crisis smoothly without any radical actions that could compromise the state infrastructure's functioning. As the report on the lessons learned states, the incident has not affected the eID usage which has kept growing steadily since then [8]. The State Information System Authority as well as Police and Border Guard Board prioritized to retain people's trust during the crisis solving [21].

The collected data shows an increasing popularity of Smart ID. Ever since the establishment of the technology, the number of its users has been growing monthly until nowadays along with the number of transactions conducted by its means. It can be said with confidence, that Smart ID shortly after its launch has become one of the most preferred authentication means of Estonians. The written comments submitted within the survey confirm this.

In the initial stage of this research, when we were requesting statistical data on eID from the issuer and the trust service provides, unfortunately, it was not possible to obtain data which could reveal what is the most often-used authentication type. However, the growth of Smart ID usage can be seen from Fig. 3 where the number of OCSP requests via Smart ID can be compared with the ones sent via Mobile ID.

A study on the adoption of Smart ID in Estonia revealed that one of the effects on a rapid growth of usage was the knowledge about it, or in other words, awareness that spread through various service providers and peer networks [28]. In the case with service providers, Estonia again presents itself as an example of successful public-private partnership [20,21].

4.3 Future Work

There is no consensus on which authentication method is the best. Depending on the purpose, service being accessed, circumstances, devices available, options offered, the choice can be different. Looking at Estonia's setting, it may as well be the case, that the status quo in identity management is satisfactory. As a step further, it is planned to continue investigating Estonian case and collect more data, possibly, by arranging focus groups where users can discuss in detail each solution, and/or get additional input from service providers.

Bearing in mind the limitations of this study, we should look for more definitive answers to support the claims made. Moreover, as these claims are derived from self-reporting of respondents rather than measurement, the individuals could deliver inaccurate evaluations. The existing research on e-identity public acceptance relies on the concepts and theories such as Technology Acceptance Model, Diffusion of Innovations and their derivatives. In order to gain more confidence and validate the list of factors specifically created to characterize eID, further research is required. More specifically, it would be beneficial to design measurements for each factor, however, this in turn calls for a more in-depth both theoretical approach as well as empirical. This way, the accuracy of interpretation and assessment would increase significantly.

5   Conclusion

This research attempted to study citizens' attitudes and perceptions of Estonian eID using factors of eID public acceptance from our previous work. We addressed the stated research questions with the analysis of survey responses. Therefore, we identified the key priorities and preferences that drive users to make their choices and decisions when they use eID and which of the available options outstand.

The study asserts the uniqueness of Estonian case that is known for the advancements in the developments of digital society and e-government. The national e-ID scheme of Estonia is now announced as part of the state critical infrastructure [20,21]. This implies numerous dependencies of e-services functioning that citizens rely on and use on a daily basis. Among the top three factors that we used to interpret respondents' opinions, the most weight was given to ease of use or convenience. Though the concept of ease of use has been already proven multiple times to be a driver of technology adoption, we nevertheless insist on its importance in the context of Estonia which case is worth to learn lessons from. Functionality and Security that were oftentimes tied together with Ease of Use close up the three leading factors. Trust and Awareness were found to be contributing factors to the public acceptance. Respondents said they trust service providers who handle their personal data despite the fact that some concerns were expressed in this regard. This allowed to conclude that the general awareness and knowledge in the given field is relatively high. This is positively an advantage that the country possesses as mostly, findings from other research report this area as a weak spot.

Estonia offers several authentication options which seems to be if not the right thing to do, but, certainly, an effective strategy. Not only is this beneficial for the stable e-state functioning, but is also appealing to users that use them in parallel depending on the ever-changing circumstances.

Among the available authentication methods, certainly, a relatively new solution of Smart ID, launched in 2017, has become popular and continues to be used more and more. However, this trend does not reflect on the usage of ID card or Mobile ID that are keeping their positions. It can be said in other words, that, once again, no "one-size-fits-all" solution exists.

The case of Estonian e-identity management positively has lessons to offer, though the application of its "know-how" should be done selectively and on a context basis. Therefore, we lay ground and point to the need of further work to be conducted in the field of public acceptance of specific technologies such as eID also in other countries.

References

1. Aichholzer, G., Strauß, S.: The Austrian case: multi-card concept and the relationship between citizen ID and social security cards. Identity Inf. Soc. **3**(1), 65–85 (2010). https://doi.org/10.1007/s12394-010-0048-9
2. Al-Hujran, O., Al-dalahmeh, M., Aloudat, A.: The role of national culture on citizen adoption of eGovernment services: an empirical study. Electron. J. e-Gov. **9**(2), 93–106 (2011)
3. Backhouse, J., Halperin, R.: A survey on EU citizens trust in ID systems and authorities. In: The European e-Identity Conference, pp. 1–31. FIDIS, Paris (2007). http://www.fidis.net/fileadmin/journal/issues/1-2007/Survey_on_Citizen_s_Trust.pdf
4. Backhouse, J., Halperin, R.: Security and privacy perceptions of e- ID: a groudned research. In: 16th European Conference on Information Systems, ECIS 2008, Galway, Ireland, 2008, pp. 1382–1393. Galway (2008)
5. Backhouse, J., Halperin, R.: Approaching interoperability for identity management systems. Future Identity Inf. Soc., 245–268 (2009). https://doi.org/10.1007/978-3-642-01820-6_6

6. Brown, L.G.: The strategic and tactical implications of convenience in consumer product marketing. J. Consum. Mark. **6**(3), 13 (1989). https://doi.org/10.1108/EUM0000000002550

7. Brugger, J., Fraefel, M., Riedl, R.: Raising acceptance of cross-border eID federation by value alignment. Electron. J. E-Gov. **12**(2), 178–188 (2014)

8. Buldas, A., et al.: ID-kaardi kaasuse õppetunnid. Technical report, Tallinn University of Technology, School of Information Technologies, Department of Software Science, Tallinn, Estonia (2018)

9. Chauhan, S., Kaushik, A.: Evaluating citizen acceptance of unique identification number in India: an empirical study. Electron. Gov. Int. J. **12**(3), 223–242 (2016). https://doi.org/10.1504/EG.2016.078416

10. Chigbu, U.E.: Visually hypothesising in scientific paper writing: confirming and refuting qualitative research hypotheses using diagrams. Publications **7**(22), 18 (2019). https://doi.org/10.3390/PUBLICATIONS7010022

11. Davis, F.D.: Perceived usefulness, perceived ease of use, and user acceptance of information technology. MIS Q. **13**(3), 319–339 (1989). https://doi.org/10.2307/249008

12. De Cock, D., Simoens, K., Preneel, B.: Insights on identity documents based on the Belgian case study. Inf. Secur. Tech. Rep. **13**(2), 54–60 (2008). https://doi.org/10.1016/j.istr.2008.06.004

13. E-Estonia: e-Estonia — We have built a digital society and we can show you how. https://e-estonia.com/

14. Gupta, N., Fischer, A.R., Frewer, L.J.: Socio-psychological determinants of public acceptance of technologies: a review, October 2012. https://doi.org/10.1177/0963662510392485

15. Halperin, R., Backhouse, J.: A qualitative comparative analysis of citizens' perception of eIDs and interoperability. Technical report 507512, FIDIS (2009)

16. ID.ee: ID.ee. https://www.id.ee/?lang=en&id=

17. Kalja, A.: The first ten years of X-Road. Est. Inf. Soc. Yearb. **2011**(2012), 78–80 (2012)

18. Kalvet, T., Tiits, M., Laas-Mikko, K.: Public acceptance of advanced identity documents. In: Proceedings of the 11th International Conference on Theory and Practice of Electronic Governance - ICEGOV 2018, pp. 429–432. ACM Press, New York (2018). https://doi.org/10.1145/3209415.3209456

19. Khatchatourov, A., Laurent, M., Levallois-Barth, C.: Privacy in digital identity systems: models, assessment, and user adoption. In: Tambouris, E., et al. (eds.) EGOV 2015. LNCS, vol. 9248, pp. 273–290. Springer, Cham (2015). https://doi.org/10.1007/978-3-319-22479-4_21

20. Lips, S., Aas, K., Pappel, I., Draheim, D.: Designing an effective long-term identity management strategy for a mature e-State. In: Kő, A., Francesconi, E., Anderst-Kotsis, G., Tjoa, A.M., Khalil, I. (eds.) EGOVIS 2019. LNCS, vol. 11709, pp. 221–234. Springer, Cham (2019). https://doi.org/10.1007/978-3-030-27523-5_16

21. Lips, S., Pappel, I., Tsap, V., Draheim, D.: Key factors in coping with large-scale security vulnerabilities in the eID field. In: Kő, A., Francesconi, E. (eds.) EGOVIS 2018. LNCS, vol. 11032, pp. 60–70. Springer, Cham (2018). https://doi.org/10.1007/978-3-319-98349-3_5

22. Ministry of Economic Affairs and Communication: Estonian populations' satisfaction with public e-services 2014. Technical report, Ministry of Economic Affairs and Communications (2014)

23. Ministry of Foreign Affairs: E-services for citizens e-Elections e-Tax Board. Technical report, Ministry of Foreign Affairs, Republic of Estonia, Tallinn, Estonia (2014). vm.ee
24. Pappel, I., Pappel, I., Tepandi, J., Draheim, D.: Systematic digital signing in Estonian e-Government processes. In: Hameurlain, A., Küng, J., Wagner, R., Dang, T.K., Thoai, N. (eds.) Transactions on Large-Scale Data- and Knowledge-Centered Systems XXXVI. LNCS, vol. 10720, pp. 31–51. Springer, Heidelberg (2017). https://doi.org/10.1007/978-3-662-56266-6_2
25. Patton, M.Q.: Designing qualitative studies. In: Qualitative Research and Evaluation Methods, 3 edn. Chap. 5, pp. 207–257. SAGE Publications, Thousand Oaks (2002)
26. Priesnitz Filho, W., Ribeiro, C., Zefferer, T.: Privacy-preserving attribute aggregation in eID federations. Future Gener. Comput. Syst. **92**, 1–16 (2019). https://doi.org/10.1016/j.future.2018.09.025
27. Robles, G., Gamalielsson, J., Lundell, B.: Setting up government 3.0 solutions based on open source software: the case of X-Road. In: Lindgren, I., et al. (eds.) EGOV 2019. LNCS, vol. 11685, pp. 69–81. Springer, Cham (2019). https://doi.org/10.1007/978-3-030-27325-5_6
28. Sai, A.A.: An exploratory study of innovation adoption in Estonia. Open J. Bus. Manag. **06**(04), 857–889 (2018). https://doi.org/10.4236/ojbm.2018.64064
29. Sjöberg, L.: Attitudes toward technology and risk: going beyond what is. Policy Sci. **35**, 379–400 (2002)
30. van Thiel, S.: A survey. In: Research Methods in Public Administration and Public Management: An Introduction, 1st edn., vol. 9780203078, Chap. 7, pp. 1–196. Taylor and Francis, London (2014). https://doi.org/10.4324/9780203078525
31. Tsap, V., Pappel, I., Draheim, D.: Key success factors in introducing national e-identification systems. In: Dang, T.K., Wagner, R., Küng, J., Thoai, N., Takizawa, M., Neuhold, E.J. (eds.) FDSE 2017. LNCS, vol. 10646, pp. 455–471. Springer, Cham (2017). https://doi.org/10.1007/978-3-319-70004-5_33
32. Tsap, V., Pappel, I., Draheim, D.: Factors affecting e-ID public acceptance: a literature review. In: Kő, A., Francesconi, E., Anderst-Kotsis, G., Tjoa, A.M., Khalil, I. (eds.) EGOVIS 2019. LNCS, vol. 11709, pp. 176–188. Springer, Cham (2019). https://doi.org/10.1007/978-3-030-27523-5_13
33. Venkatesh, M., Davis, D.: User acceptance of information technology: toward a unified view. MIS Q. **27**(3), 425 (2003). https://doi.org/10.2307/30036540
34. Yin, R.K.: Case Study Research and Applications, 6 edn. SAGE Publications Inc., Los Angeles (2019). https://doi.org/10.1017/CBO9781107415324.004

Political Parties and Internet Voting System Adoption in Ghana

Samuel Agbesi[⊠]

Electronic Systems Department, Aalborg University, Copenhagen, Denmark
sa@es.aau.dk

Abstract. The role of political parties in elections and factors that influence political parties' internet voting system adoption has hardly been explored. One of the key barriers to internet voting system adoption is the lack of trust in the technology and election management authority by political parties. The lack of trust has led to the rejection of electronic voting systems adoption by various political parties in different African countries. The main aim of this study is to examine the role political parties play in the electoral process and the factors that can influence political parties' adoption of i-voting system. Using qualitative research design data were collected from political parties' executives in the form of interviews. Themes that emerged from the analysis include "Increase Voter Turnout", "Integrity of Voting Results", "Trust in EC", "Trust in Technology", "Perceive Advantages", and "Technological Illiteracy". The implication of the research findings was also discussed in the study as well as the limitation of the research and future studies.

Keywords: Internet voting · Adoption · Political parties · Trust · Ghana

1 Introduction

Even though there has been an increase in the application of Information technology in elections [1], the intent to adopt internet voting technology in elections in several countries has not been successful so far, due to the lack of support by political parties, especially opposition parties [2–5]. Studies have shown that one of the main barriers to technology adoption is political parties and citizens' lack of trust in technology as well as the election management authority [1, 6]. A political party is a group of individuals coming together with the sole aim of capturing governmental power through an election [7]. The main interest of political parties is to gain power and to put the sitting government on its toes [7, 8]. Despite the positive roles political parties play in a country's electoral process, such as the mobilization of voters [8], they can also have a negative influence on the electoral process. According to Tobor [9], these negative influence occurs as a result of the lack of trust and disagreement between these political parties and the electoral authority. In Africa and Ghana, disagreement in electoral issues between the electoral authority and the political parties, especially the opposition parties, has resulted in several election violence [10]. To build trust between political parties and the election management authority, henceforth known as Electoral Commission (EC), it is important

© Springer Nature Switzerland AG 2020
A. Kő et al. (Eds.): EGOVIS 2020, LNCS 12394, pp. 174–186, 2020.
https://doi.org/10.1007/978-3-030-58957-8_13

to understand the role of political parties and their influence on the adoption of new technologies in elections.

The role of political parties in elections and factors that influence political parties' internet voting system adoption has hardly been explored. The lack of studies and the lack of trust in both technology and electoral authority have led to the rejection of electronic voting system adoption by various political parties in different African countries [2–5]. Previous studies on the adoption of an electronic voting system have concentrated on users and EC's perspective [11–15]. However, studies that examine the adoption of internet voting (i-voting) system from the political parties' perspective are lacking, and this call for further studies. This study contributes by examining the role political parties play in the electoral process and the factors that can influence political parties adoption of i-voting system. The study examines how trust in an internet voting system and trust in EC can influence political parties' intentions to adopt an i-voting system in an election.

2   State-of-the-Art

2.1   Introduction

This section discusses the influence of political parties in technology adoption decisions in Africa. The section further reviews literature on electronic voting system adoption and concludes with a discussion of the theoretical framework that will serve as a guide to the study.

2.2   Political Parties and Electronic Voting System Adoption in Africa

The influence of political parties on electoral activities in Africa is an area that has not been fully explored. Several misunderstandings before, during, and after elections may be attributed to how elections authority has underestimated the influence of political parties, especially opposition parties, on elections. However, in the adoption of new technologies such as an i-voting system, the role of political parties is important to its success and their involvement in the initial decision-making is crucial [16]. According to Goldsmith et al. [16], it is important to involve all stakeholders, especially opposition political parties, from the onset when an idea is conceived. But in most African countries, opposition political parties are often not included in the decision-making process which often leads to these political parties rejecting the use of those new technologies [2–5]. The perception is that the electoral authority and the government in power may use the adoption of such new technologies to gain an advantage on their opponents during the elections [4, 9]. Such assumptions are not far-fetched since there are instances where the electoral authority's attitude may seem to support those assumptions. For a country to be successful in its adoption of an i-voting system, all stakeholders such as opposition political parties must be involved from the initial decision-making process [16], and this can bring transparency in the entire process and build trust as well.

2.3 Trust and Internet Voting Adoption

Trust is one of the key determinants when it comes to i-voting adoption in an electoral process by citizens [17] and political parties [18]. There is a general lack of trust when it comes to the use of information technology in elections [19], as well as i-voting systems. Citizens and political party's lack of trust in an internet voting technology have also been strengthened by some experts' publications of the risk and vulnerabilities associated with the use of internet voting in a legally binding election [19, 20]. But it is also important to note that other countries such as Estonia and Brazil have also been able to adopt an internet voting system in their legally binding elections [21]. Studies of trust in e-government service can be viewed in two different contexts, that is, trust in the technology and trust in an entity [19, 22]. In the context of this study trust in technology refers to the internet voting system whiles trust in an entity refers to the electoral authority [22] or the government. The lack of trust by citizens and political parties has the potential to impact on i-voting adoption [11, 19, 22]. Trust has been identified to be a significant determinant in diverse online services such as e-commerce [23], and e-government services [24, 25]. Several studies [22, 26] have also examined how trust influences citizen's adoption and use of "e-government service" and i-voting systems. For example, Wahid et al. [18] examine the factors that can influence politicians trust in the use of technology in elections. The results of the study show that "institution quality" and "information quality" have a significant influence on politician's trust in the use of IT in elections [18]. The study of Warkentin et al. [22] also examines how trust and technology adoption models (TAM) impact citizens' i-voting system use intentions. The results of the findings did not show any direct influence between trust and behavioral intention to use i-voting, but there was a significant influence between trust and perceive usefulness which also has a direct influence on behavioral intention to use internet voting [22]. Even though Warkentin et al. [22] results did not show any direct correlation between trust and user i-voting adoption, the results of other studies [1, 11, 15, 27, 28], showed otherwise. For example, according to Nu'man [27], there are certain requirements such as security, usability, privacy, reliability and "equity of access", that are supposed to be met to build trust among stakeholders. When these requirements are fulfilled it increases trust among stakeholders [27]. Trust in an electronic voting system has also been identified as determinant factors to its adoption and use by voters and election authorities [15]. Security of the technology and issues of privacy are key to citizens' and stakeholders' adoption of an i-voting system in elections [15]. In the work of Carter et al. [28], trust in the internet was found to have a significant impact on citizens' intention to use an i-voting system. Trust in internet technology and trust in an entity have a significant impact on stakeholders' intention to use an electronic voting system [1, 11, 27, 28].

In the context of this study, a distinctive contribution will be made on how trust impacts on political parties' i-voting adoption intention. There are contradictions to the influence of trust in government and the use of e-government services [11, 22, 29]. In the study of Horsburgh [29], where they seek to examine the correlation between trust in government and trust in e-government services, their results did not support their hypothesis. However, other studies [6] have also found trust in government as a significant factor in the adoption and use of e-government services. This study assumes that political parties are likely to adopt an i-voting system in an election if they trust the electoral authority.

2.4 Innovation Attribute and Internet Voting Adoption

Innovation has been described as an idea that is perceived as new by its adopters [30]. In the context of this study, an internet voting system is perceived as an innovation since it is new in the context of Ghana. The adoption of innovation has been argued to be influenced by its characteristics [30]. Studies [15, 31] have shown the impact of innovation characteristics on e-government services adoption. For example, Achieng et al. [15], in investigating the factors influencing e-voting adoption in South Africa, identified "perceived relative advantage" as a significant factor in its adoption [15]. Similarly, Carter et al. [28] examine how "relative advantage" and compatibility influence the diffusion of an internet voting system. The findings showed that the perceived "relative advantage" has an impact on "use intention" of an i-voting system by users, but compatibility did not show any significant impact on users' adoption of i-voting system [28].

This study examines the influence of innovation attributes on political parties' internet voting adoption intentions. In the next section, the researcher discusses the theory that will guide the study.

2.5 Theoretical Perspective

In this study, the researcher adopts Rogers "diffusion of innovation" (DOI) theory and trust model as a theoretical guide in the qualitative exploratory study [6, 28, 30]. The main objective of this study is to examine the factors that can influence political parties' i-voting system adoption intention in Ghana. The DOI and trust model have been argued to be a suitable framework in explaining the factors that can influence an organization and stakeholder's adoption of i-voting [15, 28].

2.5.1 Diffusion of Innovation (DOI) Theory

Rogers [30], defines diffusion as "the process through which an innovation is communicated" [30]. The diffusion of innovation theory predicts the rate or speed at which innovation is adopted by the members of the social system [15, 30]. According to Rogers, one key factor that influences the speed at which innovation is adopted is the characteristics of the innovation, which he described as the "perceived relative advantage", "perceived complexity", "perceived compatibility", observability, and trialability, [30]. Relative advantage is about how innovation is seen to be better than the system it is replacing [30, 31], and complexity also describes how innovation is perceived by its adopters as difficult to understand [30, 31].

Compatibility also describes how innovation is seen to be inconsistent with existing values of potential adopters [30], and observability is defined as the degree to which the outcome of the use of the technology is visible to other stakeholders [30]. Finally, trialability also explains the extent to which an innovation can be used on trial bases before its actual adoption [30]. In the context of this study, the researcher examines "perceived relative advantage" and its influence on i-voting adoption. This construct has been identified to influence the adoption of innovation from both individual and organizational perspectives [15, 28]. The researcher is of the view that this construct can also influence political party's i-voting adoption intentions.

2.5.2 Trust Model

Trust is the belief that an organization or an entity on which one depends on, can behave in a way that is of interest and to the expectation of the trusting party [22, 32]. The two main constructs that have been identified in previous studies include trust in technology and trust in an entity [6, 22, 28, 33]. Trust in technology examines the security and risk associated with innovation such as privacy, reliability, integrity, and accuracy [20, 34]. Trust in technology has been argued to influence the adoption of various e-government services [20, 34]. Citizens and other stakeholders are skeptical in the use of e-government services such as an electronic voting system due to the uncertainty and risk associated with the technology [20, 35]. Trust in entity or government, on the other hand, refers to the trustworthiness of the institution or the government that will be responsible for managing the technology [22, 26]. In the context of this study, the researcher examines how political parties' trust in the Electoral Commission (EC) can influence their intention to adopt and use an internet voting system in Ghana. Furthermore, the study also explores how trust in internet voting technology can also influence adoption.

3 Methodology

3.1 Research Design

The purpose of this study is to get an in-depth understanding of the role political parties play in an electoral process and the factors that can influence political parties in the adoption of an i-voting system in Ghana. Hence the study adopted a qualitative research approach in the data collection and analysis [36].

3.2 Research Participant

The population of the study was political parties' executives in Ghana, and the participants include political party executives from the National Democratic Congress (NDC) and New Patriotic Party (NPP). These two parties are the leading political parties in terms of the number of seats they have in parliament and their votes gained in elections. For example in the December 2016 elections, NPP and NDC obtained over 97% of total votes (10.6 million valid votes) during the election, whiles the remaining percentage went to the other six (6) political parties [37].

Participants for the study were purposively selected based on their knowledge and involvement in the electoral process [36] and the number of years they have been involved in elections for their respective political parties. Participants whose involvement in elections is less than eight years were excluded. The assumption is that all participants must at least be involved in two general elections. A total of ten (10) participants made up of five (5) NDC and five (5) NPP were selected.

3.3 Data Collection and Analysis

The data collection was through individual interviews and online-focused group interviews. The individual interviews were carried out via phone and skype, whereas some interviewees asked for getting the questions per email. The focus group discussion was done through skype and the participants involved were four (4), made up of two (2) NPP, and two (2) NDC. The focused group discussion was very informative, but the only challenge was that the conversation could not be recorded in the form of audio or video as requested by participants. The conversations were recorded in a notebook. All the data obtained from the interviews (individual and focus group) were transcribed and uploaded into an NVIVO application. Thematic analysis was used to identify patterns in the qualitative data [38]. The data analysis was done through an initial reading of the entire transcribed data [36]. The transcribed data was read again line-by-line, and codes were assigned to statements and sentences in a process called coding [36]. After the coding process has ended all the codes were analysed and the redundant codes were merged into one single code. In the final phase of the analysis, codes were gathered into sub-themes and then into themes. To ensure reliability and validity in the process the interview transcript was given to other researchers to perform the coding again, after which the codes to be used were finalized.

4 Findings and Discussion

4.1 Introduction

This section presents the findings and discussion of the results. As specified in the introductory section, the study was to examine the role political parties play in the election and the factors that can influence political parties' adoption of an i-voting system. The first part of the section presents the findings and discussions of the role of political parties in the electoral process, and then follow by factors influencing political parties i-voting adoption intentions. Table 1 shows the various themes and sub-themes that emerged from the data analysis.

Table 1. Themes and sub-themes.

Themes	Sub-themes
Trust in technology	Mistrust among political parties, remote attack, security, accuracy of vote recording, and auditability
Trust in EC	Stakeholder consultation, political parties' involvement, and transparency
Perceived advantages	Easy accessibility, reduction in the cost of voting logistics and reduced cost and burden of polling station agents
Technological illiteracy	Technologically savvy and computer illiteracy

4.2   The Role of Political Parties in the Electoral Process

The results of the findings, with regards to the role of political parties in an electoral process, show that political parties through their representative from IPAC play important roles in the electoral process and their influence on the electoral process are well felt. IPAC is an Inter-Party Advisory Committee, that serves as an advisory body to the Electoral Commission (EC) and provides recommendations [11]. Political parties influence the electoral process in so many ways. The various themes that emerged include increase voter turnout and integrity of voting results.

Increase Voter Turnout.   Increase voter turnout in elections was identified as one way in which political parties influence the electoral process. The respondents argued that without the political parties' turnout during the election period will be low.

> *"During election political parties often transport their supporters to various voting constituencies. If political parties don't play this role during an election it affects voters' turnouts"*

The respondents assert that the turnout of district assembly elections is always low due to the non-involvement of political parties. This is because district assembly elections are supposed to be non-partisan. But with national election voter turnouts are often higher due to political parties' involvement in transporting voters, mostly students and other professionals, from their place of studies or work to their voting districts. According to Gauja [39], political parties play an important role in any democratic process such as running political campaigns [39] which in essence increase elections' visibility. These campaigns whip up enthusiasm among voters which goes a long way to increase voter turnouts.

The integrity of Voting Results.   The actions and behaviour of political parties and their supporters were also seen to impact negatively on the integrity of the election results. Some of the respondents claimed that the behaviour of other political parties during voting affects the integrity of the results which influence other losing candidates to challenge the outcome. For example, a respondent has this to say:

> *"When political party supporters misbehave and vandalize ballot box it also affects the outcome of the election results and affects the integrity of the electoral process"*

Others were also of the view that the ongoing practice where political parties bribe voters with money and other items also affects the integrity of the electoral process. The integrity of the whole electoral process can also be influenced by the behaviour and actions of political parties and their supporters during the entire election year. Various allegations come up during the voting period that accuses political parties of using various means, such as bribery, vote-buying, and unlawful tactics just to win votes at various polling stations, and these acts can influence the overall outcome [40].

4.3   Factors Influencing Political Parties Internet Voting System Adoption

With regards to political party and internet voting adoption, the study explores the factors that can influence political party's internet voting adoption intentions. Themes such as trust in technology, trust in EC, perceived advantages, and technological illiteracy emerged from the analysis.

Trust in Technology. Trust in technology was identified as one of the main determinant factors for political parties i-voting adoption intention. The respondents were of the view that there is a high level of mistrust and uncertainty when it comes to using technology in the electoral process. Several sub-themes that emerged under technological trust include mistrust among political parties, remote attack, security, the accuracy of vote recording, and auditability. The respondents were so much concerned about the possibility of a remote attack on the system during the voting period which can compromise the elections. This uncertainty or doubt surrounding the i-voting technology can hinder the adoption of an i-voting system by political parties. A respondent has this to say:

"From my perspective even though I am saying it is good, the issue that has to be addressed before it can be adopted is the fact that there is a perception of a high level of mistrust amongst political parties relative to the technologies and it being subject to remote manipulations"

Similarly, some of the respondents were not sure if their vote cast using internet voting will be recorded correctly in the system, and also if there is a possibility for audit trails. Some of their views are shared below:

"The internet is always subject to all sorts of attacks. Even the US online election was rumoured to have been compromised."

"I will vote manually because with that I am assured that my vote can be counted. I can trust that my vote can be counted in the manual one than the electronic system"

Most of the respondents agree that i-voting has numerous advantages over a paper-based system. But in their opinion, if they cannot be assured that i-voting can bring accuracy and integrity in the vote recording and counting, then they will prefer to vote with a paper-based voting system. The respondents believed that even though there are challenges with paper-based, several controls have been put in place to ensure that vote cast are accurately counted.

"With the paper one I am standing by the polling station; I have my agent who has counted the time I walk in to cast my vote. All party agents do the same and EC representatives also do the same counting. At the end of polls, we reconcile with the total counts of voters against the number of ballots in the ballot box"

The various concerns about trust in i-voting by the respondents were also in line with previous studies [19, 20] that have also raised concern about the security vulnerabilities of i-voting system adoption in elections. An i-voting system is seen to be susceptible to remote attacks and the manipulation of the election software to change the outcome of the results [20]. It's can be inferred that trust in technology is a major barrier to i-voting adoption in Ghana by political parties. The respondents are of the view that an internet voting system is susceptible to various remote attacks that can be detrimental to the integrity of the electoral process.

Trust in EC. Trust in EC also emerged as a determinant factor of political parties' adoption of an i-voting system. The sub-themes that emerged under this theme include stakeholder consultation, political parties' involvement, and transparency. With regards to stakeholder consultation, the respondents were of the view that to build trust, EC must engage the political parties from the start of the procurement process of the i-voting system. They believe that there is a lack of proper engagement and consultation between the EC and political parties when it comes to electoral issues or reforms.

> *"On the EC part, there is not enough stakeholders' engagement when they want to go and recruit whichever entity that will be the handling of implementing a technology"*

> *"But what can be done is when the processes that are involved is done in such a consultative manner that builds confidence and trust"*

From their point of view when there is total transparency, it brings trust and confidence in the entire process. This view was also shared by another respondent who has this to say:

> *"But like am saying any application from the EC being it i-voting in elections, trust me, have to come with a lot of stakeholder consultation."*

When it comes to developing countries such as Ghana, issues of distrust of the electoral authority has impacted negatively on the introduction of several electoral reforms. This from the political parties' point of view is due to the lack of broader consultation and proper engagement of various stakeholders including the political parties. The distrust of the electoral authority, that is EC, gains credence when EC and the government in power seem to push or support a particular electoral reform [41]. Issues of mistrust by political parties in developing countries in Africa have accounted for many rejections of electoral reforms and technologies by political parties, especially opposition parties [4, 9].

Perceived Advantages. The perceived advantages of i-voting were also identified by the respondents as a significant factor in i-voting adoption. Several sub-themes that emerged include easy accessibility, reduction in the cost of voting logistics, and reduced cost and burden of polling station agents. The respondents were of the view that the adoption of i-voting in Ghana's election can bring convenience into voting, and can also make it easier for the voters to cast their vote at their convenience at any location. Similarly, some were also of the view that the introduction of technology such as i-voting can reduce the cost are associated with elections at a certain point. From the perspective of political parties, it may even reduce the cost they incur as a result of training polling agents. Below are except the respondents

> *"It will reduce the cost of logistics, and concerning political parties, it will reduce the cost and burden of providing for electoral agents (polling station agents) in terms of training them to police the ballot boxes"*

"And even the tension that is even mounted at the polling stations, security-wise as a country all this can be reduced to the barest minimum with the adoption of i-voting"

Other studies [15, 28] have also identified innovation characteristics such as relative advantage as an influential factor in technology adoption. According to Carter et al. [28], an internet voting system will enhance the accessibility of voting among the citizens which will impact on the perceived relative advantage.

Technological Illiteracy. Technological illiteracy is one of the themes that emerged from the data analysis. And in the opinion of the respondents, technological illiteracy can be a barrier to the adoption of an i-voting system in Ghana by political parties. The sub-themes that emerged include "Voters not Technologically Savvy" and "Computer Illiteracy of Voters".

Voters Not Technologically Savvy. One of the respondents argued that most of the voters are not technologically knowledgeable and may be difficult for such voters to use the system.

"From the perspective of political parties, the main barriers are that we don't think the Ghanaian voters are not technologically savvy enough to be able to use the i-voting system for its intended outcome"

Computer Illiteracy of Voters. The respondents were of the view that most of the population in Ghana are computer illiterate and it can be a challenge when it comes to internet voting system. Also, some have a low educational level and cannot even read or write. The views of two of the respondents are shown below:

"Introducing this technology now for a population that does not have an appreciable knowledge of the system could be a challenge"

"We need to be mindful of the users who are going to use the technology, their competence, their educational level and their understanding of the process and how they can use it"

The respondents were of the view that i-voting can only be an additional channel for voting, and paper-based can still be maintained for other voters who may not be able to use i-voting. The study by Bélanger et al. [42] also look at the skill divide and internet voting adoption intention, but the skill divide was not found to be significantly related to internet voting adoption intention [42]. Contrary to the work of Bélanger et al. [42], the study of Alomari [43] shows the importance of the digital divide and how it can influence adoption intentions.

5   Conclusion

In this study, the researcher explores the role political parties play in elections and the factors that can influence political parties to adopt an i-voting system. The study has shown that political parties play an important role in the overall success of the electoral process. The findings show that political parties through their campaigns contribute to the high voter turnout during voting. Similarly, political parties' attitudes and behavior have a direct effect on the success and integrity of the electoral process. The findings of this study have several practical implications on the adoption of an i-voting system, and these practical implications are as follow:

5.1   Trust in EC

The findings have shown that trust in EC is a key determinant factor of political party's internet voting adoption intention, and the lack of trust can be a major barrier to its adoption. It is obvious from the findings that there is a lack of engagement and involvement of political parties in the major elections decision-making process. As such EC and Government need to have a broader consultation with all stakeholders and engage political parties on electoral issues. The study recommends that when it comes to technology adoption, EC should ensure to engage all political parties in the entire process. Even though there is an IPAC that is made of all political parties', IPAC is there as an advisory body to the EC. The study recommends for IPAC to become an integral part of the electoral commission where their decision can be binding on the EC. This will bring trust in the electoral process.

5.2   Trust in Technology

The study has also shown how the lack of trust in internet voting technology has a negative impact on its adoption. Political parties are afraid of the susceptibility of the system to remote attack and manipulation of results [20]. Hence the design of the internet voting system should have adequate controls and safeguard to able to detect and prevent such attacks to build trust and confidence among stakeholders.

5.3   Technological Illiteracy

The study also shows that technological illiteracy can pose a challenge to internet adoption. The respondents believe most of the citizens are computer illiterate and may find it difficult to use internet voting smoothly. Hence policymakers and EC need to provide enough education on the use of the technology before its adoption. Also, internet voting should be an additional voting channel but not to replace the paper-based system entirely.

6   Limitation and Future Studies

This study adopted a qualitative design approach to explore the influential factors to the adoption of an i-voting system by political parties. The focus was to have an in-depth understanding of these factors and not to make a generalization. Furthermore, due to the sensitive nature of the topic, it was difficult to obtained vital documents from the electoral authority to support other findings. Futures studies should undertake a quantitative study to cover a larger sample that can be used to generalize.

References

1. Palas Nogueira, J., de Sá-Soares, F.: Trust in e-voting systems: a case study. In: Rahman, H., Mesquita, A., Ramos, I., Pernici, B. (eds.) MCIS 2012. LNBIP, vol. 129, pp. 51–66. Springer, Heidelberg (2012). https://doi.org/10.1007/978-3-642-33244-9_4
2. Petesch, C.: Voting machines raise worries in Congo ahead of elections. https://apnews.com/1764856db1b74c7790a05a65d7a9c5b0/Voting-machines-raise-worries-in-Congo-ahead-of-elections
3. Ross, A., Lewis, D.: In Congo, voting machines raise suspicions among president's foes. https://www.reuters.com/article/us-congo-election/in-congo-voting-machines-raise-suspicions-among-presidents-foes-idUSKCN1GL13W
4. Vishnoi, A.: Indian EVMs cause furore in Botswana. https://economictimes.indiatimes.com/news/politics-and-nation/indian-evms-cause-furore-in-botswana/articleshow/64393693.cms
5. Balise, J.: BCP EVMs court challenge withdrawn. https://www.sundaystandard.info/bcp-evms-court-challenge-withdrawn/
6. Bélanger, F., Carter, L.: Trust and risk in e-government adoption. J. Strateg. Inf. Syst. (2008). https://doi.org/10.1016/j.jsis.2007.12.002
7. Kirkland, C.: Political Parties. Palgrave Pivot, Cham (2020)
8. Stokes, S.C.: Political parties and democracy. Annu. Rev. Polit. Sci. **2**, 243–267 (1999). https://doi.org/10.2307/j.ctt18fs78h.15
9. Tobor, N.: Security vulnerability concerns over the DRC's electronic voting machines. https://www.iafrikan.com/2018/07/23/voting-machines-raise-worries-in-congo/
10. Atuobi, S.: Election-related violence in Africa. Confl. Trends **1**, 10–15 (2008)
11. Agbesi, S.: Examining voters' intention to use internet voting system: a case of Ghana. Int. J. Electron. Gov. **12**, 57–75 (2020). https://doi.org/10.1504/IJEG.2020.106997
12. Agbesi, S.: Institutional drivers of internet voting adoption in Ghana: a qualitative exploratory studies. Nord. Balt. J. Inf. Commun. Technol. **1**, 53–76 (2020). https://doi.org/10.13052/nbjict1902-097X.2020.003
13. Adeshina, S.A., Ojo, A.: Factors for e-voting adoption - analysis of general elections in Nigeria (2017)
14. Adeshina, S.A., Ojo, A.: Towards improved adoption of e-voting -analysis of the case of Nigeria. In: ACM International Conference Proceeding Series (2014)
15. Achieng, M., Ruhode, E.: The adoption and challenges of electronic voting technologies within the South African context. Int. J. Manag. Inf. Technol. **5**, 1–12 (2013). https://doi.org/10.5121/ijmit.2013.5401
16. Goldsmith, B., Ruthrauff, H.: Implementing and overseeing electronic voting and counting technologies. https://www.ndi.org/sites/default/files/2.1.pdf
17. Ahmad, S., Abdullah, S.A.J., Arshad, R.B.: Issues and challenges of transition to e-voting technology in Nigeria. Public Policy Adm. Res. **5**, 95–102 (2015)
18. Wahid, F., Prastyo, D.: Politicians' trust in the information technology use in general election: evidence from Indonesia. Procedia Technol. (2013). https://doi.org/10.1016/j.protcy.2013.12.205
19. Avgerou, C.: explaining trust in IT-mediated elections: a case study of e-voting in Brazil. J. Assoc. Inf. Syst. **14**, 420–451 (2013). https://doi.org/10.17705/1jais.00340
20. Simons, B., Jones, D.W.: Internet voting in the U.S. Commun. ACM **55**, 68–77 (2012). https://doi.org/10.1145/2347736.2347754
21. Wiseman, R.: Internet voting: if not now, when? J. Japan Soc. Fuzzy Theory Intell. Inform. **29**, 100 (2017). https://doi.org/10.3156/jsoft.29.3_100_1
22. Warkentin, M., Sharma, S., Gefen, D., Rose, G.M., Pavlou, P.: Social identity and trust in internet-based voting adoption. Gov. Inf. Q. (2018). https://doi.org/10.1016/j.giq.2018.03.007

23. Kim, D.J., Ferrin, D.L., Rao, H.R.: A trust-based consumer decision-making model in electronic commerce: the role of trust, perceived risk, and their antecedents. Decis. Support Syst. (2008). https://doi.org/10.1016/j.dss.2007.07.001

24. Lallmahomed, M.Z.I., Lallmahomed, N., Lallmahomed, G.M.: Factors influencing the adoption of e-Government services in Mauritius. Telemat. Inform. (2017). https://doi.org/10.1016/j.tele.2017.01.003

25. Abdel-Fattah, M.A.K.: Factors influencing adoption and diffusion of e-Government services. In: Proceedings of the European Conference on e-Government, ECEG (2014)

26. Alzahrani, L., Al-Karaghouli, W., Weerakkody, V.: Analysing the critical factors influencing trust in e-government adoption from citizens' perspective: a systematic review and a conceptual framework. Int. Bus. Rev. (2017). https://doi.org/10.1016/j.ibusrev.2016.06.004

27. Nu'man, A.: A framework for adopting e-voting in Jordan. Electron. J. e-Gov. **10**, 133–146 (2012)

28. Carter, L., Campbell, R.: The impact of trust and relative advantage on internet voting diffusion. J. Theor. Appl. Electron. Commer. Res. **6**, 28–42 (2011)

29. Horsburgh, S., Goldfinch, S., Gauld, R.: Is public trust in Government associated with trust in E-Government? Soc. Sci. Comput. Rev. (2011). https://doi.org/10.1177/0894439310368130

30. Rogers, E.M.: Diffusion of Innovations. Free Press, New York (1983)

31. Lawson-Body, A., Willoughby, L., Illia, A., Lee, S.: Innovation characteristics influencing veterans' adoption of E-Government services. J. Comput. Inf. Syst. **54**, 34–44 (2014)

32. Gefen, D., Rose, G.M., Warkentin, M., Pavlou, P.A.: Cultural diversity and trust in IT adoption: a comparison of potential e-voters in the USA and South Africa (2005)

33. Mpinganjira, M.: Use of e-government services: the role of trust. Int. J. Emerg. Mark. **10**, 622–633 (2015)

34. Carter, L., Weerakkody, V., Phillips, B., Dwivedi, Y.K.: Citizen adoption of E-Government services: exploring citizen perceptions of online services in the United States and United Kingdom. Inf. Syst. Manag. **33**, 124–140 (2016). https://doi.org/10.1080/10580530.2016.1155948

35. Chiang, L.: Trust and security in the e-voting system. Electron. Gov. (2009). https://doi.org/10.1504/EG.2009.027782

36. Plano Clark, V.L., Creswell, J.W.: Understanding Research: A Consumer's Guide, 2nd edn. (2015)

37. EU EOM: EU EOM Ghana Presidential and Parliamentary Elections 2016 Final Report (2016)

38. Clarke, V., Braun, V.: Thematic analysis (2017)

39. Gauja, A.: Political Parties and Elections: Legislating for Representative Democracy. Routledge, London (2016)

40. Morlin-Yron, S.: Ghana elections: 5 reasons why Ghanaians don't trust the process. https://edition.cnn.com/2016/12/06/africa/ghana-election-distrust/index.html

41. City Newsroom: Arguments for and against new voters' register: The story so far. https://citinewsroom.com/2020/01/arguments-for-and-against-new-voters-register-the-story-so-far/

42. Bélanger, F., Carter, L.: The digital divide and internet voting acceptance. In: 4th International Conference on Digital Society, ICDS 2010, Includes CYBERLAWS 2010: The 1st International Conference on Technical and Legal Aspects of the e-Society (2010)

43. Alomari, M.K.: Digital divide impact on e-voting adoption in middle eastern country. In: 2016 11th International Conference for Internet Technology and Secured Transactions, ICITST 2016 (2017)

Artificial Intelligence and Machine Learning in e-Government Context

A Process Model for Generating and Evaluating Ideas: The Use of Machine Learning and Visual Analytics to Support Idea Mining

Workneh Y. Ayele$^{(\boxtimes)}$ (iD) and Gustaf Juell-Skielse (iD)

Department of Computer and Systems Sciences, Stockholm University, Stockholm, Sweden

Abstract. The significance and possibilities of idea generation and evaluation are increasing due to the increasing demands for digital innovation and the abundance of textual data. Textual data such as social media, publications, patents, documents, etc. are used to generate ideas, yet manual analysis is affected by bias and subjectivity. Machine learning and visual analytics tools could be used to support idea generation and evaluation, referred to as idea mining, to unlock the potential of voluminous textual data. Idea mining is applied to support the extraction of useful information from textual data. However, existing literature merely focuses on the outcome and overlooks structuring and standardizing the process itself. In this paper, to support idea mining, we designed a model following design science research, which overlaps with the Cross-Industry-Standard-Process for Data Mining (CRISP-DM) process and adapts well-established models for technology scouting. The proposed model separates the duties of actors in idea mining into two layers. The first layer presents the business layer, where tasks performed by technology scouts, incubators, accelerators, consultants, and contest managers are detailed. The second layer presents the technical layer where tasks performed by data scientists, data engineers, and similar experts are detailed overlapping with CRISP-DM. For future research, we suggest an ex-post evaluation and customization of the model to other techniques of idea mining.

Keywords: Idea mining · Idea generation · Idea evaluation · Text mining · Machine learning · Dynamic topic modeling

1 Introduction

The importance and possibilities of idea generation and evaluation are growing due to the increasing demands for digital innovation and the abundance of data. The accumulation of large data repositories, such as patents, could inspire people to discover and accelerate innovation from solutions to similar problems [1, 2]. Private sector organizations, as well as governmental organizations, could benefit from open and closed data repositories through extracting useful information. In this paper, we define idea mining as the process of generating and evaluating ideas from textual data using techniques of machine learning, text mining, NLP, statistics [3], information retrieval [4], and bibliometrics [5]. Idea mining could be used for supporting decision making as part of a decision support system [6].

© Springer Nature Switzerland AG 2020
A. Kő et al. (Eds.): EGOVIS 2020, LNCS 12394, pp. 189–203, 2020.
https://doi.org/10.1007/978-3-030-58957-8_14

Idea generation and evaluation are parts of cognitive processes of creativity [7], where idea generation is analogous to medicine prescription [8]. Solutions to problems could be used to conjecture solutions to analogous problems [1, 2]. The early detection of solutions from patents and publications, which is referred to as technology scouting, reduces the time-lag between the advancement of technology and its discovery [9]. Hence, the process of technology scouting could be used to find solutions to unsolved problems. Besides, ideas could be generated from networks of experts [10], scholarly literature, patents, reports, the Internet, documents [3], social media [11], and crowdsourcing [12].

Academia produces publications in large volumes [13]. Also, academia-industry collaboration nurtures the processes of innovation [14]. However, academia and the industry have different goals; the industry strives to solve problems while academia focuses on knowledge creation [15]. It is beneficial for the industry to explore and exploit the landscape of academia and its knowledge generation activities globally. Yet, it is becoming harder to find innovative ideas despite a swift growth in research findings [13]. Similarly, user-generated social media data is also growing at an unprecedented volume and speed making it hardly possible to analyze the data manually to meet companies' demands [11]. Moreover, manual analysis of scholarly literature is prone to subjectivity and bias [16]. Thus, it is natural to look for alternatives for dealing with overwhelmingly large volumes of data.

Therefore, in the wake of increasing data production and the increasing popularity of machine learning techniques, idea generation and evaluation could be done using data mining techniques. Changes in technology affect the way idea generation is performed [17]. For example, a machine learning technique, such as topic modeling, is used to elicit insights and evaluate the significance of ideas [18]. Also, unsupervised clustering of text, such as Latent Dirichlet Allocation (LDA) and Dynamic Topic Modelling (DTM) techniques (c.f. [19]), can be used to process large volumes of data. Besides, it is beneficial to follow standardized process models, such as Cross Industry Standard Process for Data Mining (CRISP-DM) to ensure reusability. Furthermore, CRISP-DM is independent of the technology used, and industry sector [20] and could be adapted for analyzing unstructured data such as social media data [21].

However, previous works related to idea mining do not integrate and map their models with the well-established CRISP-DM process model, as illustrated in [22]. Yet the work by [22] adapts CRISP-DM for Idea Mining (CRISP-IM), focusing on the task and perspectives of data scientists and data engineers. Besides, existing process models for idea mining use workflows, non-standard diagrams, and standard text mining [22]. For example, [4] used a similar measuring technique, distance measure, to identify solutions to problems. The search query and new textual corpora are used as inputs, and useful new ideas are extracted by calculating the similarity between the query phrase and potential phrases expressing solutions from the corpora [4]. Therefore, the goal of this paper is to propose the IGE (Idea Generation and Evaluation)-model as an extension of the CRISP-IM [22] for supporting idea mining using patterns generated from DTMs, and visual analytics tools.

The IGE-model is designed following design science research and is demonstrated through the evolution of topics, extracted from DTM, unsupervised machine learning [23], and visual analytics applied on scholarly articles [24]. The proposed model has two layers, a business layer, and a technical layer. The design and development were iteratively done by using 19 experts' feedback. Also, the proposed model's components are inspired by well-founded models, namely the most widely accepted process model, CRISP-DM [20], and the technology scouting process model [9], other idea evaluation techniques, presented in the next chapter, are also the foundations of the IGE-model. This paper has five chapters: Background and Previous Research, Methodology, Result, Discussion and Future Research, and finally, Conclusions.

2 Background and Previous Research

In this section, we briefly present key concepts discussed in this paper, such as "idea," sources of ideas, idea generation, idea evaluation, and finally, related research. An idea is an abstract term that is open to interpretations. On the other hand, idea mining can be used to support decisions in decision support systems [6]. Thorleuchter et al. referred to ideas as a piece of new and useful text phrase consisting of domain-specific terms from the context of technological language usage rather than unstandardized colloquial language [4]. Also, [25] defined an idea as a pair of problem-solution. In this paper, we define idea as: "a sentence or text phrase describing novel and useful information through expressing possible solution(s) to current problems".

Idea Generation. Essential sources of ideas, from which innovation could be achieved, are networks of experts [10], scholarly literature, patents [3, 26], social media [11, 27], Internet, reports, documents [3], and crowdsourcing [12]. Idea generation could be done through collaborating of persons aided by machine learning techniques [12], by finding solutions to analogous problems using machine learning on textual data [1, 2], network analysis and text mining [12], algorithms of recommendation systems [25]. Also, idea generation improves idea evaluation as part of forecasting [28].

Idea Evaluation. According to [29] idea evaluation processes consists of hierarchies of evaluation criteria with corresponding attributes such as technical (productivity, functionality, reliability, safety, ecologically, and aesthetics), customer (necessity, novelty, usefulness, and usability), market (competition, buyer, market), financial (sales volume, rate of return, and payback time), and social (importance, emphasis, commitment, and affordability). On the other hand, [30] proposed an idea evaluation hierarchy as four criteria with corresponding attributes. The criteria with corresponding attributes are novelty (originality and paradigm relatedness), workability (acceptability and implementability), relevance (applicability and effectiveness), and specificity (implicational explicitness, completeness, and clarity). An idea can be evaluated using the connectivity of a network of idea providers [10].

It is possible to evaluate ideas using Analytic Hierarchy Process (AHP), Simple Additive Weighting (SAW), and idea evaluation criteria [29]. AHP is a well-known decision-making tool that can be applied when multiple objectives are involved in judging alternatives [31]. Besides, SAW is a decision-making technique developed to solve the subjectivity of personal selection process using multi-criteria selecting [32]. Machine learning could also be used to support idea evaluation. On the other hand, [18] used topic modeling to assess the significance of ideas based on insights.

2.1 Text Mining and Natural Language Processing

Text mining is a subfield of computer science that combines techniques of Natural Language Processing (NLP), knowledge management, data mining, information retrieval, and machine learning [33]. Moreover, the techniques and tools used in text mining are used to analyze social media textual data for commercial and research purposes [34]. Natural Language Processing (NLP) covers any natural language manipulation using computers [35]. NLP can use machine learning for linguistic analysis [36].

Dynamic Topic Modeling. Capturing emerging trends is also possible using topic modeling [37]. Topic modeling is an evolving technique in machine learning which enables the identification of hidden topics from collections of textual datasets [19]. There is an increasingly growing collection of scholarly articles which demands tools such as machine learning technique to analyze [38]. DTM based on LDA is used to elicit the evolution of topics from textual data [39]. LDA is a topic modeling algorithm designed to identify latent topics without temporal patterns [40]. DTM uses multinomial distributions to represents topics. Furthermore, to infer hidden topics, DTM uses Kalman filters, vibrational approximation, and non-parametric wavelet regression [39]. DTM techniques are used to elicit and capture emerging trends [37].

2.2 Visual Analytics

According to [41], visual analytics combines a set of techniques such as automated analysis and interactive visualizations. Visual analytics is used for creating an adequate understanding, reasoning, and decision making using large and complex datasets. Also, visual analytics applied to scholarly articles enables elicitation of trends and identification of critical evidence in a flexible, repeatable, timely, and valuable way [42].

2.3 Related Research

In this section, examples of research related to computer-assisted idea generation and evaluation are presented. Thorleuchter et al. proposed a method for generating ideas using Euclidean distance measure, and the process model illustrated in their study is merely a general workflow highlighting significant steps done to achieve the desired result [4]. On the other hand, [11] proposed a process model with a scope of knowledge management, using business process modeling notation, for idea generation using social media data, and user participation. Liu et al. applied algorithms that are common in recommendation systems, such as collaborative filtering, to elicit ideas and described the process using a generic workflow [25]. Kao et al. used a simple diagram of idea mining architecture [27]. Authors proposed an idea generation framework at an abstract level using similarity measures [3, 43].

It is also possible to evaluate ideas using machine learning, text mining, NLP, and similar techniques [3]. For example, topic modeling techniques such as Latent Semantic Analysis (LSA), which is unsupervised machine learning, is used to predict the relevance of ideas and provide insight [18]. Alksher et al. used a general workflow for idea evaluation process consisting of data preparation, human judgment, statistical analysis, reliability testing, and idea evaluation [43]. An idea evaluation for contests using expert judgment, machine learning, and quality criteria was proposed by [44].

In this paper, we propose a model which combines machine learning and domain experts' judgment, and machine learning similar to [44]. CRISP-DM is a standardized process model that is technology and industry sector independent [20]. Our proposed model is also technology and sector independent and built on top of CRISP-DM.

3 Methodology

The design science approach followed in this paper consists of six activities, such as identification of problems, objectives of the solution, design and development, demonstration, evaluation, and communication [45]. Running examples and motivations for the design of the model are carried out by demonstration through DTM and visual analytics, experts' semi-structured interviews, and a literature review.

The list of respondents is presented in Table 1. The respondents were chosen based on their expertise. The IGE-model is designed for innovation agents, data and knowledge engineers, innovation accelerators and incubators, and startups dedicated to extracting useful and new ideas. Therefore, two categories of respondents were chosen. The first category of respondents consisting of all respondents (R1-R19) except R6 and R10 are business-related experts dedicated to idea generation, innovation incubation, innovation acceleration, and state-sponsored innovation catalysts. The second category of experts (R5, R6, R10, R16, R17, and R18) are professionals in data visualization and machine learning. Respondents R5, R16, R17, and R18 belong to both categories. The literature review is conducted to motivate the validity of the design, identify techniques of idea mining and corresponding processes.

3.1 Problem Identification

Problem identification was conducted using a literature review and semi-structured interviews. The thematic analysis of the selected literature and the interviews, indicated that textual data such as scholarly literature, social media data, and patents, are growing in unprecedented volume, so the manual analysis is infeasible [11, 16]. Respondents (R1–R7) suggested that it is important to support idea generation and evaluation using relevant textual data sources.

3.2 Objectives of the Solution

The proposed model, The IGE-model, aims to improve the ability to generate and evaluate ideas from, so far, untapped sources of knowledge. The IGE-model has two objectives elicited through a literature review and semi-structured interviews (R1–R19). The users of the IGE-model could be technology scouts, incubators, accelerators, data mining project managers, and technology innovation actors. The objectives are (1) to support users in generating and evaluating ideas through the use of machine learning, NLP, and similar techniques from textual data, and (2) to serve users as a guideline in structuring the task of idea generation and evaluation form textual data.

Table 1. List of respondents, where PI stands for: - Problem Identification, PD-stands for: - Problem Identification and Design and Development.

#	Respondent's organization and responsibility	#	Respondent's organization and responsibility
R1	Xlab, Hub manager (PI)	R11	ATEA, Tech scout (PD)
R2	Xlab, Community development (PI)	R12	Syntesia, CEO & Founder in Innovation and Digitization (PD)
R3	Bluemoon, Strategy leader (PI)	R13	RISE, Västra Götlandsregionen, Sustainability and innovation expert (PD)
R4	Bluemoon, Lead engineer (PI)	R14	Sahlgrenska Science Park, Business Advisor (PD)
R5	iCog, CEO and Founder (PI)	R15	Sahlgrenska Science Park, Machine learning expert (PD)
R6	ITM, Innovation fund administrator (PI)	R16	eGovlab, SU, Visualization expert (PD)
R7	ITM, Incubation manager (PI)	R17	SU, Decision Scientist (PD)
R8	SU, Idea and business advisor (PD)	R18	AAU, iCog, Machine learning, Evaluated an Incubation Process (PD)
R9	RISE, Digital innovation expert (PD)	R19	VITALIS, Strategic Advisor (PD)
R10	ATEA, Business analyst (PD)		

3.3   Design and Development, and Demonstration

The design has been informed by an established method of technology scouting [9], CRISP-DM [20], idea evaluation methods [29], and incremental development through expert feedback (R1–R19). The motivation of the relevance and the validity of the design of the IGE-model is done through a literature review, justifications of adapted models, informed demonstration of DTM using scholarly articles [23], through visual analytics of scholarly articles [24], and through 19 interviews.

3.4   Evaluation, and Communication

The ex-post evaluation of the IGE-model is left for future study. The IGE-model is communicated to business analysts, machine learning experts, decision scientists, incubators, accelerators, technology innovation agents, and public innovation centers through workshops and meetings. Also, the model will be publications.

4 Result

The IGE-model has four major phases, see Fig. 1. All phases of the IGE-model, are completely mapped with the CRISP-IM model, as illustrated in Fig. 2 below. The IGE-model is designed to structure the identification of new ideas about technological innovation and to evaluate elicited ideas. The IGE-model separates the duties of business and technical experts while the CRISP-IM serves technical experts. Furthermore, the original model was different from the model presented in this paper. R17 suggested restructuring the model to make it more understandable and usable; More specifically, R17 recommended that idea evaluation should come after idea generation. All respondents accepted the components of the model. Additionally, evaluation criteria were added, as illustrated in Fig. 3 in dotted boxes.

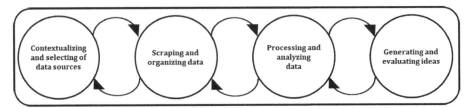

Fig. 1. IGE-model, for generating and evaluating ideas.

The description of each phase and corresponding components are described in Table 2 below. In addition to Table 2, a graphical description of the components of each phase and the illustration of the mapping of the IGE-model with the CRISP-DM model is illustrated in Fig. 2.

Table 2. Description of phases of the IGE-model

Phases	Contextualizing and selection of data sources	Scrapping and organizing data	Processing and analyzing data	Generating and evaluating ideas
Inputs	• Domain knowledge • Need for innovation and problems • Ideas from other sources e.g. contests, scouts, etc.	• Domain knowledge • Identified goals, search area, data sources, and articulated problem statement	• Domain knowledge in idea mining, machine learning, NLP, etc. • Organized datasets	• Domain knowledge • Identified trends, insights, foresight, patterns, visualizations, other sources of ideas
Activities	• Preparation • Articulate problem statement • Define goals • Identify and select search area and data sources, e.g. scholarly articles, journals, patents, social media data, etc.	• Formulate search query using identified goals and problem statements • Scrape and organize data • Based on the quality and quantity of data make decision to go back or forward	• Identify tools • Preprocessing of data, identification of trends, patterns, insights, & foresight • Statistical testing • Evaluating the result • Use statistical indicators to go back or forward	• Use of patterns to find new ideas • Evaluate ideas using evaluation criteria[a] and methods[b] • Based on the quality (statistical test) decide to finalize or to go back • Prioritize ideas for marketing
Outputs	• Defined goals • Articulated problem statements • Identified search area and data sources	• Organized dataset	• Final dataset • Trends, insight, foresight, visualization of correlation and citation analysis	• Generated ideas • Prioritized list of ideas based on evaluation • Best practices, Domain knowledge
Evaluation of Phases	• Relevance of goals, search area, and selection of data sources	• The relevance, adequacy, and quality of collected data	• Quality of trends and patterns based on interpretability and statistical tests	• Number and percentage of viable ideas identified

[a]*The evaluation of ideas, as suggested by* [29] *can be done by the rating of criteria and for additional attributes elicited from experts and literature, refer to Fig. 3 below.*
[b]*The rating of idea efficacy attributes can be done using Simple Additive Weighting (SAW)* [32] *or Analytical Hierarchy Process (AHP) method* [31].

4.1 Phase 1: Contextualizing and Selection of Data Sources

In this phase, domain knowledge, the need for innovation, and commercialization are used as inputs. Additionally, idea banks, ideas obtained from contests, ideas from scouts through formal sources (conferences, technology bulletins, etc.) and informal sources (networks of experts) are also inputs. The activities in this phase are defining goals, articulating problem statements, identifying search areas, identifying, and selecting formal data sources, e.g., scientific articles, journals, patents, social media data, etc. The outputs of this phase are defined goals, identified search area, identified data sources, and articulated problem statement.

Motivation - Defining goals and search areas, and selection of data sources are parts of technology scouting process [9]. Business understanding, which mainly focuses on technology need assessment, is the first stage of the CRISP-DM process model [20]. Also, R9 suggested preparation and planning to be added in the first phase of idea generation and evaluation.

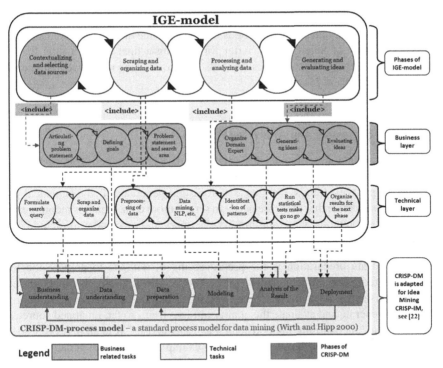

Fig. 2. IGE-model, illustrating business and technical layers, and the mapping of the IGE-model with CRISP-DM (the CRISP-DM is adapted for idea mining CRISP-IM [22], pp. 6).

Demonstration - Tasks in the process as an illustration [23] were done for the identification of goals and success criteria. Goals identified were - To be able to identify trends, to be able to identify emerging patterns, to be able to use trends to evaluate and generate ideas. Identified resources and the activities were locating datasets such as scientific literature, social media data, web forums, etc.

4.2 Phase 2: Scraping and Organizing Data

In this phase, using domain knowledge, identified goals, articulated problem statements, and identified search area search query is articulated. Data cleaning is done by reformatting data into a structured dataset by removing anomalies. Exploring and describing the data are done using Python, spreadsheet applications, etc. Finally, based on the quality and the adequacy of the data, it is decided to use the datasets and continue or go back to the previous phase to redefine the search query.

Motivation - Data collection, understanding, and identification of quality issues are parts of the CRISP-DM phase, data understanding [20]. Also, data collection is part of a technology scouting process [9]. Also, business understanding, which mainly focuses on technology need assessment, is the first stage of the CRISP-DM process model.

Demonstration - For demonstration purposes, Scopus was chosen for data collection. It is possible to use other data sources. Scopus has updated and larger datasets of scholarly literature than Web of Science [46]. After formulating a final query, a total of 5425 documents were extracted. Duplicates were also removed using reference management tools such as Zotero and Mendeley.

4.3   Phase 3: Processing and Analyzing Data

In this phase, using domain knowledge and tools, data is preprocessed to produce the final dataset to be fed to models of machine learning. Statistical testing is used to assess the quality of patterns, trends, insights, and foresight generated. If the statistical tests and evaluations indicate that there are needs to scrape more data, then it is recommended to go back to the previous phase and modify the query and reconsider to include more data sources.

Motivation - Data preparation is the preprocessing of datasets to prepare the final datasets to be fed to the modeling phase of the CRISP-DM [20]. So, the final dataset is prepared in this stage. By using machine learning techniques, it is possible to improve the ability to generate and evaluate the quality of ideas from, so far, untapped sources of knowledge. Machine learning methods, such as LDA and DTM techniques (c.f. [19]), can be used to analyze large numbers of data, for example, academic publications, patent descriptions, and social media, to identify and present topics and their relevance, and indicate the evolution of topics over time.

Demonstration - The dataset was preprocessed using Python. Preprocessing was aided by visualization of term frequency, as illustrated in [23]. After preprocessing, the final dataset was fed to the DTM, for identifying the evolution of topics. Also, trends and patterns were identified through visual analytics of scholarly articles [24]. Visualization of trends, insights, foresight, and patterns were the outputs of this phase.

4.4   Phase 4: Generating and Evaluating Ideas

In this last phase, using domain knowledge, identified trends, insights, foresight, and patterns, ideas are generated. Domain experts could decide to use quality attributes to decide to go back to the previous phase or to continue generating, evaluating, and prioritizing ideas. Ideas could be evaluated using a computer-assisted technique or simply using idea evaluation techniques available in the literature. We present available idea efficacy factors as illustrated below, see Fig. 3, but users of this model could pick more appropriate criteria and adapt the suggested criteria.

Motivation - It is possible to generate and evaluate ideas using machine learning techniques. Emerging trends elicited from topics are used for decision making in science and technology [47]. Analysis of trends results in forecasting trends in technology [48], forecasting while idea generation improves idea evaluation [28]. Machine learning, AI, and analytics can be used to elicit ideas by forecasting relevance and extracting valuable

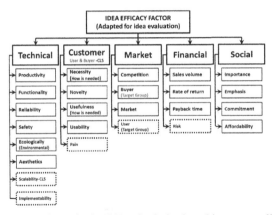

Fig. 3. Adapted idea evaluation criteria [29], criteria in dotted boxes are elicited through semi-structured interviews and a literature review.

insights [18]. Similarly, it is possible to elicit trends and identify temporal patterns using machine learning, scientometric, and visual analytics [24]. Also, [44] proposed an idea evaluation procedure for contests using expert judgment, machine learning, and quality standards [44]. Likewise, the IGE-model includes domain knowledge experts as an input in the idea generation and evaluation phases.

Idea evaluation could be done using idea efficacy factors [29]. The rating of the evaluation of each attribute could be done using the SAW method [32] or AHP [31]. Implementability is added by [30]. Risk under financial, target group (user and buyer) under market, scalability under technical, pain under customer, and finally, two types of customer characters (customer user and customer buyer) were suggested by R8. Furthermore, eliciting and analyzing evolving trends can be helpful for decision-makers and stakeholders in academia and the industry [49]. For example, elicitation of topics about emerging trends in science and technology is crucial for making decisions [47]. Trend analysis can be used for forecasting trends in technology [48].

Demonstration - Research agendas and ideas of innovation were identified using trends, insights, foresight, and other inputs [23]. Thematic analysis and visualization were used to elicit and interpret trends. Identified trends can be used to extrapolate ideas by implications, and generate a report. Also, generated ideas can be used for evaluating the relevance and timeliness of ideas being commercialized by incubators, innovators, and R&Ds. The thematic analysis of evolving topics was done to analyze, elicit trends, and report patterns and themes following [50].

5 Discussion and Future Direction

The purpose of this paper is to support idea generation and evaluation by proposing a process model following the design science approach, which could serve as a guideline for structuring the work of idea generation and evaluation. The proposed IGE-model abstracts the alignment of managerial and technical levels and maps its phases with CRISP-DM. The model is motivated by the well-founded technology scouting process model [9], in addition to CRISP-DM. Research activities, findings, and publications are increasing at unprecedented volume while it is becoming hard to find innovative ideas [13]. The need for structuring idea mining arises from the growing volume of scholarly articles, patents, social media data, etc. and with the inability of a human being to process this voluminous data without subjectivity and bias [16]. It is also difficult to be competitive in the global market with manual analysis of titanic data [11].

Previous works mainly focus on generating and evaluating ideas. Besides, existing models are merely simple workflows, or general frameworks focused on using classical data mining techniques. For example, [43] presented an idea evaluation process as a generic workflow. Also, [11] suggested a business process modeling notation, for idea generation. The IGE-model includes the use of domain experts' judgment in its critical phases, and it is also suggested that idea evaluation activities could be done using both machine learning and human involvement.

Our proposed model will enable governments and industries to upgrade their organizations to meet future challenges proactively by generating and evaluating ideas about services and products. Besides, the generation of ideas is the impetus to companies' strategic marketing positions. For example, industries could proactively update their visions and goals based on reliable future market potential and product innovation foresight. Industries, technology incubators, and technology accelerators often make decisions about production and marketing on intuition-based subjective strategists. The proposed model has not been tested in practice. Therefore, for the future, we suggest ex-ante and ex-post evaluation, adapt the model to make it applicable to other idea mining techniques.

6 Conclusions

Ideas are initiated to solve problems. Existing solutions created to address well-established problems can also be repurposed through the identification of analogous solutions to solve new problems. It is also possible to generate ideas using machine learning assisted techniques. Human involvement in the process of creative idea generation is vital. For example, [51] argued that inspiration from out-of-domain actors of innovation engaged in idea generation enables experienced innovators to have highly likely success in idea generation and an increased chance of having innovativeness in generated ideas.

Finally, idea evaluation followed by idea generation can be supported by machine learning and idea mining techniques. The IGE-model could be used to support technology scouts, innovation agents, incubators, technology accelerators, and relevant stakeholders in practice to manage idea generation processes. The use of IGE-model involves users interested in business and technical perspectives. Thus, IGE-model demands multidisciplinary expertise. We feel that the result of this study is a valuable contribution to research, especially to idea mining and idea management, which involves data and knowledge engineering research.

References

1. Hope, T., Chan, J., Kittur, A., Shahaf, D.: Accelerating innovation through analogy mining. In: 23rd ACM SIGKDD International Conference on Knowledge Discovery and Data Mining, KDD, Part F1296, pp. 235–243 (2017)
2. Hope, T., Chan, J., Kittur, A., Shahaf, D.: Accelerating innovation through analogy mining. In: 27th International Joint Conference on Artificial Intelligence, IJCAI, pp. 5274–5278 (2018)
3. Alksher, M.A., Azman, A., Yaakob, R., Kadir, R.A., Mohamed, A., Alshari, E.M.: A review of methods for mining idea from text. In: Third International Conference on Information Retrieval and Knowledge Management (CAMP), pp. 88–93. IEEE (2016)
4. Thorleuchter, D., Van den Poel, D., Prinzie, A.: Mining ideas from textual information. Expert Syst. Appl. **37**(10), 7182–7188 (2010)
5. Ogawa, T., Kajikawa, Y.: Generating novel research ideas using computational intelligence: a case study involving fuel cells and ammonia synthesis. Technol. Forecast. Soc. Chang. **120**, 41–47 (2017)
6. Thorleuchter, D., Van den Poel, D.: Idea mining for web-based weak signal detection. Futures **66**, 25–34 (2015)
7. Puccio, G.J., Cabra, J.F.: Idea generation and idea evaluation: cognitive skills and deliberate practices. In: Handbook of Organizational Creativity, pp. 189–215. Academic Press (2012)
8. Smith, G.F.: Idea-generation techniques: a formulary of active ingredients. J. Creat. Behav. **32**(2), 107–134 (1998)
9. Rohrbeck, R.: Technology scouting-a case study on the Deutsche Telekom Laboratories. In: ISPIM-Asia Conference (2007)
10. Björk, J., Magnusson, M.: Where do good innovation ideas come from? Exploring the influence of network connectivity on innovation idea quality. J. Prod. Innov. Manag. **26**(6), 662–670 (2009)
11. Kruse, P., Schieber, A., Hilbert, A., Schoop, E.: Idea mining–text mining supported knowledge management for innovation purposes. In: AMCIS (2013)
12. Rhyn, M., Blohm, I., Leimeister, J.M.: Understanding the emergence and recombination of distant knowledge on crowdsourcing platforms. In: 38th International Conference on Information Systems: Transforming Society with Digital Innovation, ICIS (2018)
13. Bloom, N., Jones, C.I., Van Reenen, J., Webb, M.: Are ideas getting harder to find? (w23782). National Bureau of Economic Research (2017)
14. Sandberg, A.B., Crnkovic, I.: Meeting industry-academia research collaboration challenges with agile methodologies. In: IEEE/ACM 39th International Conference on Software Engineering: Software Engineering in Practice Track (ICSE-SEIP), pp. 73–82 (2017)
15. Brijs, K.: Collaboration between academia and industry: KU Leuven. Cereal Foods World **62**(6), 264–266 (2017)
16. Debortoli, S., Müller, O., Junglas, I.A., vom Brocke, J.: Text mining for information systems researchers: an annotated topic modeling tutorial. In: CAIS, vol. 39, no. 1, p. 7 (2016)
17. Kornish, L.J., Hutchison-Krupat, J.: Research on idea generation and selection: implications for management of technology. Prod. Oper. Manag. **26**(4), 633–651 (2017)
18. Steingrimsson, B., Yi, S., Jones, R., Kisialiou, M., Yi, K., Rose, Z.: Big Data Analytics for Improving Fidelity of Engineering Design Decisions. SAE Technical Paper (2018)
19. Blei, D.M.: Probabilistic topic models. Commun. ACM **55**(4), 77–84 (2012)
20. Wirth, R., Hipp, J.: CRISP-DM: towards a standard process model for data mining. In: Proceedings of the 4th International Conference on the Practical Applications of Knowledge Discovery and Data Mining, pp. 29–39 (2000)
21. Asamoah, D.A., Sharda, R.: Adapting CRISP-DM process for social network analytics: application to healthcare. AMCIS (2015)

22. Ayele, W.Y.: Adapting CRISP-DM for idea mining: a data mining process for generating ideas using a textual dataset. Int. J. Adv. Comput. Sci. Appl. **11**(6), 20–32 (2020)

23. Ayele, W.Y., Juell-Skielse, G.: Eliciting evolving topics, trends and foresight about self-driving cars using dynamic topic modeling. In: Arai, K., Kapoor, S., Bhatia, R. (eds.) FICC 2020. AISC, vol. 1129, pp. 488–509. Springer, Cham (2020). https://doi.org/10.1007/978-3-030-39445-5_37

24. Ayele, W.Y., Akram, I.: Identifying emerging trends and temporal patterns about self-driving cars in scientific literature. In: Arai, K., Kapoor, S. (eds.) CVC 2019. AISC, vol. 944, pp. 355–372. Springer, Cham (2020). https://doi.org/10.1007/978-3-030-17798-0_29

25. Liu, H., Goulding, J., Brailsford, T.: Towards computation of novel ideas from corpora of scientific text. In: Appice, A., Rodrigues, P.P., Santos Costa, V., Gama, J., Jorge, A., Soares, C. (eds.) ECML PKDD 2015. LNCS (LNAI), vol. 9285, pp. 541–556. Springer, Cham (2015). https://doi.org/10.1007/978-3-319-23525-7_33

26. Rohrbeck, R.: Trend scanning, scouting and foresight techniques. In: Gassmann, O., Schweitzer, F. (eds.) Management of the Fuzzy Front End of Innovation, pp. 59–73. Springer, Cham (2014). https://doi.org/10.1007/978-3-319-01056-4_5

27. Kao, S.C., Wu, C.H., Syu, S.W.: A creative idea exploration model: based on customer complaints. In: 5th MISNC (2018)

28. McIntosh, T., Mulhearn, T.J., Mumford, M.D.: Taking the good with the bad: the impact of forecasting timing and valence on idea evaluation and creativity. Psychol. Aesthet. Creat. Arts (2019)

29. Stevanovic, M., Marjanovic, D., Storga, M.: A model of idea evaluation and selection for product innovation. In: DS 80-8 Proceedings of the 20th International Conference on Engineering Design: Innovation and Creativity, vol. 15, no. 8, pp. 193–202 (2015)

30. Dean, D.L., Hender, J., Rodgers, T., Santanen, E.: Identifying good ideas: constructs and scales for idea evaluation. J. Assoc. Inf. Syst. **7**(10), 646–699 (2006)

31. Saaty, T.L., Vargas, L.G.: Models, Methods, Concepts & Applications of the Analytic Hierarchy Process. Springer, New York (2012). https://doi.org/10.1007/978-1-4614-3597-6

32. Afshari, A., Mojahed, M., Yusuff, R.M.: Simple additive weighting approach to personnel selection problem. Int. J. Innov. Manag. Technol. **1**(5), 511 (2010)

33. Feldman, R., Sanger, J.: The Text Mining Handbook: Advanced Approaches in Analyzing Unstructured Data. Cambridge University Press. Cambridge (2007)

34. Hu, X., Liu, H.: Text analytics in social media. In: Aggarwal, C., Zhai, C. (eds.) Mining Text Data, pp. 385–414. Springer, Boston (2012). https://doi.org/10.1007/978-1-4614-3223-4_12

35. Bird, S., Klein, E., Loper, E.: Natural Language Processing with Python: Analyzing Text with the Natural Language Toolkit. O'Reilly Media, Inc. (2009)

36. Sidorov, G., Velasquez, F., Stamatatos, E., Gelbukh, A., Chanona-Hernández, L.: Syntactic n-grams as machine learning features for natural language processing. Expert Syst. Appl. **41**(3), 853–860 (2014)

37. AlSumait, L., Barbará, D., Domeniconi, C.: On-line LDA: adaptive topic models for mining text streams with applications to topic detection and tracking. In: Eighth IEEE International Conference on Data Mining. ICDM 2008, pp. 3–12 (2008). IEEE

38. Blei, D.M., Lafferty, J.D.: Topic models. In Text Mining, pp. 101–124. Chapman and Hall/CRC (2009)

39. Blei, D.M., Lafferty, J.D.: Dynamic topic models. In: Proceedings of the 23rd International Conference on Machine Learning, pp. 113–120. ACM (2006)

40. Blei, D.M., Ng, A.Y., Jordan, M.I.: Latent dirichlet allocation. J. Mach. Learn. Res. **3**, 993–1022 (2003)

41. Keim, D., Andrienko, G., Fekete, J.-D., Görg, C., Kohlhammer, J., Melançon, G.: Visual analytics: definition, process, and challenges. In: Kerren, A., Stasko, John T., Fekete, J.-D., North, C. (eds.) Information Visualization. LNCS, vol. 4950, pp. 154–175. Springer, Heidelberg (2008). https://doi.org/10.1007/978-3-540-70956-5_7

42. Chen, C., Hu, Z., Liu, S., Tseng, H.: Emerging trends in regenerative medicine: a scientometric analysis in CiteSpace. Expert Opin. Biol. Ther. **12**(5), 593–608 (2012)

43. Alksher, M.A., Azman, A., Yaakob, R., Kadir, R.A., Mohamed, A., Alshari, E.: A framework for idea mining evaluation. In: SoMeT, pp. 550–559 (2017)

44. Dellermann, D., Lipusch, N., Li, M.: Combining humans and machine learning: a novel approach for evaluating crowdsourcing contributions in idea contests. In: Multikonferenz Wirtschaftsinformatik (2018)

45. Peffers, K., Tuunanen, T., Rothenberger, M.A., Chatterjee, S.: A design science research methodology for information systems research. J. Manag. Inf. Syst. **24**(3), 45–77 (2007)

46. Aghaei, C.A., et al.: A comparison between two main academic literature collections: web of Science and Scopus databases. Asian Soc. Sci. **9**(5), 18–26 (2013)

47. Small, H., Boyack, K.W., Klavans, R.: Identifying emerging topics in science and technology. Res. Policy **43**(8), 1450–1467 (2014)

48. You, H., Li, M., Hipel, K.W., Jiang, J., Ge, B., Duan, H.: Development trend forecasting for coherent light generator technology based on patent citation network analysis. Scientometrics **111**(1), 297–315 (2017)

49. Salatino, A.A., Osborne, F., Motta, E.: AUGUR: forecasting the emergence of new research topics. In: Proceedings of the 18th ACM/IEEE on Joint Conference on Digital Libraries, pp. 303–312 (2018)

50. Braun, V., Clarke, V.: Using thematic analysis in psychology. Qual. Res. Psychol. **3**(2), 77–101 (2006)

51. Aggarwal, V., Hwang, E., Tan, Y.: Fostering innovation: Exploration is not everybody's cup of tea. In: 39th International Conference on Information Systems, ICIS (2018)

Machine Learning or Expert Systems that Is the Question, Which Is to Be Used by a Public Administration

Iván Futó[✉] [ORCID]

Multilogic Ltd., 1053 Frankel Leo u. 45, Budapest, Hungary
futoivan@t-online.hu

Abstract. The article discusses the applicability of the two key areas of Artificial Intelligence - machine learning and expert systems - in Public Administration. We classify in four categories the activities of public institutions and then assign the appropriate Artificial Intelligence tools to these activities. Finally, we provide two examples from the Hungarian state administration to support our statements: the Prime Minister's Office Knowledge Repository Project and the Flexible Tax Control Decision Support and Data Mining System of the National Tax and Customs Office.

Keywords: Artificial Intelligence · Public Administration · Machine learning · Expert systems · GDPR

1 Introduction

Artificial Intelligence is an increasingly popular concept and, as a result, has naturally appeared in the field of Public Administration (PA).

Although a study showed that for e.g. 40% of start-ups who are branded as AI application developers do not worked in this field, also shows the marketability of the concept [1]. This is why it is important to clarify the place of AI tools in public administration.

Nowadays it is primarily machine learning that comes to the forefront, but, as we will show later, only expert systems can be used for administrative decision making.

The starting point for this article is the diagram of the Hungarian Artificial Intelligence Coalition (MI Koalíció), which was presented on the first professional day of the Coalition (Fig. 1).

As can be seen from the figure, the conceptual system of AI is centered on machine learning (ML) and expert systems (ES), so we will deal with these in the article.

We categorize the activities of PA's institutions and then we show the appropriate AI tool that can be assigned to them: machine learning or expert system[1].

---

[1] Extended and modified version of *Artificial Intelligence in Public Administration: Expert Systems vs. Machine Learning*, New Hungarian Public Administration March 2020, Volume 13, Number 1, pp. 25–30. in Hungarian.

© Springer Nature Switzerland AG 2020
A. Kő et al. (Eds.): EGOVIS 2020, LNCS 12394, pp. 204–218, 2020.
https://doi.org/10.1007/978-3-030-58957-8_15

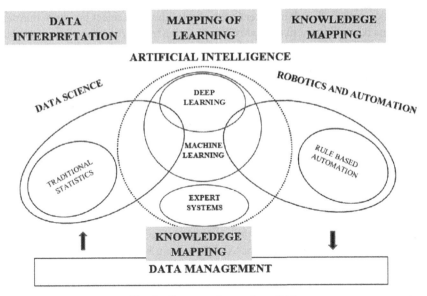

Fig. 1. Conceptual overview of AI

As expert systems have been the subject of less discussions recently, we will address these in more detail and present their capabilities with the help of the Emerald Expert System Shell [2].

The structure of the article: 1. Introduction, 2. Basic activities in the Public Administration, 3. Machine learning, 4. Expert systems, 5. Appropriate tools for the PA's institutions, 6. Example 1: making administrative decisions ex officio, 7. Example 2: administrative decisions following citizen's requests, information provision, 8. Conclusions, 9. References.

2   Basic Activities in the Public Administration

Institutions of public administration essentially perform the following activities:

1. Definition of institutional policy/strategy
2. Making administrative decisions:

   (a) as a result of a citizens' initiative
   (b) ex officio

3. Providing information services

The administrative decision has two forms:

1. Nondiscretionary (normative case): the decision to be taken is clearly prescribed by the law and the decision maker has no choice to take an alternative solution.

2. Discretionary: the decision maker has a certain liberty to select between alternative solutions depending on his/her previous experience, or recommendations provided by the institutions' policy.

In Section 5 we assign to each activity the appropriate AI tool: machine learning or expert system.

Furthermore, we will show why these tools are not "interchangeable, but before doing that, we shortly introduce Machine Learning (ML) and expert systems.

3   Machine Learning

A possible definition of machine learning (ML) is [3]:

"In ML, the computer receives input data as well as the answers expected from the data, and the ML agent needs to produce the rules. These rules can then be applied to new data to produce original answers. An ML system is trained rather than explicitly programmed".

When we talk about machine learning, we mean primarily four types of machine learning algorithms: supervised, unsupervised, reinforced, and deep learning [4, 5].

Main characteristics of each machine learning method is shortly presented in the following paragraphs.

3.1   Supervised Learning

Definition of supervised learning according to [6]:

"Supervised learning algorithms try to model relationships and dependencies between the target prediction output and the input features such that we can predict the output values for new data based on those relationships which it learned from the previous data sets".

Supervised learning is generally associated with two kinds of problems: regression and classification. Regression helps to predict the numerical value of a target variable, whereas classification (also called categorization) helps to predict the category to which the new data point will pertain.

Supervised learning requires human intervention, it is necessary to specify what output variables - values, classes - belong to the input data of the learning set - "tagged data".

3.2   Unsupervised Learning

A possible definition of unsupervised learning according to [7]:

"When using unsupervised learning, no labels are given to the learning algorithm, leaving it on its own to find structure in its input. Unsupervised learning can be a goal in itself (discovering hidden patterns in data) or a means towards an end (feature learning)".

Forms of unsupervised learning are clustering, association rule mining and principal component analysis.

When clustering, we try to find clusters of data in the dataset that are not immediately obvious to the human observer due to high number of variables.

Association rule mining attempts to find rules and relationships between elements of large data sets.

Principal component analysis is a process that converts multiple independent variables into a smaller number of new independent variables than the original.

3.3 Reinforcement Learning

Reinforcement learning works by having an agent (computer) complete a task by interacting with an environment. Based on these interactions, the environment will provide feedback that causes the agent to adapt its behavior. In other terms, the agent learns through trial and error, where error is penalized by the environment and success rewarded. It then automatically adjusts its behavior over time producing more refined actions.

3.4 Deep Learning

The main difference between deep learning and the previous three methods is that the concept of deep learning algorithms is inspired by the biology of the human brain, so deep learning is often referred to as the Artificial Neural Network (ANN).

"Depth" refers to the number of hidden layers of the artificial neural network (Fig. 2) and generally uses nets with two or more hidden layers.

Input level   Hidden levels   Output level

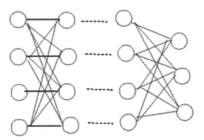

Fig. 2. Artificial Neural Net

Neurons are divided into three distinct groups: input layer, hidden layer(s), output layer.

The input layer receives the input data, each neuron one kind of data. Hidden layers perform mathematical calculations on their inputs, usually adding up their values.

The challenges in neural network design is to determine the number of hidden layers and their neurons.

The output layer specifies the output data and values.

4 Expert Systems

A definition of the expert system could be the following:

An expert system is a computer application that emulates the human expert's decision-making ability. Expert systems are designed to solve complex problems where knowledge, is represented by *if then* rules.

This definition is too general and those who use rule based programming would tend to say "yeah, we make expert systems too".

That's why we're narrowing the definition introducing the notion Expert System 4.0:

An Expert System 4.0[2] on request, can show how it has reached a question/result and can present the part of the used law or regulation.

Development of expert systems is done by the use of so called Expert System Shells, which automatically provide the functions mentioned above (Emerald [1], Exsys Corvid [8], OPA [9]).

This means that it is not necessary to program them for each application.

In the rest of the paper, under expert systems we will understand expert system 4.0.

Applications developed by the use of an Expert System Shell can support the work of an institution of PA in three different ways:

1. Serving citizens directly online.
2. Supporting the work of front-office, in many cases even replacing the official in charge.
3. Implementation of back-office systems.

Expert systems that make a decision—as opposed to helping a decision maker make a decision—would generally be suitable only for decisions involving nondiscretionary elements.

The most important services provided by an expert system (Expert System Shell) are the following (Emerald):

1. Document repository
2. Thesaurus
3. Annotation
4. Semantic search
5. Consultation

4.1 Document Repository

The central infrastructure element of the aforementioned services is the document repository. Documents in the repository have a standard structure (XML) and descriptive data (e.g. author, issuer, period of validity, etc.). The standard structure and the descriptive data set is designed for easy processing with IT tools (e.g. version management, connection analysis, and information extraction) and uniform appearance. The applicable

---

[2] In the rest of the paper by expert system we will understand Expert System 4.0.

XML structure makes it possible to combine information (expert applications, terminology dictionaries) formulated with IT tools with the usual natural language representation, and to interpret them together. The XML structure also enables easy integration with other systems (for e.g. MetaLex [10]). Documents that serve as a basis for building the knowledge base are stored in the document repository: books, articles, expert formulations, study materials, etc. The document library has a time machine and maintains chronologically the different versions of documents (Fig. 3).

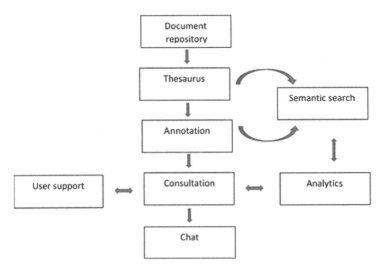

Fig. 3. The functions of an expert system developed in Emerald

4.2 Thesaurus

Thesaurus allows create common notions, and link notions of different organizations thus supporting a common understanding of concepts. It allows to use data from – structured and unstructured – sources and supports the integration with different systems (e.g. DMS, CMS, Wiki, etc.). The representation is based on the World Wide Web Consortium (W3C). The solution used allows the glossaries of different organizations to be linked and analyzed together, thus improving communication between individuals and organizations and the interpretation of legislation. The use of RDF [11] and SKOS [12] concepts-based dictionaries (thesauri, concept classifications, ontologies) allows complex glossaries to be built, maintained and published either on the Internet or intranet. It can also provide an explanation of the notions used in the documents, as well as an understanding and visual representation of the relationships between the concepts (e.g. narrower/broader concepts). The applied IT knowledge representation OWL [13] enables mathematical modeling of the meaning of concepts. It automatically checks the consistency and completeness of the glossary.

4.3 Annotation

The ability to annotate documents ensures that the notions in the documents can be linked to the elements of the dictionary, or thesaurus. In this way, we can facilitate the interpretation of the document and highlight occurrences of notions. In addition, it makes possible for the expert system to refer to relevant parts of the documents in support of the (partial) results, contributing to a deeper understanding of the consultation.

4.4 Semantic Search

The semantic search service is an advanced search service. The search engine supports structure-sensitive search in addition to standard free-text search. Unlike keyword search, semantic search can be used to search synonyms and homonyms, and for narrower and broader concepts by the use of a thesaurus. It uses also a grammatical parser and allows also to make a search using Boolean operators.

4.5 Consultation

Consultation is a rules-based expert application that enables human knowledge to be replaced in some cases by artificial intelligence solutions. Using semantic technologies OWL and SWRL [14] it is possible to model the rules formulated by the field experts using IT tools.

Rules
Rules are central to logical inference based expert systems. The knowledge is basically formulated in the form of rules, see Fig. 4.

Original text

(2) The notification specified in Subsection (1) above may be filed if the taxpayer wishing to enter the simplified taxation system meets all of the eligibility criteria set out in this Act at the time the notification is filed (including the requirements prescribed for the tax year of eligibility) and has no tax debt owed to the state tax authority, the customs authority or any municipal tax authority in excess of one thousand forints. Taxpayers are required to declare these circumstances on the official notification form.

The program

Then
 client 'can be registered under the scope of SET'
If
 client 'meets all of eligibility criteria'
 NOT client 'has tax debt owed to state tax authori excess of one thousands forints'
 NOT client 'has tax debt owed to customs authori excess of one thousands forints'
 NOT client 'has tax debt owed to municipal tax authority in excess of one thousands forint:

Fig. 4. A rule of Act XLIII of 2002 on Simplified Entrepreneurial Tax (SET)

Law is often not very well structured, the use of "or" and "and" is often "confused" and does not correspond to the usual interpretation in mathematical logic. This makes it difficult to model, so it is often needed to create "auxiliary rules" to make each paragraph more structured.

Rule Graphs

If we match the precondition of each rule (if part) with the consequence (then part) of other rules then the result is a so-called rule graph. By selecting a vertex of a rule graph, we can get the part of the law corresponding to the rule, or the rule itself (Fig. 5). Conversely, pointing to the appropriate point of the law, if it is properly modelled, we will get the corresponding rule back (Fig. 6).

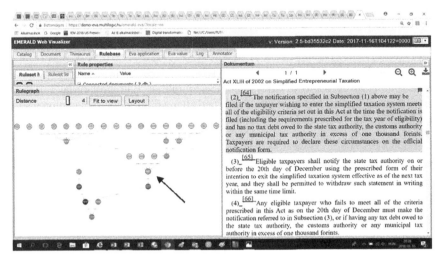

Fig. 5. The rule graph and the part of the law corresponding to a rule.

Advantages of Using a Rule Graph

The full range of statutory rules is automatically created. When a part of the law is

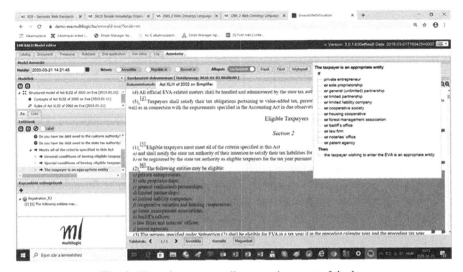

Fig. 6. The rule corresponding to a given part of the law

changed the affected rule/rules is/are immediately seen with the other rules that could be affected too. This is especially important for system maintenance. It is possible to compare each version of the law automatically and in case of differences the relevant rules are presented.

If a rule is not connected to another rule or to a rule no other rules are linked, then there is a legislative or modelling problem.

Legislative changes can be automatically displayed after recording a new version in the document library, and prior knowledge rules - traditionally program segments - of the changed legislative parts, if any, can be automatically presented and modified as needed.

Inference and Explanation
Suppose that a citizen wants to enter under the Simplified Entrepreneurial Tax (SET). The expert system refuses to accept the query and after a request for explanation it shows the reason (Fig. 7).

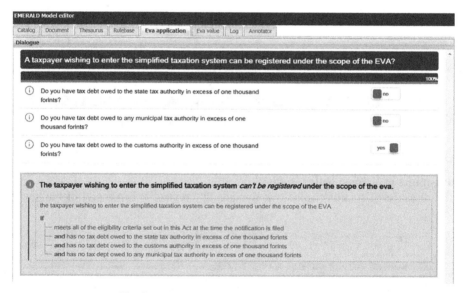

Fig. 7. Explanation of the decision – reasoning

The cause of refusal is that the applicant answered "yes" for the question "Do you have debt to the customs authority in access of one thousands forints?"

The left part of Fig. 8 shows the path leading to the result, the right part is the corresponding segment of the law applied.

If the consultation is over then a request for the explanation can be formulated (*how*, *why* and *why not* services). It is also possible to examine the effect of modifying an earlier given answer and look the new outcome of the consultation (*what if* service).

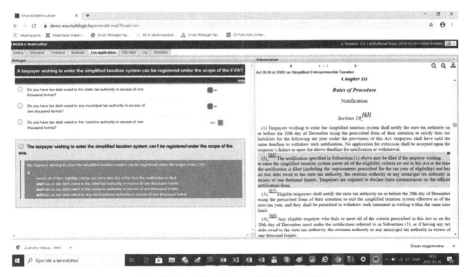

Fig. 8. Legal background of the decision

5 Appropriate AI Tools for the PA's Institutions

In Sect. 2 we introduced the three basic activities of PA's institutions. Now we assign the appropriate AI tools to each of them.

5.1 Supporting the Definition of Institutional Policy/Strategy

The definition of institutional policy/strategy can be supported mainly by machine learning systems but in certain cases expert systems could be also suitable for this purpose.

For example, an unsupervised learning systems can help transform institutions' large, but unused, data into data-driven decisions.

They can identify groups that exhibit common behaviors, so they can be targeted by specific programs.

Combined with field and temporal data, aggregating data can lead to new insights in areas such as emergency response, environmental monitoring, and crime prevention.

On the other hand, by the use of an expert system one can predict the potential effect of a planned law by simulation. Simulation means "playing" with the model and trying different possibilities by modifying it, that is modifying the planned version of the law. Depending on the results, the "best" version could be selected [15].

5.2 Supporting Administrative Decision Making

The concept of decision is defined in Hungary by CL 2016. Section 81 of the General Administrative Order (Ákr) Act. (1) (the part of interest to us is highlighted in italics):

"The decision shall contain all the information necessary to identify the determining authority, the clients and the case, including the facts, the evidence, the reasons for the opinion of the authority, *the reasons for the decision and the documents on which it is based*".

Since, as we have seen, systems using machine learning cannot justify the results – they are black boxes – so in principle they are not suitable for administrative decision making.

In the future, serious efforts are planned to expand the potential of machine learning to explain the results [16].

Unlike machine learning, expert systems can be used for administrative decision making in the following ways:

1. Providing automated decision
2. Providing recommendations to the decision maker
3. Guiding decision maker showing relevant facts, legislation to be taken in account in process of decision and excluding irrelevant cases
4. Providing useful commentaries to explain decisions

Making Administrative Decisions as a Result of a Citizens' initiative
These are the cases when citizens make a request to the administration to solve their problems.

In this case, where the procedure is based on normative regulation, an expert system is able to act correctly and lawfully, replacing the activities of decision maker (case 1).

In other words in case of nondiscretionary decisions expert systems are the suitable tools to be used for decision making. If the expert system model is well defined, no agent could make any other decision.

In case of discretionary decision making the expert system can be used to support the civil servant in the process of decision making (5.2. 2–4).

The services of an Expert System 4.0, meet the requirements of Section 81 (1) of CL Act 2016 and also fulfil the GDPR requirement prescribed for electronic decision support systems to provide explanations on request.

Making Administrative Decisions Ex Officio
In this case, the decision making consists of two phases:

1. Definition the scope of those involved in the administration
2. Individual treatment of each case

The affected group can be defined by machine learning, while later the individual administration can be done with expert system support (see Sect. 6).

5.3   Providing Information Services

Both expert and machine learning systems may be suitable for providing information. In fact, the real solution is the combination of these.

With the help of machine learning based natural language understanding, speech recognition, and machine vision information services could be implemented and these solutions facilitate the task of citizens.

However, because the base of these solutions is machine learning – and as we have seen no explanation of the solution can be given – these applications can't be used for administrative decision.

They are very useful for giving information concerning working times, organizing appointments or defining the case to be dealt by an officer.

The real service can be provided by a citizen/agent communication interface - chatbot - with the above three features (natural language understanding, speech recognition, machine vision) and the expert system behind them, where the machine learning application asks the user to define exactly what the problem is and then calls the appropriate expert system to explain the solution of the problem.

In this case, the expert system is not linked to the back-office systems, it only provides information and does not start to handle the case itself.

6   Example 1: Making Administrative Decisions Ex Officio

Following the Hungarian Tax Office's (today National Tax and Customs Administration - NTCA) strategic plans, large-scale projects have been launched since 2008, to develop risk assessment models to increase the effectiveness of selection for auditing.

The development of the Flexible Tax Control Decision Support System (RADAR) was a major step forward in achieving this goal [17].

The following objectives have been formulated as a condition for the implementation of a modern risk management activities:

1. Risk analysis and selection cannot be left solely to the subjective judgment of those who carry it out.
2. National databases should be available for efficient selection. This required the integration of data, often in decentralized, county-level systems, into a national repository.
3. Query applications based on data markets that allow flexible use should be introduced and learned to use them at a skill level.

In addition to the above requirements, the project aimed primarily to develop a software for risk analysis, decision support and modelling, which would enable regular and automatic mathematical-statistical and AI methods to assess the riskiness of taxable persons subject to VAT.

The RADAR system supports selection for auditing – first step - with data of collected by varying frequency - daily, weekly, monthly, and on-demand - from different data sources. In total, about 100 different types of data are included in RADAR.

The evaluation of data in brief – first step:

1. Logistic regression on 2/3 part of the database
2. Automatic selection of variables with highest explanatory power (15–20)

3. Application of the methodology most commonly used in bank credit rating (Basel II)
4. Validation for the remaining 1/3 part of the database

To support the audit – second step - NTCA also uses the ESCORT expert system [18]. The first version was acquired in 1999.

7   Example 2: Administrative Decisions Following Citizens' Requests, Information Provision

In 2019, more than 12 million cases were handled by the "Government Windows", the offices managing citizens' claims.

There are 2300 type of cases. The Government's Knowledge Repository supporting the work of Government Windows contains information about the case types to be handled divided into twenty-two life situations.

The information stored is: responsible, description of regulations, institutions concerned, workflow, etc. - all over around 90 data.

Thousands of civil servants were trained in the use of the Knowledge Repository, including knowledge modelers – knowledge engineers - and help desk staff.

The implemented chat service helps to find the appropriate case type, based on the dialogue with the users, then initiates the adequate expert system to start the administration or information provision.

As the Knowledge Repository virtually covers the entire public administration, in principle, instead of developing island-like specific expert systems, it gives an opportunity for the gradual development based on a unified approach and conceptual framework [19].

8   Conclusions

Machine learning systems and expert systems use different techniques to solve different types of problems:

1. Machine learning:

   (a) categorization of cases into clusters or groups of interest.
   (b) no explanation is given how the solution was found.

2. Expert system:

   (a) solution of individual cases based on *if then* rules and logical inference.
   (b) explanation is given for the solution, together with the documents – parts of knowledge base - used during the reasoning.

Due to the different approaches and types of solutions, there is no possibility to replace one with the other.

Concerning the Public Administration, different AI tools can be used for different purposes:

1. Defining institutional policy/strategy: machine learning, expert system (simulation)
2. Administrative decision

   (a) as a result of a citizens' initiative - expert system
   (b) ex officio - machine learning first, then expert system

3. Information provision:

   (a) machine learning - natural language understanding, speech recognition, machine vision.
   (b) expert system - solutions only, no explanation.

References

1. Shulze, E.: 40% of A.I. start-ups in Europe have almost nothing to do with A.I., CNBC. https://www.cnbc.com/2019/03/06/40-percent-of-ai-start-ups-in-europe-not-related-to-ai-mmc-report.html. Accessed Mar 06 2019
2. Förhécz, A., Kőrösi, G., Strausz, Gy.: Versioned linking of semantic enrichment of legal documents: Emerald: an implementation of knowledge-based services in a semantic web approach. In: Conference Artificial Intelligence And Law 21, pp. 485–519, November 2013
3. Craglia, M.: Artificial Intelligence A European Perspective. European Commission, Joint Research Centre (JRC), p. 140 (2018). https://doi.org/10.2760/11251. ISBN 978-92-79-97217-1, ISSN 1831-9424
4. James, L.: The 10 algorithms machine learning engineers need to know. KDNugetts, August 2016
5. Berryhill, J., Kok Heang, K., Clogher, R., McBride, K.: Hello, world: artificial intelligence and its use in the public sector. In: OECD Working Papers on Public Governance No. 36, OECD, p. 185 (2019)
6. Fumo, D.: Types of Machine Learning Algorithms You Should Know. Towards Data Science, 15 Jun 2017. https://towardsdatascience.com/types-of-machine-learning-algorithms-you-should-know-953a08248861?gi=e40b1318ccd8
7. Sanatan, M.: Unsupervised Learning and Data Clustering. Towards Data Science, 19 May 2017. https://towardsdatascience.com/unsupervised-learning-and-data-clustering-eeecb78b422a
8. EXSYS: Exsys Corvid Knowledge Automation Expert System. Exsys Inc. 2011–2016. http://www.exsys.com/exsyscorvid.html
9. ORACLE: Oracle Policy Automation. https://www.oracle.com/applications/oracle-policy-automation/index.html
10. METALEX: CEN MetaLex, Open XML Interchange Format for Legal and Legislative Resources. http://www.metalex.eu/
11. RDF: RDF – Semantic Web Standard. https://www.w3.org/RDF/
12. SKOS: SKOS Simple Knowledge Organization System. https://www.w3.org/2004/02/skos/

13. OWL: OWL 2 Web Ontology Language, Document Overview, 2nd edn. W3C Recommendation, 11 December 2012. http://www.w3.org/TR/owl2-overview/. Accessed 12 Mar 2020
14. SWRL: SWRL: A Semantic Web Rule Language Combining OWL and RuleML Member Submission, 21 May 2004. http://www.w3.org/Submission/SWRL/. Accessed 11 Mar 2020
15. Futó I., Várkonyi J.: Legal expert systems as simulation tools. In: Proceedings of the SCS Winter Conference 1993, Los Angeles, pp. 1259–1263 (1993)
16. Era Learn: CHIST-ERA call 2019, Explainable Machine Learning-based Artificial Intelligence (XAI). https://www.era-learn.eu/network-information/networks/chist-era-iv/chist-era-call-2019
17. Vikarius, G.: Priority Audit Tasks in, Particularly Intentional Fraud, Tax Avoidance (2012). https://docplayer.hu/19964184-Featured-laboratory-Tasks-2012-ben-collateral-view-a-sandex-csalasra-adoelkerulesre.html. (in Hungarian)
18. Lethan, H., Jacobsen, H.: ESKORT – an expert system for auditing VAT accounts. In: Proceedings of Expert Systems and Their Applications – Avignon 87, Avignon, France (1987)
19. Futó, I.: The use of Artificial Intelligence tools – expert systems – in the Public Administration, Dialóg Campus Publisher, Budapest, p. 165 (2019). (In Hungarian)

Modelling GDPR-Compliant Explanations for Trustworthy AI

Francesco Sovrano[1(✉)], Fabio Vitali[1], and Monica Palmirani[2]

[1] DISI, University of Bologna, Bologna, Italy
{francesco.sovrano2,fabio.vitali}@unibo.it
[2] CIRSFID, University of Bologna, Bologna, Italy
monica.palmirani@unibo.it

Abstract. Through the General Data Protection Regulation (GDPR), the European Union has set out its vision for Automated Decision-Making (ADM) and AI, which must be reliable and human-centred. In particular we are interested on the Right to Explanation, that requires industry to produce explanations of ADM. The High-Level Expert Group on Artificial Intelligence (AI-HLEG), set up to support the implementation of this vision, has produced guidelines discussing the types of explanations that are appropriate for user-centred (interactive) Explanatory Tools. In this paper we propose our version of Explanatory Narratives (EN), based on user-centred concepts drawn from ISO 9241, as a model for user-centred explanations aligned with the GDPR and the AI-HLEG guidelines. Through the use of ENs we convert the problem of generating explanations for ADM into the identification of an appropriate path over an Explanatory Space, allowing explainees to interactively explore it and produce the explanation best suited to their needs. To this end we list suitable exploration heuristics, we study the properties and structure of explanations, and discuss the proposed model identifying its weaknesses and strengths.

Keywords: Interactive explanatory tool · General Data Protection Regulation · Trustworthy artificial intelligence

1 Introduction

The academic interest in Artificial Intelligence (AI) has grown together with the attention of countries and people toward the actual disruptive effects of Automated Decision Making (ADM [27]) in industry and in the public administration, effects that may affect the lives of billions of people. Thus, GDPR (General Data Protection Regulation, UE 2016/679) stresses the importance of the Right to Explanation, with several expert groups, including those acting for the European Commission, have started asking the AI industry to adopt ethics code of conducts as quickly as possible [5,9]. The GDPR draws a set of expectations to meet in order to guarantee the Right to Explanation (for more

© Springer Nature Switzerland AG 2020
A. Kő et al. (Eds.): EGOVIS 2020, LNCS 12394, pp. 219–233, 2020.
https://doi.org/10.1007/978-3-030-58957-8_16

details see Sect. 2). These expectations define the goal of explanations under the GDPR and thus describe requirements for explanatory content that should be "adapted to the expertise of the stakeholder concerned (e.g.. layperson, regulator or researcher)" [11]. Analysing these requirements we found a minimal set of explanation types that are necessary to meet these expectations: causal, justificatory and descriptive.

Most of the literature on AI and explanations (e.g. eXplainable AI) is currently focused on one-size-fits-all approaches usually able to produce only one of the required explanation types: causal explanations. In this paper we take a strong stand against the idea that static, one-size-fits-all approaches to explanation (explainability) have a chance of satisfying GDPR expectations and requirements. In fact, we argue that one-size-fits-all approaches (in the most generic scenario) may suffer the curse of dimensionality. For example, a complex big-enough explainable software can be super hard to explain, even to an expert, and the optimal (or even sufficient) explanation might change from expert to expert. This is why we argue that an explanatory tool for complex data and processes has to be user-centred and thus interactive. The fact that every different user might require a different explanation does not imply that there might be no unique and sound process for constructing user-centred explanations. In fact we argue that every interactive explanatory tool defines and eventually generates an Explanatory Space (ES) and that an explanation is always a path in the ES. The explainee explores the ES, tracing a path in it, thus producing its own (user-centred) explanation.

This is why we assert that a more nuanced approach must be considered, where explanations are user-centred narratives that allow explainees to increase understanding through sense-making and articulation, in a manner that is fit to specified explainees, their goals, and their context of use. Upon these considerations, and following the High-Level Expert Group on Artificial Intelligence (AI-HLEG) Ethics Guidelines for Trustworthy AI, we propose here a new model of a User-Centred Explanatory Tool for Trustworthy AI, compliant with GDPR. To this extent we propose a definition of user-centred explanations as Explanatory Narratives, based on concepts drawn from ISO 9241. We present a formal model of an Interactive Explanatory Process consequently identifying 4 fundamental properties (the SAGE properties) of a good explanation and 3 heuristics for the exploration of the ES. Finally, we define the structure of the ES, combining the SAGE properties and the identified exploration heuristics, thus showing an application of the model to a real-case scenario.

This paper is structured as follows: in Sect. 2 we provide some background information. In Sect. 3 we discuss over the GDPR, introducing our definition of Explanatory Narratives. In Sect. 4 we analyse existing work. While in Sect. 5 we propose a simple model of a User-Centred Narrative Explanatory Process. Finally in Sect. 6 we discuss the strengths and the weaknesses of our model, and in Sect. 7 we conclude pointing to future work.

2   Background

2.1   Explanations in Literature

In literature, many types of possible explanations have been thoroughly discussed, and it is not clear whether a complete and detailed taxonomy may exist. In the field of Explainable Artificial Intelligence (XAI), the most discussed type of explanations is probably the causal one. We can say that explanations can be causal or non-causal. Causal explanations may have many different shapes and flavours [16], including explanations based on *causal attributions* (or chains), on *causal reasoning*, etc. Similarly, non-causal explanations can be of several different types, including (but not limited to):

- Descriptive: explanations related to conceptual properties and characteristics: hypernyms, hyponyms, holonyms, meronyms, etc.
- Justificatory: explanations of why a decision is good.
- Deontic: justifications of the decision based on permissions, obligations and prohibitions [15]. In this sense, deontic explanations are a subset of justificatory explanations.
- Contrastive: counterfactual explanations on events instead of the causes of events.

2.2   The GDPR and the Right to Explanation

The GDPR is technology-neutral, so it does not directly reference AI, but several provisions are highly relevant to the use of AI for decision-making [13]. The GDPR defines the "Right to Explanation" as a right that individuals might exercise when their legal status is affected by a solely automated decision. In order to put the user in the conditions to be able to contest an automated decision and thus to exercise the right to explanation, the insights of the decisions have to be properly explained.

The GDPR defines (indirectly) two modalities of explanation: explanations can be offered before (*ex-ante*; artt. 13-14-15) or after decisions have been made (*ex-post*; art. 22, paragraph 3). For each modality, the GDPR defines goals and purposes of explanations, thus providing a set of explanatory contents. From a technical point of view, there are technology-specific information to consider in order to fully meet the GDPR explanation requirements. Fundamentally, ex-ante we should provide information that guarantees the transparency principle, such as describing:

- The algorithms and models pipeline composing the ADM.
- The data used for training (if any), developing and testing the ADM.
- The background information (e.g. the jurisdiction of the ADM).
- The possible consequences of the ADM on the specific data subject.

Ex-post the data subject should be able to fruitfully contest a decision, so he/she should be given access to:

- The justification about the final decision.
- The run-time logic flow (causal chain) of the process determining the decision.
- The data used for inferring.
- Information (metadata) about the physical and virtual context in which the automated process happened.

In this scenario, law and ethics scholars have been more concerned with understanding the internal logic of decisions as a means to assess their lawfulness (e.g. prevent discriminatory outcomes), contest them, increase accountability generally, and clarify liability. For example, [26] propose counterfactuals as a reasonable way to lawfully provide *causal* explanations under the GDPR's right to explanation. [26] takes strength from the Causal Inference theory, in which counterfactuals are hypothesised to be one of the main tools for Causal Reasoning [20].

2.3   Transparency and the AI-HLEG Guidelines for Trustworthy AI

The AI-HLEG has been charged by the European Union to identify a set of Ethics Guidelines for Trustworthy AI, published in April 2019 [11]. The AI-HLEG vision for a user-centred AI appears to incorporate the GDPR principles, trying to expand them into a broader framework based on 4 consolidated ethical principles, including: respect for human autonomy, fairness, explicability. From the aforementioned principles they derive seven key requirements for Trustworthy AI, including: transparency, diversity, non-discrimination and fairness, accountability.

The ethical principle of Explicability [9] is associated to the requirements of Transparency and Accountability. The Transparency requirement, in turn, is clearly inspired by articles 13-14-15–22 of the GDPR. In a way, the AI-HLEG applies the technologically neutral GDPR by defining relevant guidelines on how Transparency can be achieved in Trustworthy AI systems, also through accessibility and universal design. The "Accessibility and Universal Design" requirement puts user-centrality at the core of Trustworthy AI systems. While the Transparency requirement encompasses transparency of elements relevant to an AI system (the data, the system, the business models), including: Traceability, Explainability, and Communication.

3   GDPR-Compliant Interactive Explanatory Tools for Trustworthy AI

In this section we will discuss over the GDPR and the AI-HLEG guidelines, identifying a minimal set of required explanation types, thus proposing a new User-Centred Explanatory Tool based upon a definition of Explanatory Narratives aligned to ISO 9241.

3.1   Explanations Under GDPR

The GDPR clearly draws a set of expectations to meet, in order to guarantee the Right to Explanation. These expectations are meant to define the goal of explanations and thus an explanatory content that may evolve together with technology. This explanatory content identifies at least 3 different types of explanations: causal, descriptive, justificatory. We will refer to them as the minimal set of explanations required, for explaining ADM under the GDPR. In fact, in the case of GDPR, we see that:

- Descriptive explanations are mostly required in the *ex-ante* phase, to explain business-models, the possible effects of ADM on user, and characteristics and limitations of the algorithms.
- Causal explanations are mostly required in the *ex-post* phase, to explain the causes of a solely automated decision.
- Justificatory explanations are required in both the *ex-ante* and *ex-post* phase, to justify decisions through permissions, obligations and so on.

The aforementioned explanations can be provided to the user through one or more explanatory tools as part of the whole AI system. This is why the AI-HLEG has defined some characteristics that these AI systems (and consequently their explanatory tools) should possess for trustworthiness. These characteristics include (among other things) transparency and user-centrality.

3.2   User-Centred Explanatory Tools

According to the AI-HLEG and the ICO [13], user-centrality implies that (in the most generic scenario) explanations following a One-Size-Fits-All approach (OSFA explanations) are not user-centred by design. For example, static symbolic representations where all aspects of a fairly long and complex computation are described and explained are one-size-fits-all explanations. OSFA explanations have intuitively at least two problems. The first problem is that if they are small-enough to be simple, it is impossible that in a complex-enough domain they would contain enough information to satisfy the explanation appetite of every user. The second problem is that if they contain all the necessary information, in a complex-enough domain they would contain an enormous amount of information and every user interested in a specific fragment of the explanation might look for it within hundreds of pages of explanations mostly irrelevant to her/his purposes.

At this point one might observe that OSFA explanations could be useful for simple domains, but according to [22] the complexity of a domain is exactly what motivates the need for explanations. In other terms, explanations are more useful to be given in complex domains.

What are OSFA explanations? Static explanations are OSFA explanations by design, but sometimes OSFA explanations can also be interactive. In fact, intuitively, simply adding naive ways of interaction to a static explanatory tool does not imply that the new interactive tool is no more following a one-size-fits-all approach. This is why we argue that interactivity is not a sufficient property for user-centred explanatory tools.

What are the sufficient properties for user-centred explanatory tools? A user-centric explanatory tool requires to provide goal-oriented explanations. Goal-oriented explanations implies explaining facts that relevant to the user, according to its background knowledge, interests and other peculiarities that make her/him a unique entity with unique needs that may change over time. If the explanations have to be adapted to users, does this imply that we should have a different explanatory tool for every possible user?

3.3   Explanatory Narratives

The fact that every different user might require a different explanation does not imply that there might be no unique and sound process for constructing user-centred explanations. In fact we argue that every interactive explanatory tool defines and eventually generates an Explanatory Space (ES) and that an explanation is always a path in the ES. The explainee explores the ES, tracing a path in it, thus producing its own (user-centred) explanation. We are going to give a more formal definition of the ES and the other components of an explanatory process, later.

Actually, being able to construct useful explanations is one of the main challenges of making science. This is why a lot of literature exist on how to construct scientific explanations. Constructing scientific explanations and participating in argumentative discourse are seen as essential practices of scientific inquiry (e.g., [8]), that according to [4] involves 3 different practices: sense-making, articulating, evaluating. In fact a scientist should use evidence to make sense of phenomenon, articulating understandings into explanatory narratives. These explanatory narratives should be validated, e.g., defending them in a public debate against the attacks of scientific community. We believe that similarly to scientific explanations, constructing lawful explanations involves the same practices. For example, legal evidential reasoning can be seen as reasoning on evidences (sense-making) in order to justify/prove an hypothesis (articulating), in a way that the resulting arguments can be defended from opponents and accepted by judges during a debate (evaluating) [21]. This is why we argue that a user-centred explanatory tool should be an instrument for sense-making, articulating and evaluating information into an explanatory narrative. If we focus on user-centred explanatory tools, then we are focusing on tools for sense-making through creating an explanatory narrative. What is an explanatory narrative? We consider an explanatory narrative as a sequence of information (explanans) to increase understanding over explainable data and processes (explanandum), for the satisfaction of a specified explainee that interacts with the explanandum having specified goals in a specified context of use. Our definition takes inspiration from [14,17,19], integrating concepts of usability defined in ISO 9241, such as the insistence on the term "specific", the triad "explainee", "goal" and "context of use", as much as the identification of a specific quality metric, which in our case are effectiveness and satisfaction. The qualities of the explanation that provide the explainee with the necessary satisfaction, following the categories provided by [17], can be summarized in a good choice of narrative appetite, structure and purpose.

The problems of a user-centred approach is that fully-automated explainers are unlikely to target quality parameters that guarantee the satisfaction of each specified explainee. Even if an AI could be used to generate such user-centred explanations, this would only shift the problem of explaining from the original ADM to another ADM – the explanatory AI used to explain the original ADM. As such we believe that, in the case of user-centred explanations, the simplest solution is to require that reader (explainee) and narrator (explainer) are the same, generating the narration for themselves by selecting and organizing narratives of individual event-tokens according to the structure that best caters their appetite and purpose. In this sense, a tool for creating explanatory narratives would allow users to build intelligible sequences of information, containing arguments that support or attack the claims underlying the goal of a narrative explanatory process defined by explainee/explainer and explanandum.

4   Related Work

Apparently most of the tools for explaining ADM are static (e.g.. AIX360 [1]). Interactive tools also exist [6,7,10,28], but: 1) they do not consider to offer descriptive explanations, but other types of explanations on pre-defined aspects of the ADM; 2) or they generate explanations automatically (e.g. from static argumentation frameworks), using templates. Completely automated sense-making or understanding articulation is possible only with very specific ADMs, or by pre-defining narrative scenarios that can be as powerful as dangerous [3,25]. Furthermore, a solely automated explainer is an ADM process itself, that might require to be explained as well.

Actually, as far as we know, there is no tool for explanatory narratives of ADMs, but more generic tools for teaching exist such as [23,24]. There are some interesting similarities between our work and the two aforementioned works, including the assumption that highlighting the structural elements of the explanandum is necessary in the articulation of an understanding.

5   A User-Centred Narrative Explanatory Process

In this section we present our model of User-Centred Narrative Explanatory Process under the GDPR. We start modelling a generic explanatory process, giving a formal definition of explanandum, explanans and Explanatory Space. Concurrently to modelling we show, step-by-step, an application of the model in a real-case scenario.

5.1 Real-Case Scenario

We present here a real-case scenario we will continuously refer to when defining our user-centred narrative explanatory process. This real-case is about the conditions applicable to child's consent in relation to information society services. The art. 8 of GDPR fixes at 16 years old the maximum age for giving the consent without the parent-holder authorization. This limit could be derogated by the domestic law. In Italy the legislative decree 101/2018 defines this limit at 14 years. In this situation we could model legal rules in LegalRuleML [2,18] using defeasible logic, in order to be able to represent the fact that the GDPR art. 8 rule is overridden with the Italian's one. The SPINDle legal reasoner processes the correct rule according to the jurisdiction (e.g., Italy) and the age. Suppose that Marco (a 14 years old Italian teenager living in Italy) uses Whatsapp, and his father, Giulio, wants to remove Marco's subscription to Whatsapp because he is worried about the privacy of Marco when online. In this simple scenario, the ADM system would reject Giulio's request to remove Marco's profile. What if Giulio wants to get an explanation of the automated decision? To answer this question we have to pick an explanatory process.

5.2 The Interactive Explanatory Process

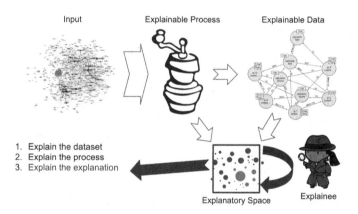

Fig. 1. Stylized interactive explanatory process.

According to the definition given in Sect. 3.3, a user-centred (interactive) narrative explanatory process is a process explaining an explanandum to an explainee (reader and narrator), thus producing as output an explanans (explanatory narrative) that is meaningful for the specific explainee. As shown in Fig. 1, an explanatory process is a function p for which $p(D, E_t, i_t) = E_{t+1}$, where:

- D is the explanandum.
- E_t is the input explanans, at step $t \geq 0$.

- i_t is the user interaction at step t.
- E_{t+1} is the output explanans, thus at step $t + 1$.

We can iteratively apply p, starting from an initial explanans E_0, until satisfaction. The user interaction i is a tuple made of an action a taken from the set A of possible actions, and a set of auxiliary inputs required by the action a.

5.3 The Explanandum

As defined by AI-HLEG guidelines, in this setting the explanandum is a collection of context-dependent information, made of one or more: datasets, processes, business models (that are higher-order processes). Naturally, the explanandum has to be *explainable* in order to be explained. In this scenario, datasets and processes are said to be explainable when they have a clear and not ambiguous symbolic representation, i.e., when their data items and rules are aligned with meaningful ontologies[1] for the end-users. The context-dependency implies that, in the most generic scenario, the information contained in datasets and processes is not sufficient to understand their nature without external knowledge. This external knowledge is commonly assumed to be part of the explainee knowledge (e.g. the knowledge about how to interpret a natural language). We will refer to this external common knowledge as the *explanandum context*, considering it as a dataset implicitly part of the explanandum.

In our real-case the explanandum is made of: a rule-base (the LegalRuleML one), a dataset of premises (the information about the involved entities), a dataset of conclusions obtained by applying the premises to the rule-base, a causal chain (the ordered chain of rules involved in the production of the dataset of conclusions).

What are datasets and processes?

A dataset is a tuple $\langle X, N, S \rangle$ where:

- X is a set of data-items.
- N is the set of (possibly informal) ontologies describing X.
- S are the (possibly unstructured) sources used to derive N and X.

A process is a tuple $\langle D_1, D_2, D_3 \rangle$ where:

- D_1 is the dataset of the process *inputs*, i.e. the domain.
- D_2 is the dataset of the process *function*.
- D_3 is the dataset of the process *outputs*, i.e. the codomain.

When D_1 is a collection of processes, the process is said to be higher-order.

In our real-case the sources of the function/rule-base are the GDPR (art. 8) and the Italian legislative decree 101/2018, while the source of the inputs/premises and the outputs/conclusions is the textual description of the case. The main ontology of the rule-base is a representation of the knowledge behind the SPINDle legal reasoner, while the ontologies for the premises and the conclusion might include the Dublin Core Schema, etc.

---

[1] These ontologies do not have necessarily to be explicit, formal or complete.

5.4   The Explanans and the Explanatory Space

The explanans is a particular type of dataset, in fact it is an ordered sequence of arguments (contained in the explanandum) useful to the explainee to reach its goals. The set of all the possible explanans reachable by an explainee interacting with the explanatory process, given an explanandum and an initial explanans, is called *Explanatory Space* (ES). The explanatory space is defined by:

- p (the explanatory process),
- A (the set of actions),
- D (the explanandum),
- the initial explanans E_0.

Thus, following the formalizations previously presented, the components of an explanatory process are the: Explainee, Instances (X), Ontologies (N), Sources (S).

This is why we say that a good explanans (explanation) has to be bound to both the explainee and the explanandum. In other words, a good ES is:

- Sourced: bound to the sources.
- Adaptable: bound to the specific explainee.
- Grounded: bound to the instances.
- Expandable: bound to the ontologies.

We will call to these properties: the SAGE properties of a good ES.

5.5   Heuristics for Exploring the Explanatory Space

Assuming that the explanandum D is provided as defined above, then:

1. How do we define the explanatory process p?
2. How do we pick the initial explanans E_0?
3. How do we pick the set of actions A?

The answers to these questions are highly dependent to the constraints that the explanatory space is supposed to have. In our scenario, we want to define an explanatory space sufficient to provide user-centred explanations of ADMs for trustworthy AI.

Considering that the narrative explanatory process p consists in exploring an Explanatory Space, in order to define p we identify 3 policies for exploring the ES, namely: the *Simplicity*, the *Abstraction*, and the *Relevance* policies.

Simplicity is mentioned in recommendation 29.5 of the AI-HLEG Policy and Investment Recommendations [12]: "Ensure that the use of AI systems that entail interaction with end users is by default accompanied by procedures to support users [...]. These procedures should be accompanied by simple explanations and a user-friendly procedure". In fact, the amount of information that can be effectively provided to a human is limited by physical constraints. Thus simple explanations about something are more likely to be accepted and understood and they are better than complicated ones and should be presented earlier than complex ones.

The **Abstraction** policy maintains that preferring abstract concepts over their concretizations helps in keeping the explanation as direct as possible. This is because there might be many concretizations of the same abstract concept. In other words, exploring concretizations before abstractions would generate longer paths in the explanatory space rather than the opposite. If we explore abstractions before concretizations, it is more likely that the ES is less complicated, without losing informative content.

The **Relevance** policy bounds further the explanatory process to the purposes/objectives of the explainee. It states that the information that is more likely to be relevant for the explainee (to reach its objective) should be presented earlier than the less relevant one. One of the expected effects of the relevance policy is that explanations will be shorter.

The Simplicity, Abstraction and Relevance policies shape the explanatory process p, putting significant constraints on the initial explanans E_0 and the set of actions A. Simplicity implies that in the explanatory process we start from a very minimal explanans and iteratively we add information to it in order to make it more detailed and complex. Simplicity also implies that simple representations of the explanandum (e.g. natural language descriptions) should be presented before the original representations (the "Ground"; e.g. XML, JSON, etc.). Abstraction implies that the explanans should start from generic and conceptual information about the explanandum (e.g. its size and other meta-data), going toward more specific and concrete information (the "Ground"). Relevance implies (among other things) that E_0 should contain the most relevant information possible, and that further details should be firstly about the entities directly involved in E_0. The other entities should be explored/presented in a second moment, if needed.

5.6   The Initial Explanans

The initial explanans E_0 should contain an overview of the underlying Explanatory Process (EP), giving explicit information about the purposes (e.g. to give insights about a sequence of events, to verify an hypothesis, etc.) of the EP.[2] E_0 should also provide an overview of the explanandum, pointing to information about the metadata (e.g. size, language, knowledge representation conventions). We will refer to the information contained in E_0 as the "incipit" or "background" of the EP.

In the case of explanations under the GDPR, E_0 should specify (among other things) whether the EP is operating ex-ante or ex-post, and the explanandum referred by E_0 should contain all the information mentioned in Sect. 2.2. A succinct justification about the automated decision (required in the ex-post phase)

---

[2] It is not excluded that the original purposes might change during the explanatory process.

can be generated through a static explanatory tool such as AIX360 [1], and should be given as part of the EP overview.

In our real-case, the justification about the automated decision states that Giulio's request has been rejected because of the Italian decree.

5.7   The High-Level Actions and the Structure of the Explanatory Space

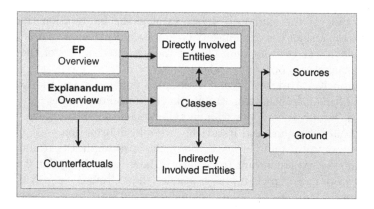

Fig. 2. Structure of the explanatory space: arrows show the flow of information, while every rectangle represents a different sub-stage in the explanatory space.

The explainee explores the Explanatory Space through a set of pre-defined actions meant to be used to build explanations respecting the SAGE properties. For every SAGE property, we identify a set of commands that may be used by the explainee during the Explanatory Process:

- **Source-ability** (commands): used to show the source of a model (a law, a paper, etc.).
- **Adapt-ability**: used to keep track of important information while exploring the explanatory space, building an argumentation framework.
- **Ground-ability**: used to refer and show specific parts of the explanandum in their original format (e.g. XML, JSON, SQL, etc.), and used for generating counterfactuals.
- **Expand-ability**: used to deepen concepts, aligning them to other concepts available in the explanandum context.

Defining the explanatory process p, the (high-level) set of commands/actions A and the initial explanans E_0, we have also defined the structure of the Explanatory Space. The resulting structure (shown in Fig. 2) is made of 6 main stages: Incipit (EP and Explanandum Overview), Core Information (Classes and Directly Involved Entities), Marginal Information (Indirectly Involved Entities),

Ground, Sources, Counterfactuals. Each stage of the structure is involved in a different step of the explanans construction.

In our real-case the explainee (Giulio) wants to get an explanation of SPIN-dle's conclusions (the process' decision). Giulio uses the Explanatory Process (EP) on the explanandum. The EP starts from the "Incipit" stage (the initial explanans) showing:

- A succinct *ex-post* justification of the process' decision, and that the justification is related to known concepts that can be easily explored.
- The explanandum is made of a knowledge base and a process having a set of inputs that can be changed by Giulio in order to understand whether the justification is valid and useful for him (maybe it is not).

The first level result of EP is too shallow, thus Giulio asks to EP to go down to the "Core Information" stage showing more information about the explanandum. Now Giulio sees that the data is composed by: a set of logical conclusions, the hierarchy of rules used to get those conclusions (the causal chain), the premises on which the rules have been applied. Giulio wants to get more information about the rules, thus it moves to the "Marginal Information" stage, finding out that the Italian decree 101/2018 has rebutted the GDPR and it is responsible for the final decision, thus it marks that information as an argument that supports the process' decision. Furthermore, Giulio sees that every rule is ground-able to a LegalRuleML component, and linkable to the pertinent source of law that justifies the rule. Giulio can also see rebuttals, and if he would ask the EP to tell more about the GDPR rebuttal he would find out that the "Lex specialis derogat generali" is applied, causing the activation of the rule associated to the Italian decree instead of the rule associated to the GDPR.

6   Discussions

With an explanatory tool based on our model, the user can explore the explanatory space and build its own explanatory narrative through a set of pre-defined actions. The explanatory narrative can be built through the adapt-ability commands, by defining an argumentation framework. The exploration of the explanatory space can be performed through the expand-ability, source-ability and ground-ability commands. The resulting tool is user-centred by design and can be used for finding evidence to make sense of phenomena (sense-making), articulating understandings into an explanatory narrative. Furthermore, we claim that the structure of Explanatory Space we identified is sufficient to produce the descriptive, causal and justificatory explanations required by the GDPR. In fact, assuming that the information at the "Background" stage defines the initial explanans, we have that: Descriptive explanations can be obtained by reasoning over the "Core and Marginal Information" stages of the ES, Causal explanations over the "Counterfactuals" stage mainly, and Justificatory explanations over the "Incipit" and "Sources" stages mainly. It is possible to apply logical rules in order to automatize the production of reasonable explanations. In fact,

Description Logic can be used for reasoning over descriptions, Causal Inference [20] for reasoning over causations, Defeasible Deontic Logic for reasoning over justifications.

Despite this, our model has some limitations. Because it is meant to be effective in building user-centred explanations, but not community-centred ones. In fact, constructing strong, effective and non-over-fitted explanations is historically an iterative and community-centred process.

7   Conclusions and Future Work

We have introduced a model of a User-Centred Narrative Explanatory Process, based on concepts drawn from ISO 9241, as a promising contribution to Trustworthy AI compliant with the GDPR. To this end, we identified a minimal set of required explanation types and we converted the problem of generating explanations into the identification of an appropriate path over an Explanatory Space (ES) defined and eventually generated by every user-centred (interactive) explanatory tool. Finally we provided a reasonable structure of the ES through the identification of the SAGE properties and of some space exploration heuristics. Building a working prototype based upon our model is the next natural step. We are also considering to extend the current model in order to make it suitable also for community-centred explanatory tools.

References

1. Arya, V., et al.: One explanation does not fit all: a toolkit and taxonomy of ai explainability techniques. arXiv preprint arXiv:1909.03012 (2019)
2. Athan, T., Boley, H., Governatori, G., Palmirani, M., Paschke, A., Wyner, A.Z.: OASIS LegalRuleML. In: ICAIL, vol. 13, pp. 3–12 (2013)
3. Bennet, W.L., Feldman, M.S.: Reconstructing Reality in the Courtroom. Quid Pro Books, Tavistock (1981)
4. Berland, L.K., Reiser, B.J.: Making sense of argumentation and explanation. Sci. Educ. **93**(1), 26–55 (2009)
5. Cath, C., Wachter, S., Mittelstadt, B., Taddeo, M., Floridi, L.: Artificial intelligence and the 'good society': the US, EU, and UK approach. Sci. Eng. Ethics **24**(2), 505–528 (2017). https://doi.org/10.1007/s11948-017-9901-7
6. Cocarascu, O., Rago, A., Toni, F.: Extracting dialogical explanations for review aggregations with argumentative dialogical agents. In: Proceedings of the 18th International Conference on Autonomous Agents and MultiAgent Systems, pp. 1261–1269. International Foundation for Autonomous Agents and Multiagent Systems (2019)
7. Čyras, K., et al.: Explanations by arbitrated argumentative dispute. Expert Syst. Appl. **127**, 141–156 (2019)
8. Driver, R., Newton, P., Osborne, J.: Establishing the norms of scientific argumentation in classrooms. Sci. Educ. **84**(3), 287–312 (2000)
9. Floridi, L., et al.: Ai4People–an ethical framework for a good AI society: opportunities, risks, principles, and recommendations. Minds and Machines **28**(4), 689–707 (2018)

10. Fox, M., Long, D., Magazzeni, D.: Explainable planning. arXiv preprint arXiv:1709.10256 (2017)

11. Hleg, A.: Ethics guidelines for trustworthy AI (2019)

12. Hleg, A.: Policy and investment recommendations (2019)

13. ICO: Project explain interim report (2019). https://ico.org.uk/about-the-ico/research-and-reports/project-explain-interim-report/. Accessed 05 Jan 2020

14. Lipton, P.: What good is an explanation? In: Hon, G., Rakover, S.S. (eds.) Explanation. Synthese Library (Studies in Epistemology, Logic, Methodology, and Philosophy of Science), vol. 302, pp. 43–59. Springer, Dordrecht (2001). https://doi.org/10.1007/978-94-015-9731-9_2

15. Meyer, J.J. C.: Deontic logic: a concise overview. In: Deontic Logic in Computer Science: Normative System Specification, pp. 3–16. Wiley (1993)

16. Miller, T.: Explanation in artificial intelligence: insights from the social sciences. Artif. Intell. **267**, 1–38 (2018)

17. Norris, S.P., Guilbert, S.M., Smith, M.L., Hakimelahi, S., Phillips, L.M.: A theoretical framework for narrative explanation in science. Sci. Educ. **89**(4), 535–563 (2005)

18. Palmirani, M., Governatori, G.: Modelling legal knowledge for GDPR compliance checking. In: JURIX, pp. 101–110 (2018)

19. Passmore, J.: Explanation in everyday life, in science, and in history. Hist. Theory **2**(2), 105–123 (1962)

20. Pearl, J.: The seven tools of causal inference, with reflections on machine learning. Commun. ACM **62**(3), 54–60 (2019)

21. Prakken, H.: An argumentation-based analysis of the Simonshaven case. In: Topics in Cognitive Science (2019)

22. Raymond, A., Gunes, H., Prorok, A.: Culture-based explainable human-agent deconfliction. arXiv preprint arXiv:1911.10098 (2019)

23. Sandoval, W.A., Reiser, B.J.: Explanation-driven inquiry: integrating conceptual and epistemic scaffolds for scientific inquiry. Sci. Educ. **88**(3), 345–372 (2004)

24. Suthers, D.D., Toth, E.E., Weiner, A.: An integrated approach to implementing collaborative inquiry in the classroom. In: Proceedings of the 2nd International Conference on Computer Support for Collaborative Learning, pp. 275–282. International Society of the Learning Sciences (1997)

25. Verheij, B., et al.: Arguments, scenarios and probabilities: connections between three normative frameworks for evidential reasoning. Law Probab. Risk **15**(1), 35–70 (2015)

26. Wachter, S., Mittelstadt, B., Russell, C.: Counterfactual explanations without opening the black box: automated decisions and the GPDR. Harv. JL Tech. **31**, 841 (2017)

27. WP29: guidelines on automated individual decision-making and profiling for the purposes of regulation 2016/679 (wp251rev.01). European Commission (2016)

28. Zhong, Q., Fan, X., Luo, X., Toni, F.: An explainable multi-attribute decision model based on argumentation. Expert Syst. Appl. **117**, 42–61 (2019)

Author Index

Printed in the United States
By Bookmasters